FOCUS 3
ON THE PAST

BEN Looney

GW00633847

THE MODERN WORLD

Gerard Brockie
Raymond Walsh

Gill and Macmillan

Published in Ireland by
Gill & Macmillan Ltd
Goldenbridge
Dublin 8

with associated comapnies throughout the world

© Gerard Brockie and Raymond Walsh 1991
© Artwork, Gill and Macmillan 1991

Original design   Design Works, Dublin
Additional artwork   Denis Baker
Cover illustration   Cathy Henderson
Picture research   Anne-Marie Ehrlich
Print originated in Ireland by
Seton Music Graphics, Bantry.

0 7171 1845 2

Acknowledgments:
For permission to reproduce photographs and colour transparencies grateful acknowledgment is made to the following: E.T. Archive; Mary Evans Picture Library; Archiv für Kunst und Geschichte, Berlin; National Maritime Museum; Office of Public Works, Dublin; Novosti; Popperfoto; Hulton-Deutsch Picture Library; Military Archive and Research Service; Hutchison Library; John Topham; RTE/Cashman Collection; Associated Press; Camera Press; Gamma; George A. Duncan; Lensmen; George Morrison; National Gallery of Ireland; National Library of Ireland; Public Record Office, Belfast; Dr Garret Fitzgerald T.D.; Ulster Museum; Network; Pacemaker; Peter Newark's American Pictures; Bettman Archive; Rod Tuach; Kobal Collection; Bord Failte; Anne Ronan Picture Library. The poem 'Base Details' by Siegfried Sassoon is reproduced by kind permission of George T. Sassoon.

Contents

Using this book

Students taking the Higher Level course must cover the following three sections of the book:

A.   Chapters 1-10 (Peace and War in Europe)
                         and either
        Chapters 11-13 (The Rise of the Superpowers)
                or
        Chapters 14-16 (Moves towards European Unity)

B.   Chapters 17-30 (Political Developments in Ireland)

C.   Chapters 31-37 (Social change in the Twentieth Century)

Students taking the Ordinary Level course can cover the following two sections:

A.   Chapters 1-10 **and either** chapters 11-13 **or** chapters 14-16

B.   Chapters 17-30

Alternatively Ordinary Level Students can cover the following two sections:

A.   Chapters 1-10 **and either** chapters 11-13 **or** chapters 14-16

C.   Chapters 31-37

INTERNATIONAL RELATIONS
IN THE TWENTIETH CENTURY

FROM WAR TO PEACE

WAR AND PEACE

Whether countries live together in peace or go to war was once only the concern of kings, governments and armies. Until around 1800, countries in Europe were often at war with one another. However, the fighting was mostly confined to the summer months and civilian populations were usually spared.

Following the Industrial Revolution, warfare changed as new weapons were invented and generals made use of railways to transport their armies.

After 1900, however, it became clear that future wars could not be limited to armies and navies. Ordinary civilians, including women and children, would become victims of new weapons of mass destruction.

In the twentieth century, issues such as war and peace became vitally important in the lives of ordinary people. Since 1900, two world wars have been fought. They resulted in the deaths of millions of soldiers, sailors and civilians. Because of these conflicts, the continent of Europe has lost its position as the most powerful area in the world.

In order to understand how the world as we know it today took shape, we must look at peace and war since 1900.

The world in 1900: European countries had vast empires throughout the world

British

French

German

THE WORLD IN 1900

Take a close look at the map of the world in 1900. You will notice many differences between it and a map of the world today. In the first place, some of the powerful countries or Great Powers of Europe such as Great Britain and France once had vast overseas empires, especially in Asia and Africa. These overseas possessions often led to tension and rivalry between the European powers. In particular, the German emperor, Wilhelm II, was jealous of the vast colonies of Britain and France. Germany arrived late in the search for colonies and had to be content with a small number of fairly poor areas.

You will also notice from the map that, unlike today, Eastern Europe in 1900 was divided among three large empires.

Europe in 1900. By 1914 it had become divided into two armed camps, the Triple Alliance and the Triple Entente.

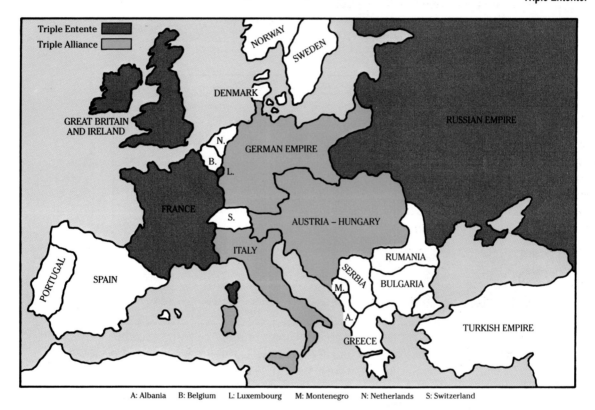

Triple Entente
Triple Alliance

NORWAY
SWEDEN
DENMARK
GREAT BRITAIN AND IRELAND
RUSSIAN EMPIRE
N.
GERMAN EMPIRE
B.
L.
FRANCE
S.
AUSTRIA – HUNGARY
ITALY
PORTUGAL
SPAIN
RUMANIA
SERBIA
M.
BULGARIA
A.
TURKISH EMPIRE
GREECE

A: Albania   B: Belgium   L: Luxembourg   M: Montenegro   N: Netherlands   S: Switzerland

- The *Russian Empire* was ruled by Tsar Nicholas II from his capital at St Petersburg.
- The *Austro-Hungarian Empire* was ruled by Emperor Franz-Joseph from his capital in Vienna.
- The *Turkish* or *Ottoman Empire* was ruled by the Sultan of Turkey from his capital at Constantinople.

As the Turkish empire was very weak, the Russians and Austrians hoped to gain land lost by the Turks. However, people living in the Balkan areas of Eastern Europe wished to be ruled by neither Turks, Austrians or Russians. Instead, they wanted to rule themselves. These tensions made the Balkans a trouble spot and a serious danger to world peace.

THE PATH TO WAR

From 1900 onwards, rivalry between the Great Powers of Europe grew stronger and stronger. The emperor of Germany, Kaiser Wilhelm II, expanded the German navy by building huge battleships. This angered the British government, which responded by building even more battleships than the Germans.

Alarmed by the growth of the German navy, the British government built a fleet of new battleships known as dreadnoughts.

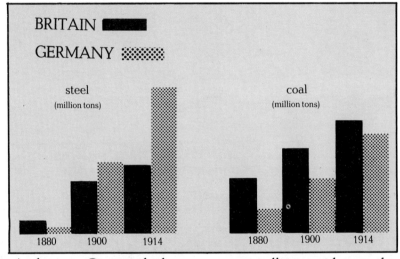

BRITAIN

GERMANY

steel
(million tons)

coal
(million tons)

1880 1900 1914   1880 1900 1914

Between 1880 and 1914 Germany became Britain's greatest rival in the production of steel and coal.

At the time, Germany had an agreement or alliance with two other European powers, Austria-Hungary and Italy. It was known as the *Triple Alliance*. In response to this, Great Britain, France and Russia developed their own alliance which became known as the *Triple Entente*. The danger facing Europe and the world was clear: if two of these Great Powers became involved in a war, all the others would soon become involved as well. This was exactly what happened in the summer of 1914 when conflict broke out in the Balkans.

DEATH AT SARAJEVO

On 28 June 1914, the heir to the Austrian throne, Archduke Franz Ferdinand, and his wife were shot and killed in the town of Sarajevo in Bosnia, a Balkan province of the Austro-Hungarian Empire. When Austria blamed the neighbouring independent country of Serbia,

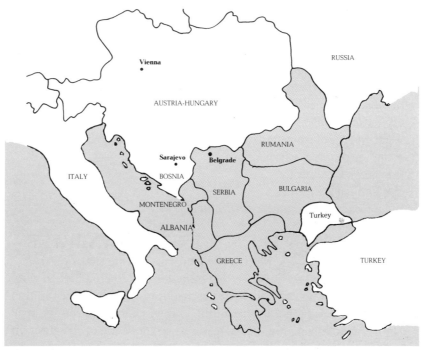

The Balkan lands

Serbia's ally, Russia, came to her assistance. Germany then agreed to support Austria and attacked Russia's ally, France. When German armies attacked neutral Belgium, Great Britain entered the war. By 4 August 1914, most of Europe was at war.

Many people in various countries welcomed the outbreak of war. They believed that their own armies would be victorious by Christmas 1914. However, the war was to last for over four years. In September 1914, the Germans had almost reached Paris, the French capital. They were halted by British and French troops at the Battle of the Marne.

Cheering crowds in Berlin welcome the outbreak of war on 4 August 1914. There were similar scenes in London and Paris.

5

1 *Why did issues of war and peace become so important for ordinary people during the twentieth century?*

2 *Name two European countries which had overseas empires in 1900.*

3 *Why was the German emperor, Kaiser Wilhelm II, jealous of Great Britain and France?*

4 *List the three empires in Eastern Europe in 1900.*

5 *What type of government was desired by the people in the Balkan region?*

6 *Name the countries which formed:*
   (a) The Triple Alliance
   (b) The Triple Entente

7 *What took place at Sarajevo on 28 June 1914?*

THE WESTERN FRONT: TRENCH WARFARE

After the Battle of the Marne, the Germans on one side, and the British and French on the other, dug trenches and erected barbed wire defences. Soon, a line of trenches stretched from the North Sea in the north to the Swiss border in the south. This was known as the *Western Front*. In the following four years, it was to be the scene of slaughter on a scale never experienced before.

Conditions on the Western Front were appalling. The trenches were rat-infested and water-logged and men were constantly subjected to the barrage of enemy gunfire. Countless numbers of soldiers perished as they went 'over the top' into 'no man's land'

In 1915, a terrible new weapon – poison gas – made its first appearance on the Western Front. The wind often blew this gas back into the faces of those who had used it in the first place. Gas masks were later worn for protection. Despite numerous attacks and heavy casualties the Western Front hardly moved more than a few kilometres throughout the war. The two most famous battles fought on the Western Front took place in 1916, at Verdun and the Somme.

Defending the trenches against enemy attack.

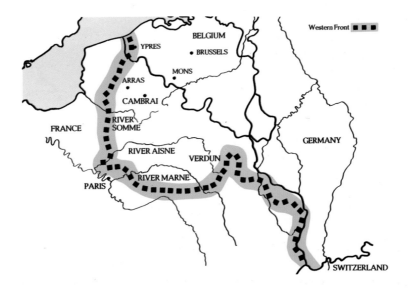

The Western Front, 1914-1918 stretched from the Belgian coastline in the north to the Swiss border in the south.

What does this illustration tell us about conditions in the trenches during World War I?

Soliders cutting through the barbed wire defences of enemy trenches.

THE EASTERN FRONT

In August 1914, two Russian armies advanced on German territory in the East. Under the command of generals Hindenburg and Ludendorff, the Germans trapped the Russians and managed to split the two armies. The Germans defeated the Russian armies separately at the battles of Tannenberg and Masurian Lakes in August and September 1914. Over 500 Russian guns were captured and a quarter of a million Russians were either killed or taken prisoner.

However, Germany's ally, Austria, was less successful against the Russians. When Russian armies defeated the Austrians, the Germans had to come to their assistance. By the end of 1914, there was a stalemate on the Eastern Front as well as the West. Unlike the Western

Front, however, the German, Russian and Austrian armies in the East would advance a certain distance every now and then, only to be beaten back again because of lack of equipment and poor communications.

The Russian losses continued on a massive scale. In 1916, Tsar Nicholas II himself went to the front as Commander-in-Chief. Russian casualties continued to rise, however, leading to the revolutions of 1917. After the Communists came to power in October of that year, they took Russia out of the war on harsh terms which were dictated by Germany in the *Treaty of Brest-Litovsk*.

TEST YOUR KNOWLEDGE
1 *Describe the conditions in the trenches along the Western Front.*
2 *What new and terrible weapon made its first appearance there in 1915?*
3 *Name two famous battles fought along the Western Front.*
4 *List three countries which fought on the Eastern Front in World War I.*
5 *Name two battles which were fought there in August and September 1914.*
6 *How did the fighting on the Eastern Front differ from the fighting on the Western Front?*
7 *When did Russia pull out of World War I?*

The fighting on the Eastern Front took place between Austria and Germany on one side and Russia on the other.

THE WAR AT SEA

There was great rivalry between the British and German navies. The British navy blockaded Germany and the Germans responded with a U-boat (submarine) campaign against British shipping. In 1915, a famous American liner, the *Lusitania*, was sunk by a German submarine off Kinsale, Co. Cork, resulting in the deaths of over 1000 people.

The sinking of the Lusitania

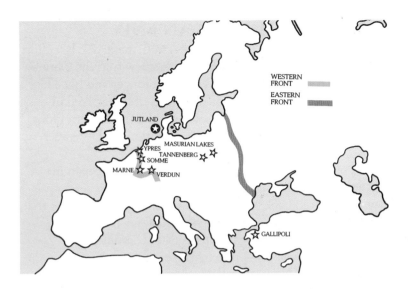

WESTERN FRONT

EASTERN FRONT

JUTLAND

MASURIAN LAKES
YPRES
TANNENBERG
SOMME
MARNE   VERDUN

GALLIPOLI

The main sea battle of World War I was the Battle of Jutland which took place off the coast of Denmark in May 1916. Under Admiral von Scheer, the Germans confronted the British fleet under the command of Admiral Jellico. Fierce fighting occurred in misty conditions.

Although British losses were higher than German ones, the German fleet was lucky to escape back to port under cover of night. After this encounter, the German navy never again risked open battle with the British Royal Navy. Britain continued to control the seas and blockaded Germany until the end of the war.

AMERICA ENTERS THE WAR

On 6 April 1917, the United States of America, under President Woodrow Wilson, entered the war on the side of Britain and France. America entered the war because German submarines continued to sink ships with Americans on board. Germany, however, ignored repeated American warnings over this interference with their shipping.

America's entry brought great hope to Britain and France. The huge might of America in terms of men and weapons was to play an important part in the eventual Allied victory.

American troops on their way to fight in France.

1918: THE WAR COMES TO AN END

In March 1918, the German general, Ludendorff, made one last effort to break the deadlock on the Western Front. He knew that the German civilian population could not stand the war much longer and hoped for a breakthrough before large numbers of American troops arrived in France. He was able to release German soldiers from the Eastern Front as Russia had made peace on harsh German conditions in December 1917.

Ludendorff's plan was known as *The Spring Offensive*. It began in March 1918 and at first, the Germans advanced well. However, by August they were beaten back to their earlier positions. It was clear that the German army would soon collapse before the force of the Allies. Realising this, Kaiser Wilhelm II gave up his throne and fled to Holland, leaving a new government to make peace.

On the morning of 11 November 1918, fighting on the Western Front ended when Germany surrendered unconditionally. An *armistice* or cease-fire was signed, bringing four and a half years of war and destruction to an end. The victors now had the task of drawing up a peace treaty which they hoped would prevent war from breaking out again in Europe.

TEST YOUR KNOWLEDGE
1 *What campaign did the German navy carry out against British ships?*
2 *Name the famous liner sunk off Kinsale in 1915.*
3 *What important sea battle was fought in May 1916?*
4 *Why did the United States of America enter the war in 1917?*
5 *When did fighting on the Western Front end?*

IRISH INVOLVEMENT IN WORLD WAR I

At the beginning of the war in 1914, there were almost 50,000 Irishmen in the British army. By the end of the war in 1918, over 300,000 had volunteered to fight. Famous Irish regiments included the Royal Irish Rifles, the Royal Dublin Fusiliers, the Connaught Rangers and the Royal Munster Fusiliers. Irish regiments suffered heavy casualties at Gallipoli in Turkey (1915) and on the Western Front. The Ulster Division in particular experienced appalling losses at the Battle of the Somme (1916). Two famous Irishmen killed in World War I were the poet, Francis Ledwidge, and the scholar, Thomas Kettle. By the end of the war, around 50,000 Irishmen had been killed in action. Thousands more returned home wounded.

The War Memorial at Islandbridge, Dublin, which commemorates the Irishmen who died fighting on the Allied side in World War I.

THE LEGACY OF WORLD WAR I

World War I resulted in death, destruction and change on a scale never before experienced.

- Millions were killed as a direct result of the war.
- Countless soldiers returned home maimed and wounded, never to forget the horrors of war. Millions of women and children were widowed and orphaned.
- Four main empires came to an end as a result of the war: Germany, Russia, Austria and Turkey.
- Economic depression set in all over Europe when demobilised soldiers returned home to face unemployment and poverty.

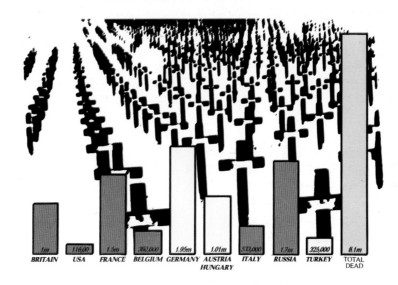

1m	116,00	1.5m	300,000	1.95m	1.01m	533,000	1.7m	325,000	8.1m
BRITAIN	USA	FRANCE	BELGIUM	GERMANY	AUSTRIA HUNGARY	ITALY	RUSSIA	TURKEY	TOTAL DEAD

Military casualties in World War I

Chapter 1: Review

- From around 1900 onwards, it was clear that, in future, war would not be limited to armies and navies. Ordinary civilians, including men, women and children, would become caught up in widespread suffering and death.

- In 1900, the most powerful countries in the world were in Europe. They were known as the Great Powers.

- Britain and France owned vast overseas empires especially in Africa and Asia. Under Kaiser Wilhelm II, Germany had also begun to build up an overseas empire.

- In 1900, Eastern Europe was divided into three large empires: the Russian Empire, the Austro-Hungarian Empire and the Turkish Empire.

- There was tension in the Balkans, an area of Eastern Europe where both the Russians and Austrians wanted to gain territory at the expense of the weak Turkish Empire.

- Between 1900 and 1914, there was strong rivalry between Britain and Germany. This developed into a naval race centred on the size of their navies and the number of battleships each country possessed.

- By 1914, Europe was divided into two hostile camps: the Triple Alliance of Germany, Austria-Hungary and Italy; and the Triple Entente between Great Britain, France and Russia.

- On 28 June 1914, the heir to the Austrian throne, Archduke Franz Ferdinand, was assassinated at Sarajevo. This began a chain of events which led to the outbreak of World War I.

- During World War I, there was trench warfare on the Western Front. The huge casualties amid horrific conditions created strong anti-war feeling in Europe during the 1920s and 1930s.

- Although trench warfare was avoided, there was also a stalemate on the Eastern Front from the end of 1914 onwards. This was only broken when the new Communist government in Russia withdrew from the war and agreed to harsh German peace terms at the end of 1917 (Treaty of Brest-Litovsk).

- There was a war fought at sea between the British and German navies. The main sea battle of World War I was the Battle of Jutland. It was fought off the coast of Denmark in May 1916.

- In April 1917, the United States of America, under President Woodrow Wilson, entered the war on the Allied side. This greatly assisted the Allied war effort and helped bring about their victory in November 1918.

- World War I resulted in death and destruction on a scale never witnessed before. Millions were killed and wounded and four powerful empires came to an end.

ACTIVITIES

1 Complete the following sentences.
   (a) Around 1900, Eastern Europe was divided up between _____.
   (b) There was a race to build larger battleships between _____.
   (c) The first shots of World War I were fired in June 1914 in a town called _____.
   (d) The Treaty of Brest-Litovsk (1918) was signed by _____.
   (e) World War I came to an end on _____.

2 Match an item in Column 1 with an item in Column 2.

COLUMN 1	COLUMN 2
Ludendorff	A battle on the Western Front
The Somme	An area in Eastern Europe
Jutland	A German general
The Balkans	A battle on the Eastern Front
Tannenberg	A sea battle

3 Imagine that you were a soldier in a trench on the Western Front during World War I. Write a speech that you would make to a peace rally during the 1920s.

4 During World War I, many poets fought with the various armies. Much of their poetry reflected the horrors of war. Read the following extracts by two British poets and answer the questions which follow.

(a)   Base Details

> If I were fierce and bald, and short of breath,
> I'd live with scarlet Majors at the Base,
> And speed glum heroes up the line to death.
> You'd see me with my puffy petulant face,
> Guzzling and gulping in the best hotel,
> Reading the Roll of Honour. 'Poor young chap',
> I'd say – 'I used to know his father well.
> Yes we've lost heavily in this last scrap'.
> And when the war is done and youth stone dead,
> I'd toddle safely home and die – in bed.

Siegfried Sassoon

(b)   From Anthem for Doomed Youth

> What passing-bells for these who die as cattle?
> – Only the monstrous anger of the guns.
> Only the stuttering rifles' rapid rattle
> Can patter out their hasty orisons.
> No mockeries now for them; no prayers nor bells;
> Nor any voice of mourning save the choirs –
> The shrill, demented choirs of wailing shells;
> And bugles calling for them from sad shires.

Wilfred Owen

(i)   Give examples of how the generals are mocked in 'Base Details'.
(ii) Would you agree that Sassoon stresses the suffering of young people? Support your answer.
(iii) Show how Wilfred Owen paints a picture of the horrors of dying in trench warfare.
(iv) Explain how poems like these helped in the creation of anti-war feeling in Europe after 1918.

CHAPTER 2

PEACE-MAKING AT VERSAILLES

In January 1919, the victorious Allied leaders met at Versailles outside Paris. Millions had fought in World War I, believing it to be 'the war to end all wars'. For the first time in history, war had influenced the everyday lives of whole populations. Millions of men lay buried in the battlefields of Europe and many more returned home wounded. Therefore, when the statesmen assembled at Versailles, they had a mission to draw up a peace settlement that would prevent war in the future.

THE LEADERS OF VERSAILLES
WOODROW WILSON OF THE UNITED STATES

President Wilson came to the peace conference with his own *Fourteen-Point Plan*. This plan declared that the people of each nation should have the right to choose their own government – *self-determination*; Germany should be treated fairly; the arms race should be ended; and a *League of Nations* should be set up to preserve peace in the world.

GEORGE CLEMENCEAU OF FRANCE

Clemenceau was known as 'The Tiger'. He had been Prime Minister of France during the last years of the war. His main interest was that France should never again be invaded by Germany. He proposed that Germany pay a huge sum as compensation for the damage done to French territory and that steps be taken to make the border between France and Germany secure. He was determined to deal harshly with Germany.

DAVID LLOYD GEORGE OF GREAT BRITAIN

Lloyd George had fought and won an election in December 1918 on the promise to make Germany pay. Like Clemenceau, he was determined to make the Germans compensate the Allies for the destruction caused by the war. Britain had gone heavily into debt in order to finance her war effort. As a result, anti-German feelings ran very high in the country.

VITTORIO ORLANDO OF ITALY

Orlando, the Italian Prime Minister, represented his country at Versailles. Italy entered the war on the Allied side in 1915, although it had earlier been part of the Triple Alliance with Germany and Austria-Hungary. Italy now hoped to gain some Austrian territory at the peace conference.

TEST YOUR KNOWLEDGE
1 *Name the four main leaders at the Versailles Peace Conference.*
2 *Which two shared common views on the treatment of Germany?*
3 *What plan did President Wilson bring to the conference?*
  Outline some of its provisions.

THE TREATY OF VERSAILLES

Discussions continued among the Allied leaders at Versailles between January and June 1919. *The Treaty of Versailles* between the Allied powers and Germany was finally signed on 28 June 1919, exactly five years after the first shot of the war had been fired at Sarajevo.

The signing of the Versailles Peace Treaty on 28 June 1919.

Read the following extracts from the Treaty of Versailles.

WORKING WITH EVIDENCE

Article 231
  The Allied governments affirm, and Germany accepts, the responsibility of Germany and her allies for causing all the loss and damage to which the Allied governments and their peoples have been subjected as a result of the war.

Article 232
  The Allied governments require, and Germany undertakes, that she will make compensation for all the damage done to the civilian population of the Allied powers and to their property during the war.

Article 428

As a guarantee that the treaty shall be carried out, the German territory to the west of the Rhine will be occupied by Allied troops for fifteen years.

Article 160

The German army must not comprise more than seven divisions of infantry and three divisions of cavalry. The total number in the army must not exceed 100,000 men. The army shall be devoted exclusively to the maintenance of order within the territory and the control of frontiers.

1 Article 231 was known as the 'War Guilt' Clause. Explain why.
2 Would you consider that this clause was totally fair to Germany?
3 What did Germany undertake to do under Article 232?
4 What limit was set on the size of the German army?
5 Explain the precautions taken by the Allies to make sure that the Germans would carry out the terms of the treaty.

As well as having its army reduced, Germany's navy was to be reduced to six small battleships. The German airforce was abolished.

However, all of these conditions were overshadowed by the main results of the Treaty of Versailles – huge losses of territory by Germany. As well as losing all their overseas colonies, the Germans lost about one-eighth of their land and population in Europe.

As well as losing Alsace-Lorraine to France, Germany lost land to Poland in the east, Denmark in the north and the new state of Czechoslovakia in the south.

What view of the Versailles Treaty is shown in this German cartoon?

As the delegates left Versailles for home, many of them failed to grasp that decisions taken at the Conference would lead to serious problems in the future.

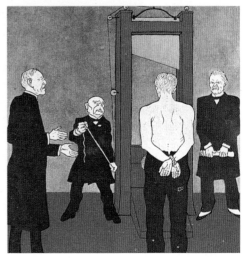

New States created at Versailles

Germany was reduced in size

Note the breaking up of the Austrian Empire (Austria–Hungary) into several independent countries. Austria and Hungary were made into two smaller independent states, while the rest of the empire was divided between three new states: Yugoslavia, Czechoslovakia and Poland. The Treaty which broke up the Austrian Empire was known as the Treaty of Saint–Germain.

A: Albania B: Belgium D: Denmark L: Luxembourg N: Netherlands S: Switzerland

Territorial changes in Europe after the Versailles Conference, 1919.

CHANGES IN CENTRAL AND EASTERN EUROPE

As a result of the Versailles Conference, there were vast changes in central and eastern Europe. As you can see from the map, the old empire of Austria-Hungary, defeated in the war, was completely broken up. Austria and Hungary became two small independent states, while two completely new states ruled by Slav peoples were established. These were Czechoslavakia, with its capital at Prague, and Yugoslavia, with Belgrade as its capital city. As part of the Versailles settlement, any future union of Germany and Austria was strictly forbidden.

Poland, which had ceased to be a separate state around 1800, now recovered its independence from Austria, Germany and Russia.

Despite President Wilson's ideas on national self-determination, there were many national minorities in the new states set up at Versailles. Since many different races had settled in central and eastern Europe, this could not be avoided. It was to be a source of tension and conflict in the years ahead.

THE LEAGUE OF NATIONS

The statesmen at Versailles accepted President Wilson's idea for an international peace-making organisation and in 1920, the League of Nations was founded. Its headquarters was at Geneva in Switzerland. The League was organised as follows:

The Assembly – It met once a year. Each member country had one vote and looked after the League's main business.

The Council – A smaller body than the Assembly, it had some permanent members such as Britain and France and some who were elected every year. It met a few times a year to deal with business when the Assembly was not meeting.

The Secretariat – A permanent body of officials was the League's 'Civil Service'.

The organisation of the League of Nations.

ASSEMBLY
(Representative of all member states)
USA never joined.
Germany was allowed to enter in 1926 but left in 1933.
Russia did not join until 1934.

COUNCIL
4 large powers
(Britain, France, Italy and Japan)
+ representatives from 9 other countries

SECRETARIAT
(Civil Service of League)

Although the League carried out important work in areas such as health and justice, it was to fail in its main aim of preventing future war. It was weakened from the outset when the most powerful nation in the world, the United States of America, failed to join. President Wilson toured America trying to persuade his fellow countrymen and women that the US should join the League. He prophesied what would happen if they did not join:

'I can predict with absolute certainty that within another generation there will be another world war.'

A meeting of the League of Nations at Geneva.

However, the American Senate voted to stay out of the League of Nations, a policy known as *Isolationism* (that is, Americans wished to remain 'isolated' or apart from European disputes).

As well as lacking American participation, the League of Nations had no armed force to put its decisions into operation. With the US refusing to take part, Great Britain began to spend less money on defence and to keep out of continental European affairs. This left France to face a bitter and resentful Germany without much international support.

The future of peace in Europe was not based on any secure foundations, despite all the promises that World War I would be 'the war to end all wars'.

What weakness of the League of Nations is highlighted in this contemporary cartoon?

TEST YOUR KNOWLEDGE

1 *What did the Treaty of Versailles contain regarding:*
   (a) The German navy?
   (b) The German airforce?
2 *Name two countries which gained former German territory in 1919.*
3 *List five new states on the map of Europe in 1919.*
4 *Did the Versailles settlement introduce complete national self-determination? Explain your answer.*
5 *List the three main parts of the League of Nations.*
6 *Give two reasons why it failed to prevent war in the future.*

Chapter 2: Review

- In January 1919, the victorious Allied leaders met at Versailles outside Paris to draw up peace treaties with Germany and the other defeated countries and to plan the shape of the post-war world.

- President Woodrow Wilson represented the United States of America. He came with a Fourteen-Point Plan which included the right of each people to choose their own government and a proposal for a League of Nations.

- France was represented by her Prime Minister, Georges Clemenceau, who wanted to impose harsh conditions on Germany to make sure that she was never in a position to invade France again.

- David Lloyd George, the Prime Minister, represented Great Britain. Like Clemenceau, he was determined to make Germany pay for the destruction caused by the war.

- In the Treaty of Versailles, Germany was made to accept responsibility for the war – War Guilt Clause; had to pay huge sums of money to the winning countries – Reparations: and lost a lot of territory including Alsace-Lorraine.

- Germany also lost its airforce and most of its army, and the navy was to be strictly limited in size. German troops were not to be allowed in the Rhineland and all German overseas colonies were lost to the Allies.

- The Austrian Empire was broken up into a number of small countries including Austria, Hungary, Czechoslovakia and Yugoslavia.

- Poland, which had been divided between Austria, Germany and Russia, became an independent country.

- The League of Nations was set up as an international organisation with its headquarters at Geneva. It did not succeed in its main aim of preventing future war.

ACTIVITIES

1 *Multiple choice*
   (a) *The Fourteen-Point Peace Plan was developed by:* (i) *Lloyd George;* (ii) *Orlando;* (iii) *Wilson;* (iv) *Clemenceau.*
   (b) *The Reparations Clause in the Treaty of Versailles concerned:* (i) *changes in borders;* (ii) *payments of compensation;* (iii) *war-guilt;* (iv) *disarmament.*
   (c) *As a guarantee that Germany would carry out its obligations under the Treaty, the Rhineland was to be occupied by Allied troops for:* (i) *fifteen years;* (ii) *twenty years;* (iii) *five years;* (iv) *ten years.*
   (d) *The powerful country which failed to join the League of Nations was:* (i) *France;* (ii) *Great Britain;* (iii) *Italy;* (iv) *the US.*

2 *Fact or opinion?*
   Which of the following statements are facts and which are opinions?
   (a) *France recovered Alsace-Lorraine in 1919.*
   (b) *The French leader, Clemenceau, argued for harsh treatment of Germany.*
   (c) *The Germans lost too much territory under the Versailles settlement.*
   (d) *The war-guilt clause was completely fair.*
   (e) *The German navy was reduced in size under the treaty.*

3 *Draw a chart on the Versailles settlement and list entries under the following headings:*
   (a) *New States established*
   (b) *Territory lost by Germany*
   (c) *Other conditions imposed on Germany.*

4 *Write out a short speech which you would make for or against the motion that 'The Versailles settlement offered a good opportunity for peace in the future'.*

CHAPTER 3

WAR AND REVOLUTION IN RUSSIA

RUSSIA AROUND 1900

A traveller to Russia in 1900 would have been struck by the many differences between that country and the rest of Europe. The huge Russian Empire contained over 150 million people. It stretched for over 6000 kilometres from Poland in the west to Asia in the east. Many different races of people lived within its borders. The great majority of the people were peasants who depended on the land for a living. Russia had been barely affected by the Industrial Revolution. The standard of living of both peasants and workers was very low.

The government of the Russian Empire was an *autocracy* – all power rested in the hands of one ruler, the *tsar*, who ruled without a parliament. Any opposition to the government was ruthlessly put down by the tsar's secret police. Several revolutionary groups were set up in Russia with the aim of overthrowing the tsar and his government. The most famous of these was the Bolshevik Party led by Vladimir Ulyanov, better known as Lenin.

Poor people gather around a street fire during a harsh Russian winter.

Lenin (1870-1924).

LENIN

Lenin was born in 1870, the son of a school inspector. From an early age he came into contact with revolutionary groups through his brother, Alexander, who was executed for his part in a plot to kill the tsar in 1887. Lenin increased his revolutionary involvement while at university and was expelled because of this. After a period of imprisonment in the 1890s, he fled to exile in Switzerland where he continued his revolutionary activities. By this stage, Lenin had become a committed Communist and was greatly influenced by the ideas of Karl Marx.

Lenin was determined to organise a workers' revolution in Russia. In the meantime, he published a newspaper, ISKRA, aimed at spreading his revolutionary ideas throughout Russia.

In 1903, the Russian Communists split over the type of party they wanted. The minority, known as the *Mensheviks*, wanted a mass party composed of all the working classes. However, the majority, known as the *Bolsheviks*, supported Lenin. They wanted a small, organised party consisting of professional revolutionaries.

Lenin and the Bolsheviks waited for the right opportunity to overthrow the tsarist government. This was to come with Russia's involvement in World War I.

TEST YOUR KNOWLEDGE
1 When was Lenin born? Who was his first revolutionary influence?
2 Whose revolutionary ideas did Lenin adopt?
3 What party did Lenin form? What was the aim of this party?
4 What newspaper did Lenin found? What was its aim?

RUSSIA AND WORLD WAR I

Russian involvement in World War I proved a costly error for the tsar and his government. From the beginning, Russian armies suffered heavy losses, due largely to bad leadership and poor equipment. Between 1914 and 1916, nearly two million Russians were killed in action while countless others were wounded. Tsar Nicholas II made a serious error in going to command the army as he was now blamed for Russia's continuing losses.

The war also had serious effects at home where food supplies were disrupted and prices soared. This state of affairs led to increasing resentment throughout the country. Matters became worse when, in the absence of the tsar, the government was in the hands of his wife the Tsarina Alexandra, and Rasputin. Rasputin was a strange Siberian monk who promoted his followers and had great influence on the government of the country. By the time Rasputin was assassinated in December 1916, the people had lost all faith in the tsar's government.

THE FEBRUARY REVOLUTION OF 1917

By early 1917, the tsar's government, greatly weakened by the war, was on the brink of total collapse. Riots took place in St Petersburg and the February Revolution began when the tsar's soldiers refused to fire on the demonstrators and joined them instead. Nicholas II was now persuaded to *abdicate* (give up his throne) and Russia became a republic.

Workers marching in Moscow during the February Revolution, 1917.

This February Revolution had been a bloodless event. It led to the establishment of a provisional government, first under Prince Lvov and then under Alexander Kerensky. This government was to last from February until October 1917.

LENIN RETURNS TO RUSSIA

Conditions in Russia continued to worsen under the provisional government. Kerensky had made a serious error of judgment by keeping Russia in the war. He had failed to understand that the war had been largely responsible for toppling the tsar's government.

Meanwhile, Lenin was watching events from abroad and awaiting an opportunity to return to Russia. Hoping that he would stir up revolution, the Germans helped him to return to Russia from Switzerland in April 1917. In an effort to gain the support of the people, Lenin, along with another leading Communist, Leon Trotsky, called for 'Peace, Bread and Land' – promising immediate peace, land for the peasants and an end to food shortages. By October 1917, Lenin's promises had won him the support of many people within Russia – the starving workers, the land-hungry peasants and the war-weary soldiers.

THE OCTOBER REVOLUTION, 1917

In October 1917, armed workers in St Petersburg stormed the government buildings, overthrowing Kerensky and his provisional government. In a matter of hours, this October Revolution had brought Lenin and the Bolsheviks to power as the government of the Union of Soviet Socialist Republics (USSR). Lenin had now achieved his life's aim. Holding on to power, however, was to prove a far more difficult task than seizing it in the first place.

A workers' council or soviet meeting in a factory in October 1917.

Revolutionaries attacking an office in St Petersburg in October 1917.

A convent being set on fire during the Russian Revolution. The Bolsheviks closed down all churches, monasteries and convents throughout Russia.

TEST YOUR KNOWLEDGE

1 What was the result of the February Revolution in Russia?
2 What error of judgment did Alexander Kerensky make?
3 What did Lenin call for on his return to Russia in April 1917?
4 What was the result of the October Revolution?

CIVIL WAR IN RUSSIA

One of Lenin's first actions on achieving power was to take Russia out of World War I. In March 1918, he signed the Peace Treaty of Brest-Litovsk with Germany. This treaty was particularly harsh on Russia, as she was forced to give up a quarter of her European territory including the Ukraine.

Many Russians were dissatisfied with this humiliating treaty while others feared the changes which the Communists would introduce. Some of those opposed to Lenin formed themselves into armies known as the 'Whites', while the Communist forces were known as the 'Reds'. From 1919 to 1921, a bitter civil war took place in Russia between these two groups. Some foreign countries such as Britain and France, who were shocked at the Communist revolution in Russia, sent armies to aid the Whites. Despite this, the Communists or Reds won the civil war for a number of reasons:

- Most people supported Lenin and the Bolsheviks.
- The Communists were very closely united, while deep divisions existed among the White Russians.
- Under Leon Trotsky, the Red Army was developed into a highly efficient fighting force.
- The Communists controlled the main industries and lines of communication.

Years of war and famine had left Russia in a weak and devastated condition. Having defeated his opponents in a civil war, Lenin was now faced with the challenge of building up a new state in Russia. By the time of Lenin's death in 1924, the Communist government was firmly established in Russia. The immediate problem now was a choice of leader to succeed Lenin.

TEST YOUR KNOWLEDGE
1 By what treaty did Russia make peace with Germany in 1918?
2 Who were the Whites? Why did they oppose the Communist regime?
3 State three reasons why the Bolsheviks won the civil war.

Chapter 3: Review

- In 1900, Russia was a vast empire containing over 150 million people. The great majority of the inhabitants were peasants who earned their living on the land.

- Total power in Russia was in the hands of one man – the emperor or tsar who ruled without the advice of an elected parliament.

- One of the main opponents of the tsar's rule was the Communist leader Lenin (1870-1924).

- Lenin was greatly influenced by the ideas of Karl Marx. From his exile in Switzerland, he ran the Bolshevik Party and waited for an opportunity to start a revolution in Russia.

- World War I helped to bring about the fall of the tsar's government which was blamed for the huge Russian losses in battle and the food shortages and soaring prices.

- While Nicholas II was away at the war, the government was in the hands of his wife, the Tsarina Alexandra, and the monk Rasputin. As a result people lost all confidence in the Russian government.

- In February 1917, a revolution broke out in Russia. The tsar was forced to abdicate and a provisional government under Kerensky took over the running of the country.

- The provisional government did not solve the country's problems. Lenin saw his opportunity and returned to Russia in April 1917. His popularity rapidly increased because he promised the people Peace, Bread and Land.

- In October 1917, Lenin and the Bolsheviks brought about a successful Communist revolution in Russia when they overthrew the provisional government.

- Lenin signed the Treaty of Brest-Litovsk with Germany in March 1918. This treaty got Russia out of the war, but on harsh German terms.

- A bitter civil war took place between the Bolsheviks known as the Reds and the Russians opposed to Lenin – the Whites – between 1919 and 1921. Countries like Britain and France sent aid to the White armies. However, the Red Army organised by Leon Trotsky proved successful in the end.

ACTIVITIES

1 Fill in the blanks with the words from the box.

| executed | school inspector | revolutionary | Karl Marx |
| ISKRA | the Bolsheviks | Switzerland | |

Lenin was born in 1870, the son of a _____. His older brother Alexander was _____ for plotting against the tsar. After a period of imprisonment, Lenin fled to _____ where he continued his _____ activities and studied the writings of _____. He published a newspaper called _____.

In 1903, the Russian Communist party split and Lenin gained control over the majority known as _____.

2 Complete the following sentences.
(a) In Russia, the all-powerful ruler was known as the _____.
(b) During World War I, Tsar Nicholas II made a serious error when he _____.
(c) Rasputin was _____.
(d) Nicholas II abdicated during _____.
(e) Alexander Kerensky's main mistake was _____.

3 Write a paragraph on the civil war in Russia between 1919 and 1921.

RUSSIA UNDER STALIN

JOSEPH STALIN

In 1879, Joseph Stalin was born into a peasant family in the southern Russian region of Georgia. At an early age he became interested in revolutionary ideas and joined Lenin's Bolshevik Party. Stalin spent most of the period between 1907 and 1917 in prison for his political activities. He played a small part in the October Revolution of 1917, but was unknown at this time.

In 1922, Stalin was appointed General Secretary of the Russian Communist Party. This was to mark the beginning of his extraordinary rise to power. Through this position he became familiar with the workings of the party and was able to build up vital contacts within it.

Lenin was deeply suspicious of Stalin's ambition. In his final testament or will, written shortly before his death, Lenin tried to warn the party against choosing Stalin as leader:

'Comrade Stalin, having become General Secretary, has concentrated an enormous power in his hands; and I am not sure that he always knows how to use that power with sufficient caution . . . Stalin is too coarse, and this fault is insupportable in the office of General Secretary. Therefore I propose to the comrades to find a way to remove Stalin from that position and to appoint to it another man who in all respects differs from Stalin – more patient, more loyal, more polite, more attentive to comrades.'

Joseph Stalin (1879-1953).

Lenin (left) was deeply suspicious of Stalin and he did not want him to be the next leader of the USSR.

This document was suppressed by Stalin and it did not become publicly known until many years later. After Lenin's death in 1924, Stalin engaged in a power struggle to succeed Lenin as leader.

Stalin's main rival and the person most favoured by Lenin was Leon Trotsky. By 1926, Stalin had outwitted his rival and in that year he had Trotsky and his wife expelled from Russia. By 1928, Stalin had become dictator of the Soviet Union.

During the following years, Stalin set about crushing all opposition to his rule. He believed in a policy called *Socialism in One Country*. All efforts should be made to make the USSR fully socialist before attempting to spread revolution throughout the world. Making the USSR fully socialist would involve drastic changes in Soviet agriculture and industry.

THE COLLECTIVISATION OF AGRICULTURE

At the time of Lenin's death, Russian agricultural methods were primitive and levels of production were low. Stalin saw that better farming methods and higher levels of production would provide more capital which could then be channelled into industrial development. Workers could also be transferred from the land to the cities where they would be employed in industry.

Stalin set about modernising Russian agriculture through a policy known as *collectivisation*: the peasants were required to join their farms together and work the land collectively as state-employees. The wealthy peasants known as *Kulaks* fiercely resisted collectivisation. Some destroyed their property and livestock rather than surrender their possessions to the state. Stalin, however, ruthlessly enforced his policy of collectivisation and put down all resistance. While some 25 million one-family farms were now replaced by 300,000 collective farms, the cost in human terms was huge. It is estimated that around five million families disappeared during the years of collectivisation.

The introduction of tractors on the collective farms greatly improved the levels of production.

Women returning from work on a collective farm.

TEST YOUR KNOWLEDGE
1 *What was collectivisation?*
2 *Why did Stalin adopt this policy?*
3 *Who were the Kulaks? How did they react to Stalin's policy of collectivisation?*

THE INDUSTRIALISATION OF RUSSIA: FIVE YEAR PLANS

The industrialisation of Russia was Stalin's greatest achievement. He transformed a backward agricultural land into a modern industrialised country by means of three *Five Year Plans*. They were designed to increase industrial production, especially in iron and steel, and they resulted in great achievements:

- New industries were set up.
- Many workers were transferred from the land to the factory.
- New power stations were constructed.
- Transport was vastly improved, with the Moscow Underground Railway being one of the greatest achievements.
- Education, especially literacy levels, was greatly improved.

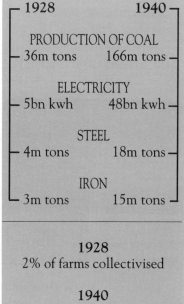

Results of Stalin's Five Year Plans in Russia

	1928	1940
PRODUCTION OF COAL	36m tons	166m tons
ELECTRICITY	5bn kwh	48bn kwh
STEEL	4m tons	18m tons
IRON	3m tons	15m tons

1928
2% of farms collectivised

1940
62% of farms collectivised

Massive hydro-electric power stations like this were built in Russia during the Five Year Plans.

Building the Moscow Underground Railway during the 1930s.

Hard work was encouraged and rewarded while lack of effort was dealt with severely. Propaganda was constantly used to encourage higher levels of production. One young miner named Alexei Stakhanov was set up as a model for other Soviet workers to imitate.

> *In August 1935, a miner, Alexei Stakhanov, pondered over his highly skilled task of operating a pneumatic drill or coalcutting machine. He had the idea that he could cut more coal if he could concentrate all his effort and attention on cutting, while the operation of removing the coal was performed by other members of the team, who were also concentrating on their own particular processes.*
>
> *The result was immediately amazing. Instead of the usual six or seven tons per shift, Stakhanov began to cut 102 tons in one shift. The idea spread to other industries.*

Forced labour was widely used in the drive to industrialise the USSR.

Within a short period of ten years, Russia had experienced dramatic industrial growth. By 1930 she was ranked among the great industrial powers of the world. Russia's industrial revolution had been achieved at tremendous cost, however. Forced labour had been widely used, overall living standards remained very low, and consumer goods were in very short supply.

TEST YOUR KNOWLEDGE
1 *How did Stalin set about industrialising Russia?*
2 *State four steps introduced under the Five Year Plans.*
3 *'Russia's Industrial Revolution had been achieved at tremendous cost.'*
   Do you agree with this statement? Explain your answer.
4 *Give an example of how propaganda was used to encourage high levels of production among workers.*

THE PURGES AND SHOW TRIALS OF THE 1930s

Stalin had shown his terrible ruthlessness in dealing with those who in any way resisted his policies of collectivisation and industrialisation. By the 1930s, he had become deeply suspicious of those around him and was determined to exterminate all possible enemies, especially anyone who had associations with Trotsky. In 1933, therefore, he began a great purge of all his enemies.

Stalin used his secret police, the Cheka (NKVD), to carry out this policy of extermination. During the 1930s, countless numbers of people were visited by the NKVD in the middle of the night. They were taken away and never seen again. Others were arrested and made to face 'show' trials where they were forced to confess to crimes which they had never committed. Leading Russian politicians, beaten up and threatened beforehand, confessed to plotting the overthrow of Stalin. They were then found guilty on the basis of their own confessions and executed.

This is one victim's account of the interrogation methods used by the secret police.

> *'The torture began . . . The five men beat viciously. They beat with fists, feet, birch rods, tightly braided towels; they beat with anything anywhere . . . The more they beat the more brutal they became . . . How long they beat me I don't know . . .*
>
> *My shirt had turned to bloody shreds. I lay on the floor in a pool of blood. My eyes were swollen. With difficulty I raised my eyelids and as if in a fog saw my torturers. They were smoking, taking a rest. Someone came up to me and just then something very painful burned my body. I was convulsed with pain. And they laughed. Then it burned again, again, again . . . I understood. They were putting out their cigarettes on my body.'*

Millions of people died in the great purges while countless others were sent to forced labour camps in Siberia. Read the following description of life in such a camp.

> *'It took twenty to thirty days to turn a healthy man into a wreck. Working in the camp mine sixteen hours a day, without any days off, with systematic starvation, ragged clothes, sleeping in a torn tent at sixty below zero, did the job. Beatings by the foremen, by the ringleaders of the thieves, by the guards, speeded up the process.*
>
> *Prisoners were taken out to work during the worst frosts. The barracks were not given enough heat, clothing would not dry out. Prisoners were given third-hand clothing, mere rags, and often had only cloth wrapping on their feet. Their torn jackets did not protect them from the bitter frost, and people froze in droves.'*

By the time the purges eased in 1938, nearly half the officers in the Red Army had been killed on the orders of Stalin.

Chapter 4: Review

- After Lenin died in Russia in 1924, a leadership struggle took place between Leon Trotsky and Joseph Stalin. Stalin won this struggle and by 1928 he was the undisputed ruler of the Soviet Union.

- Stalin believed that all efforts should be made to make Russia fully Communist before attempting to spread revolution throughout the world. This policy was known as Socialism in One Country.

- Stalin set about bringing all farms under state control. This was known as collectivisation and led to fierce resistance from the larger Russian peasants known as Kulaks.

- In a series of Five Year Plans, Stalin set about changing the Soviet Union from a backward agricultural country into a modern industrial one.

- Although by 1939 the Soviet Union ranked among the great industrial powers of the world, this was achieved at great human cost – forced labour had been widely used.

- During the 1930s, Stalin eliminated all opposition in the great purges and show trials which resulted in the death or imprisonment of millions of people.

ACTIVITIES

1 *True or False?*
State whether each of the following sentences are true or false.
(a) Joseph Stalin was born in the Ukraine in 1879.
(b) In 1922, Stalin was appointed Secretary General of the Russian Communist Party.
(c) In 1926, Stalin had Trotsky and his wife placed in prison.
(d) Stalin set about modernising Russian agriculture with a policy known as collectivisation.
(e) He was opposed by Kulaks who were poor peasants on small farms.

2 *Complete the following sentences.*
(a) Stalin believed in a policy known as 'Socialism _____.
(b) During the Five Year Plans, Stalin transformed a backward agricultural land into _____.
(c) To carry out the extermination of his enemies, Stalin made use of _____.
(d) 'Show trials' were _____ .
(e) The purges of the 1930s damaged the Red Army by _____.

3 *Stalin defended his modernisation policy in the following speech. Read it and answer the questions which follow.*

> *'We must increase the speed as much as it is within our powers and possibilities. This is dictated to us by our obligations to the working class of the world. To slacken the speed would mean to fall behind and those who fall behind get beaten. No, we refuse to be beaten. One feature of the history of the old Russia was the continual beatings she suffered because of her backwardness . . .*
> *Such is the law of the exploiters – to beat the backward and the weak. It is the jungle law of capitalism. That is why we must no longer lag behind.*
> *We are fifty or a hundred years behind the advanced countries. We must make good this distance in ten years. Either we do it or we shall be crushed. This is what our obligations to the workers and peasants of the USSR dictate to us.'*

(a) What argument does Stalin use to justify increasing speed of production?
(b) How do you think he viewed the condition of Russia before the revolution?
(c) What view did Stalin have concerning capitalism?
(d) What time scale does he set for the modernisation of Russia?
(e) Pick one example of propaganda from this extract.

BENITO MUSSOLINI AND THE RISE OF FASCISM

THE FASCIST DICTATORS

In the 1920s and 1930s, a new form of government emerged in some important European countries. Existing democratic governments were replaced by dictatorships. In a democracy, a government is elected by the people, controlled by a parliament and can be replaced in a general election. In a dictatorship, however, one man rules without the control of parliament and cannot easily be removed from power.

The three principal dictators in Western Europe between the two World Wars were Mussolini in Italy, Hitler in Germany and Franco in Spain. These dictatorships had a number of characteristics in common:

- The dictators outlawed all opposition to their rule, exercising complete control over the lives of the people. This system was known as *totalitarianism*.
- Everything centred on the personality of the dictator himself who demanded the full loyalty and obedience of every citizen. The army and the police were used to enforce this loyalty.
- The dictators were extremely nationalistic: they encouraged all citizens to love their country without question.
- The dictators were strongly anti-Communist and were determined to rid their countries of any Communist influences.

There were a number of reasons why dictators came to power in Europe in these years:

- In a time of economic depression with high unemployment, people lost faith in their existing democratic governments and turned to the dictators in despair.
- Many people feared the spread of Communism and looked to the dictators to prevent this from happening.
- After World War I, many countries, especially Italy and Germany, felt that they had been wronged by the Versailles settlement. The dictators exploited this resentment and promised a return to national greatness.

TEST YOUR KNOWLEDGE
1 *What new form of government emerged in some European countries between the two World Wars?*
2 *What do you understand by the terms: (a) democracy, (b) dictatorship and (c) totalitarianism?*
3 *Name the three most important dictators in Western Europe and the countries they ruled.*
4 *State any three features which the dictators had in common.*
5 *Why did so many people support dictators between the wars?*

THE LIFE AND TIMES OF MUSSOLINI
THE EARLY YEARS

Benito Mussolini was born in northern Italy in 1883, the son of a blacksmith and a schoolmistress. He started his career as a teacher but soon turned to journalism. He showed an early interest in politics and became a socialist. Mussolini later turned away from socialism and in 1915 he joined the Italian army to fight in World War I. He was wounded in 1917 and returned to his work as a journalist.

Along with most Italians, Mussolini believed that Italy had been badly treated at the Versailles Peace Conference. Italy had hoped to gain more territory at Austria's expense, but was bitterly disappointed.

In addition, Italy suffered a severe economic depression after the war. Prices soared, unemployment increased, and strikes and street disturbances were widespread. Weak Italian governments were unable to cope with this crisis. Mussolini saw the need for a new political movement to deal with this situation.

On 23 March 1919 he founded the Fascist Party – *Fascio di Combattimento* – in Milan. This party stood for the following:

- Strong, decisive leadership under the party leader.
- Law and order – the movement got its name from the *fasces*, a bundle of rods carried before a governor in ancient Rome as a symbol of authority.
- A belief in Italy's greatness and the need to build up her armed strength.
- Mussolini's party was deeply anti-Communist and brought itself into the public view by clashing with Communist strikers.

Mussolini addressing a meeting of his followers.

34

MUSSOLINI'S PATH TO POWER

Between 1919 and 1922, Mussolini and the Fascists went from strength to strength. Mussolini organised a series of meetings and demonstrations throughout Italy. At these he was surrounded by his armed followers who were known as *Blackshirts* due to the colour of their uniform. These Blackshirts fought in the streets with the Communists and other opponents. Mussolini claimed that Communists were not loyal Italians but followers of Russian Communist rulers. Industrialists and businessmen supported Mussolini's party because they came to see it as the only means of preventing a Communist takeover.

In October 1922, the Fascists took part in the famous *March on Rome* in an effort to seize power. Their plans succeeded when King Victor Emmanuel invited Mussolini to form a government. Mussolini organised a huge victory celebration in Rome on 31 October 1922 in which some 25,000 Blackshirts marched.

Mussolini leading the Fascist March on Rome in October 1922.

TEST YOUR KNOWLEDGE
1 *Where and when was Mussolini born?*
2 *Give two reasons why Mussolini saw the need for a new political party in Italy in the years after World War I.*
3 *What new party did Mussolini found? State two beliefs which it had.*
4 *Who were the Blackshirts? Why were they so named?*
5 *Why did many industrialists and businessmen come to support Mussolini's party?*
6 *What was the 'March on Rome' and what was its result?*

MUSSOLINI: THE YEARS OF POWER

Once Mussolini was safely in power, he set about creating a Fascist dictatorship in Italy. He gradually eliminated all opposition to his rule. The Socialist leader, Matteotti, was murdered by Fascist Blackshirts in 1924. In the following year, all political parties, except the Fascist Party, were banned.

By then Italy had become a *police state* – Mussolini's police and Fascist followers dealt violently with any opponents of the government. The Italian parliament no longer had any power in running the country. Free trade unions were abolished and strikes outlawed. Italy had become a one-party state ruled by a dictator.

In the early years of his rule, Mussolini had the support of most Italians. Propaganda played a large part in his popularity. He became known as *Il Duce*, the leader who could do not wrong. His portrait was displayed in all public places. Fascist slogans were seen everywhere and schoolchildren were instructed to admire and be loyal to Il Duce.

Activity
Identify examples of Fascist propaganda in the following pictures.

A Fascist demonstration in Milan.

The triumphant arrival of Mussolini in Turin.

Fascist women
march past
Mussolini.

While Mussolini had set up a totalitarian state in which the government had full control, he had a number of important achievements to his credit:

- Unemployment was greatly reduced.
- A huge programme of public works was implemented by the government: new motorways were built; railways were electrified and wasteland reclaimed (the most famous project was the draining of the Pontine Marshes near Rome).
- Food production, especially wheat, was greatly increased.
- In 1929 an agreement or concordat called the *Lateran Pact* was signed between Mussolini and the pope. The independent Vatican City State was set up in Rome with the pope as its ruler. This finally brought an end to many years of disagreement between the pope and the Italian government.

Mussolini dressed as a peasant takes part in a festival to celebrate the harvesting of wheat in the reclaimed land of the Pontine Marshes. In what way is this another example of Fascist propaganda?

A meeting between
Pope Pius XI and
Mussolini.

THE BUILDING OF AN EMPIRE

Building up an overseas empire for Italy was one of Mussolini's deepest ambitions. He was determined to expand and equip the Italian armed forces so that they could rival the best in the world. One of his first priorities was to gain revenge for the defeat of an Italian army by Abyssinia (Ethiopia) back in 1896. As leader of Italy, he still had vivid memories of that defeat:

> 'That day I was ill. At about ten o'clock one of my school friends ran into the dormitory with an open newspaper shouting "Read! Read!". I grabbed the newspaper. From the first page to the last it talked of nothing but the disastrous battle – ten thousand dead and 72 cannons lost. Those figures are still hammering in my skull.'

In October 1935, Mussolini realised his life's ambition when Italian forces invaded Abyssinia. Although that country's ruler, Emperor Haile Selassie, appealed to the League of Nations for help, no decisive action was taken against Italy.

The Abyssinians resisted the Italian invasion, but they were no match for Mussolini's forces who used modern methods of warfare, including bombing and poison gas.

By this time, a new Fascist dictator had emerged in Germany – Adolf Hitler. Over the next few years, Mussolini and Hitler were to become close allies.

TEST YOUR KNOWLEDGE
1 *Outline three steps taken by Mussolini to make Italy a dictatorship.*
2 *How did Mussolini use propaganda to increase his popularity?*
3 *By what name did Mussolini become known?*
4 *What forms of public work did Mussolini implement?*
5 *What was the Lateran Pact?*
6 *State one of Mussolini's deepest ambitions.*
7 *Why did Italian forces invade Abyssinia in 1935?*

Chapter 5: Review

- In Western Europe during the 1920s and 1930s, democracy was replaced by dictatorships in a number of countries. Under a dictatorship, all opposition was outlawed and the state exercised complete control over people's lives.

- The three main dictators in Western Europe in these years were Adolf Hitler, Germany; Benito Mussolini, Italy; and Francisco Franco, Spain.

- These dictators were all strongly anti-Communist. They were also extremely nationalist – that is, they encouraged their citizens to live and die for their country without question. They were also Fascist – a word which originated in Italy and came to mean a government which allowed no opposition to its rule.

- Bad economic conditions and the threat of Communism were used by the dictators as a means of gaining power.

- In 1919, Mussolini founded the Fascist Party in Milan. This stood for strong, decisive government and Italy's return to greatness. Mussolini was surrounded by a group of armed followers known as Blackshirts.

- Following a threat of a march on Rome, Mussolini came to power in 1922. He quickly set about creating a Fascist dictatorship in Italy. Before long, Italy had become a one-party police state ruled by a dictator. Propaganda played a large part in accounting for Mussolini's early popularity.

- One of Mussolini's deepest ambitions was to build up an overseas empire for Italy. In 1935 Italian forces invaded Abyssinia in revenge for Italy's defeat by that country in 1896.

ACTIVITIES

1 *Mutiple Choice*
   (a) *Benito Mussolini was born in northern Italy in: (i) 1883; (ii) 1873; (iii) 1893; (iv) 1903.*
   (b) *In March 1919 he founded the Fascist Party at: (i) Genoa; (ii) Rome; (iii) Milan; (iv) Naples.*
   (c) *The main enemies of Mussolini's Fascist Party were: (i) the employers; (ii) the Catholic Church; (iii) the Austrians; (iv) the Communists.*
   (d) *Armed bands of Italian Fascists were known as: (i) Blackshirts; (ii) Brownshirts; (iii) Blueshirts; (iv) Redshirts.*
   (e) *In October 1922, Mussolini was invited to form a government in Italy by: (i) King Umberto; (ii) King Victor Emmanuel; (iii) Pope Pius XI; (vi) King Alfonso XIII.*

2 *Complete the following sentences.*
   (a) *Mussolini condemned the Versailles Peace Conference (1919) because _____.*
   (b) *The March on Rome (1922) was _____.*
   (c) *In 1924, Fascist Blackshirts murdered the Italian Socialist leader _____.*
   (d) *Mussolini became popularly known as _____.*
   (e) *The Lateran Pact (1929) was _____.*

3 *List some of the changes which the Fascist government brought about in Italy after 1922.*

4 *Write out a short speech which you would make in favour of the idea that Mussolini's form of Fascism contained some strong nationalistic beliefs.*

GERMANY UNDER HITLER

THE WEIMAR REPUBLIC: 1919-33

In 1919, Germany's leading politicians met in the town of Weimar to decide how their country should be governed. They drew up a new constitution which provided for the establishment of a democratic republic. This form of government, known as the *Weimar Republic,* was to rule Germany until 1933. Its *Reichstag* or parliament was elected by the people. The head of the government was known as the *chancellor*. There was also a head of state elected by the people and known as the *president*.

The new government faced a number of serious problems in the years ahead:

- Some Germans blamed the politicians of the Weimar Republic for accepting the humiliating Treaty of Versailles.
- The German economy was in a state of depression after the war. Unemployment was very high, prices continued to rise and vast reparation payments crippled the economy. The worst year was 1923, when inflation reached huge levels and money became almost worthless.

For the most part, Weimar politicians were weak and indecisive and failed to face the country's problems. However, one politician, Gustave Stresemann, emerged head and shoulders above the others. Under his direction, the German economy began to recover with the aid of American loans.

Stresemann died in 1929 at a time when his country needed him most. The coming of the Great Depression in 1929 threw the German economy into another decline. American loans were withdrawn and the German people once again faced soaring inflation and unemployment. They now lost all faith in the Weimar Republic and turned increasingly towards more extreme groups which were offering them a way out of the Depression.

One such group was the Nazi Party. Its leader was Adolf Hitler.

TEST YOUR KNOWLEDGE
1 *What type of government was set up in Germany in 1919?*
2 *Why was this government known as the Weimar Republic?*
3 *State two problems facing German politicians in the 1920s.*
4 *Who was the most able politician in Weimar Germany? What contribution did he make to his country?*
5 *Why did the fortunes of the German economy experience a new drop in 1929?*

ADOLF HITLER: THE EARLY YEARS

Adolf Hitler was born in Austria on 20 April 1889, the son of a customs officer. Both his parents died while he was still at school. After leaving school Hitler applied for a place in the academy of art in Vienna. Although he was not accepted in the art school, he still went to live in Vienna. While there, Hitler became interested in politics and for many years lived the life of a 'down-and-out' in Vienna. It was here that he developed much of his hatred of the Jews, whose wealth he resented.

**Adolf Hitler
(1889-1945)**

When World War I broke out, Hitler joined the German army and fought for four years on the Western Front where he was decorated three times for bravery. After the war, he was employed as a government spy in Munich with the task of keeping an eye on revolutionary groups. It was here that he came in contact with a small group known as the *National Socialist German Workers Party (Nazi party)*. Hitler joined this group and quickly became its leader. In 1923 he organised a rebellion against the government in Munich. This failed and he was imprisoned for over a year as a result.

HITLER'S POLITICAL IDEAS

While in prison, in 1924, Hitler wrote his famous book called *Mein Kampf (My Struggle)*. In this book he set out his main ideas for the future of Germany:

- Hatred of the Jews – Hitler blamed the Jews for all of Germany's problems, especially its defeat in World War I.
- Hatred of Communism – He was determined to rid Germany and the world of Communism which he saw as a great threat.
- The Master Race – Hitler believed that the Germans were the Master Race, or Aryans, who were destined to rule the world. He wanted Germany to expand eastwards and use the local people as slaves.
- A belief in Germany's greatness – Hitler was determined that Germany should become a great power again and that the Versailles Treaty should be wrecked.
- All Germans should be reunited under one single leader.

TEST YOUR KNOWLEDGE

1 When and where was Hitler born?

2 What ideas did Hitler develop while in Vienna?

3 How did Hitler come to join the Nazi Party? What was the full name of that party?

4 Why was Hitler imprisoned in 1923?

5 What famous book did Hitler write in 1924?

6 Write down three ideas outlined by him in that book.

A Nazi demon-stration 1924.

HITLER'S PATH TO POWER

Between 1924 and 1929, Hitler and the Nazi party were almost unknown in Germany. Owing to economic improvements at home, these were good years for most Germans. Hitler's great opportunity came, however, when severe economic depression hit Germany after the Wall Street Crash in America in 1929. Massive unemployment and soaring prices led to a crisis in Germany. The existing democratic government was unable to deal with these serious problems. More and more, Germans turned in desperation to the Communists or the Nazis to find an answer to their problems.

GERMAN ELECTIONS 1928-32	
1928 Nazis win 12 seats	**1932 (July)** Nazis win 230 seats
1930 Nazis win 107 seats	**1932 (November)** Nazis win 196 seats

Hitler played especially on people's fears and promised a way out of the crisis. He was a powerful public speaker who was able to stir the emotions of an audience. This is one Nazi's recollection of the power of Hitler's oratory.

'I don't know how to describe the emotions that swept over me as I heard Adolf Hitler. His words were like a scourge. When he spoke of the disgrace of Germany, I felt ready to spring on any enemy. His appeal to German manhood was like a call to arms; the gospel he preached, a sacred truth. I forgot everything but the man. Then, glancing around, I saw that his magnetism was holding these thousands as one. The intense will of the man, the passion of his sincerity, seemed to flow from him into me. I experienced an exultation that could be likened only to religious conversion.'

Like Mussolini, Hitler used propaganda in the form of massive rallies and cinema newsreels to gain more support. He was surrounded by groups of armed followers or storm troopers known as the SA and the SS. These groups terrorised all opposition, especially Communists and Jews.

Hitler addressing a Nazi rally at Nuremberg.

Joseph Goebbels as minister of propaganda organised many of the Nazi rallies. He is seen here in a group of Hitler's supporters.

Many industrialists and businessmen supported Hitler because of his opposition to Communism. In total despair, many Germans now came to see Hitler as their only hope. In the election of July 1932, the Nazi party won more seats than any other party. Six months later, Hitler was invited by President Hindenburg to form a government. The 'down-and-out' of Vienna had now become the Chancellor of Germany.

Hitler with President Hindenburg.

TEST YOUR KNOWLEDGE
1 *Why were the Nazis almost unknown in Germany between 1924 and 1929?*
2 *Why did Hitler's fortunes begin to turn after 1929?*
3 *What methods did Hitler use to increase his support?*
4 *Why did many industrialists and businessmen come to support Hitler?*
5 *Why was the election in July 1932 so important for Hitler?*

A victory march of Hitler's brown-shirted supporters after he became chancellor.

Members of the Nazi Youth Movement, organised by Hitler throughout Germany.

HITLER IN POWER

Once in power, Hitler was determined to set up a dictatorship in Germany. His first opportunity came when the Reichstag building was burned to the ground on 27 February 1933. Hitler blamed the Communist party for this act and accused them of plotting against the state. As a result, some 4000 Communist party officials were arrested.

In March 1933, Hitler forced parliament to pass the *Enabling* Act. This allowed him to rule without the aid of parliament for a period of four years. He was now firmly on the road towards becoming a dictator. All other political parties were soon banned. By the summer of 1933, the Nazi party was the only legal political organisation in Germany. Newspapers, radio and cinema were strictly censored and forced to present Nazi views.

Hitler's position was further strengthened when President Hindenburg died on 2 August 1934. Hitler now became both president and chancellor of Germany. From then on, Hitler was known as *Der Führer* (the leader) and his motto became *Ein Reich, Ein Volk, Ein Führer* – One Empire, One People, One Leader. He called his government the *Third Reich*, or the Third Empire, which, he boasted, would last a thousand years.

Young people were instructed to be loyal to the German state and the Führer from an early age. A *Hitler Youth Movement* was organised for this purpose. The following order, which was issued by the Ministry of the Interior, stated the purpose of education in the Third Reich.

'The principal task of the school is the education of youth in the service of manhood and the state in the National Socialist spirit. At the beginning of every lesson, the teacher goes to the front of the class, which is standing, and greets it by raising his right arm, with the words "Heil Hitler"; the class returns the salute.'

Hitler set up a police state in Germany with his infamous secret police – *the Gestapo* – dealing ruthlessly with all opposition. During the 1930s, concentration camps were opened to deal with enemies of his rule, especially Communists and Jews. The Jews were to suffer most at the hands of the Nazi state.

THE JEWS

What does this picture tell you about the treatment of Jews in Nazi Germany?

In November 1935, the *Nuremberg Laws* were passed. These deprived Jews of all citizenship rights, forbade a Jew to marry a German, and forced all Jews to wear a special badge (the Star of David) to identify themselves. As a result of these laws, many Jews such as the famous scientist, Albert Einstein, fled from Germany.

Jews, fleeing from Germany on board a train, are caught trying to take their valuables with them.

Worse, however, was yet to come. In Berlin on 9-10 November 1938, Jewish property was attacked and burned. This incident, which caused the massive destruction of shops and synagogues, became known as 'the Night of the Broken Glass' (*Kristallnacht*).

The following eye-witness account tells about this dreadful night.

'*Jewish buildings were smashed into and the contents demolished or looted. In one of the Jewish sections, an eighteen-year-old boy was hurled from a third storey window to land with both legs broken. Jewish shop windows by the hundred were smashed throughout the entire city. Three synagogues were fired by incendiary bombs. Having demolished dwellings and burned most of the moveable effects on the streets, they threw many of the trembling inmates into a small stream, commanding horrified spectators to spit at them, defile them with mud, and jeer at their plight. There is much evidence of physical violence, including several deaths.*'

In the years ahead, Hitler was to put his plan for the total elimination of the Jews into operation. It was known as *the Final Solution*.

The destruction caused to a Jewish shop in Berlin on the 'Night of the Broken Glass'. Describe the reaction of the onlookers.

TEST YOUR KNOWLEDGE
1 *What was the Enabling Act?*
2 *What name did Hitler adopt? What was his motto? What do you understand by this motto?*
3 *Who were the Gestapo?*
4 *How did Hitler deal with enemies of his rule?*
5 *What were the Nuremberg Laws?*

Chapter 6: Review

- Between 1919 and 1923, Germany was ruled by the Weimar Republic, a democratic form of government. The greatest statesman of these years was Gustave Stresemann who helped Germany to recover after the defeat of World War I.

- However, the economic depression which hit Germany in 1929 helped Adolf Hitler and the Nazi party come to power in January 1933.

- Hitler's main beliefs included a commitment to Germany's greatness, a hatred of Jews and Communists, and the idea that the Germans were a Master Race, superior to other peoples.

- Hitler was a powerful speaker who was able to stir the emotions of an audience. Like Mussolini, he used propaganda in the form of massive rallies and cinema newsreels to gain support.

- Once in power, Hitler banned all other political parties as well as trade unions. When President Hindenburg died in August 1934, he took over that office and became known as Der Führer (the leader). Under the 1935 Nuremberg Laws, Jews were deprived of their civil rights.

46

ACTIVITIES

1 *Fill in the blanks using words in the box*

art	hatred of Jews	Vienna	Austria
Corporal		Western Front	Munich

Hitler was born in _____ in 1889. As a young man he went to live in _____ in order to study _____. While there he developed a _____. During World War I, he fought bravely on the _____ and rose to the rank of _____. In 1923, he organised an unsuccessful rebellion against the German government in _____.

2 *Fact or opinion?*
Which of the following are statements of fact and which are opinions?
(a) While in prison, in 1924 Hitler wrote his famous book, Mein Kampf.
(b) The German army was betrayed by civilians at the end of World War I.
(c) Communists burned down the German parliament buildings in 1933.
(d) By the summer of 1933, the Nazi party was the only legal political group in Germany.
(e) While he was building up a totalitarian state, Hitler improved the standard of living for most Germans.

3 *Imagine that you were a Jew growing up in Germany during the 1930s. Write out three short entries which you would have made in your diary on different occasions.*

4 *In 1934, a young English author, Patrick Leigh Fermor, went on a walking tour through Germany. Read his account of a Nazi rally in a small town and answer the questions which follow.*

> *'The town was hung with National Socialist flags and the window of an outfitter's shop next door held a display of party equipment: swastika arm-bands, daggers for the Hitler Youth, blouses for the Hitler Maidens and brown shirts for the grown-up SA men; swastika buttonholes were arranged in a pattern which read* **Heil Hitler** *...*
>
> *The crunch of measured footfalls and the rhythm of a marching song sounded in a side street. Led by a standard bearer, a column of the SA marched into the square ... It was dark now and the snowflakes began falling across the lamplight. The SA men wore breeches and boots and stiff brown ski-caps. Their shirts, with a red arm band on the left sleeve, looked like brown paper but as they listened to an address by their commander they had a menacing and purposeful look ... When his speech had died away, the speaker clapped his left hand to his belt buckle, his right arm shot out, and a forest of arms answered him in concert with a three-fold "Heil!" to his clipped introductory "Sieg!"'*
>
> *from Patrick Leigh Fermor,* **A Time of Gifts**

(a) List some of the Nazi emblems on sale in the town.
(b) How did the writer first become aware that a rally was about to begin?
(c) Describe the appearance of the SA men.
(d) How did the rally end?
(e) Do you think that this is a biased or an unbiased account? Why?

CIVIL WAR IN SPAIN

THE PATH TO WAR

Between 1936 and 1939, a fierce civil war took place in Spain. In 1931, the king of Spain had been overthrown and a republic was set up. For the next five years, the Republican government tried to bring in reforms to improve the lot of the poorer people.

- In towns and cities, workers' conditions were improved.
- In the country, attempts were made to divide large estates among the peasants.

Many of those supporting the Spanish Republic were Communists or Socialists who wanted to introduce sweeping changes to Spain. They wished to take land from the rich landowners and place it under the control of the peasants. They wanted workers to control the factories. And above all, they wished to reduce the power and influence of the Catholic Church. These groups joined together to form the *Popular Front* and won an election in February 1936.

The success of this group greatly alarmed the old ruling class made up of rich landowners, businessmen, army officers and Church leaders. These people now looked to the Spanish Fascist Party (Falange) for protection. In July 1936, General Francisco Franco, leader of the Fascists, led a revolt in Spanish Morocco against Spain's Republican government. This revolt soon spread to Spain itself – the Spanish Civil War had begun.

General Francisco Franco.

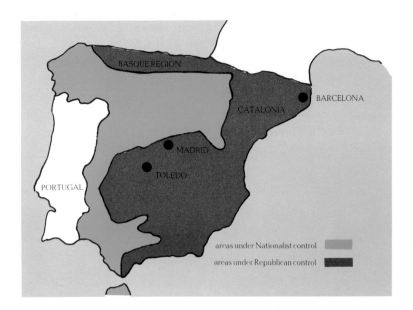

Spain was deeply divided between Nationalist and Republican areas during the Civil War, 1936-39.

THE WAR RAGES

Many army garrisons in Spain supported Franco – his followers became known as the *Nationalists*. Franco's opponents, the *Republicans* – mostly Communists and Socialists – had their strongest support in the province of Catalonia where industrial workers were most numerous.

The war was fought with great cruelty on both sides. The Republican forces were strongly opposed to the Church's influence in Spain. They murdered many priests and nuns and burned churches. The Nationalists conducted ruthless mass killings of their captured opponents.

Fighting in a village in Catalonia during the Spanish Civil War.

A Catholic priest being crucified by Republicans during the war.

Hitler and Mussolini sent arms and soldiers to their fellow-Fascist, General Franco. From Soviet Russia, Stalin sent aid to the Republicans. An International Brigade was organised in which men from all over the world (including Ireland) went to Spain to fight for the Republicans in an effort to defeat Franco and Fascism. But many others, strongly opposed to Communism, supported Franco. Ireland's Eoin O'Duffy and some of his followers went to Spain to fight for Franco.

Republicans marching in Madrid in July 1936. Notice the women carrying guns.

Members of the International Brigade setting off from Madrid to go to the battlefront to fight for the Republic.

THE BOMBING OF GUERNICA

One of the most horrific incidents of the war was the German bombing of the town of Guernica on 26 April 1937. The following account, written by a local priest, gives us a vivid report of that terrible event.

'Late in the afternoon of 26 April I was going by car to rescue my mother and my sister. We reached the outskirts of Guernica just before six o'clock. The streets were busy with the traffic of market day. Suddenly we heard the siren and trembled.

Soon, an aeroplane appeared over Guernica, followed by a squadron of seven planes, followed a little later by six more, and this in turn by a squadron of five more. All of them were Junkers (German aircraft). Meanwhile, Guernica was seized by a terrible panic. For more than an hour these eighteen planes dropped bomb after bomb on Guernica. The sound of the explosions and of the crumbling houses cannot be imagined. Bombs fell by thousands. Later we saw the bomb craters. Some were sixteen metres in diameter and eight metres deep.

The aeroplanes left around seven o'clock and then there came another wave of them, this time flying at immense altitude. They were dropping incendiary (fire) bombs on our martyred city. The new bombardment lasted thirty-five minutes, sufficient to transform the town into an enormous furnace. Even then I realised the terrible purpose of this new act of vandalism. They were dropping incendiary bombs to try to convince the world that the Basques had fired their own city.

When it grew dark, the flames of Guernica were reaching the sky, and the clouds took on the colour of blood, and our faces too shone with the colour of blood.'

What view of Guernica is conveyed in Picasso's famous painting?

THE WAR ENDS

In the spring of 1939, Franco's Nationalist army was finally victorious. Its soldiers had been better trained and it had received more foreign aid than the Republicans. Furthermore, while the Nationalist side was totally united under Franco, there had been deep divisions in the Spanish Republic between various political parties.

Franco's troops fighting for control of Madrid at the end of the Civil War.

Once in power, Franco set up a Fascist dictatorship, outlawing all political parties except his own. Free trade unions were banned and a strict censorship was imposed on the press and the radio. Under the Republic, regions like the Basque country and Catalonia were given a certain amount of freedom. Franco, however, ruled all of Spain centrally from Madrid.

1 *Who were the Republicans?*

2 *What groups of people were against the Republic?*

3 *By what name was the Spanish Fascist Party known? Who was its leader?*

4 *Name the two sides in the Spanish Civil War.*

5 *What part did Mussolini, Hitler and Stalin play in the Spanish Civil War?*

6 *Why did many people go to Spain to fight for: (a) the Republicans; (b) the Nationalists?*

7 *Give three reasons why Franco won the Civil War.*

8 *How did Franco go about setting up a dictatorship in Spain?*

9 *What do you think Franco's Spain had in common with Mussolini's Italy and Hitler's Germany?*

Chapter 7: Review

- In Spain, a fierce civil war took place from 1936 until 1939 between supporters of the Republican government and the Nationalist forces under General Francisco Franco. The Republic was largely supported by Communists and Socialists, while Franco had the backing of rich landowners and the Catholic Church.

- There was much international involvement in the Spanish Civil War. Hitler and Mussolini sent arms and soldiers to help their fellow Fascist, Franco. From Soviet Russia, Stalin sent aid to the Republicans.

- The war ended in the spring of 1939 when Franco's forces were finally victorious. His soldiers had been better trained and the Nationalist side had received more aid than the Republicans.

- Once in power, Franco set up a Fascist dictatorship in Spain, outlawing all political parties except his own.

ACTIVITIES

1 *Match an item in Column 1 with an item in Column 2*

COLUMN 1	COLUMN 2
A Basque town	The Falange
Franco's party	Italy
An ally of the Republic	Guernica
A strongly Republican province	The Soviet Union
An ally of Franco	Catalonia

2 *Write a paragraph on the causes of the Spanish Civil War.*

3 *Draw a map of Spain and colour in the following:*
(a) Republican towns and areas;
(b) Nationalist towns and areas.

CHAPTER 8

THE STEPS TOWARDS WAR

HITLER'S FOREIGN POLICY

Hitler's foreign policy had four main aims:

- To make Germany a great power again
- To gain revenge for the humiliation of the Versailles settlement
- To unite all German-speaking peoples under one leader
- To expand eastwards and enslave the Jews and the Communists

HITLER DISMANTLES THE TREATY OF VERSAILLES

In the 1930s, Hitler set about making Germany a strong nation again. He particularly wanted to reverse the humiliating aspects of the Treaty of Versailles. Although the treaty had set strict limits on the size of Germany's army and navy, Hitler ignored it. He introduced *conscription* in 1935 and Germany soon had an army far greater than the 100,000 soldiers permitted under the Treaty of Versailles. Hitler also built up the German navy and the airforce (the *Luftwaffe*).

In 1933, Hitler took Germany out of the League of Nations. When Mussolini invaded Abyssinia, Hitler formed an alliance with him known as the *Rome-Berlin Axis* (1936). Around the same time, Germany also formed an alliance with Japan. Relations between Germany, Italy and Japan were now firmly established in the form of the *Rome-Berlin-Tokyo Axis*.

Hermann Goering became head of the German airforce, the *Luftwaffe*.

A newspaper illustration showing Mussolini's visit to Hitler after the formation of the Rome-Berlin Axis.

Celebrations in Tokyo following the alliance between Germany, Italy and Japan.

German troops, although forbidden to do so by the Treaty of Versailles, enter the Rhineland in March 1936. What is the reaction of the local people?

THE RHINELAND IS REOCCUPIED

Under the Treaty of Versailles, Germany was forbidden to station soldiers in the Rhineland zone. Hitler defied this and sent troops into the zone in March 1936. The French were both angered and frightened by this move. The British, on the other hand, were not prepared to take action because they regarded the Treaty of Versailles as being too harsh on Germany. As a result of Hitler's move into the Rhineland, the French built a line of forts along their border with Germany – the *Maginot Line*. The Germans, in turn, built the *Siegfried Line* of defensive forts along their side of the border. Meanwhile, Hitler's successful reoccupation of the Rhineland encouraged him to expand further.

TEST YOUR KNOWLEDGE
1 State three steps taken by Hitler to dismantle the Treaty of Versailles.
2 How did the French and British react to Hitler's invasion of the Rhineland?
3 What were: (a) the Maginot Line; (b) the Siegfried Line?

- By 1935 Hitler had increased the size of the German army and had built up the navy and airforce.
- Hitler enters the Rhineland (1936)
- Hitler annexes Austria (The Anschluss) (March 1938)
- Hitler takes over the Sudetenland area of Czechoslovakia (September 1938)
- Hitler takes over all of Czechoslovakia (March 1939)
- Hitler invades Poland (1 September 1939)

The expansion of Germany under Hitler

GERMANY ANNEXES AUSTRIA

It was now clear to Hitler that the League of Nations could do nothing to prevent German expansion. The League had already failed to take action when Italy invaded Abyssinia and when Japan invaded part of China. This encouraged Hitler to make his next move: the takeover of Austria, the land of his birth.

Hitler believed that all German-speaking people should be united under one leader. Many Austrians also desired union with Germany. This policy was known as the *Anschluss*. There was a powerful Nazi party in Austria and Hitler put pressure on the Austrian government to give important positions to members of that party. Finally, in March 1938, Hitler invaded Austria, having first secured Mussolini's agreement.

Britain and France did not interfere, although the Anschluss was forbidden by the Treaty of Versailles. Hitler made a triumphant visit to Austria and announced that the county would become a part of the Third Reich.

The man who had once been a down-and-out artist in Vienna had now returned as the city's victorious ruler.

Nazi troops marching in Vienna after the German annexation of Austria in March 1938.

TEST YOUR KNOWLEDGE
1 *What was meant by Anschluss?*
2 *When did Hitler annex Austria?*
3 *What was Britain's reaction to this move?*

THE MUNICH CONFERENCE AND THE GERMAN INVASION OF CZECHOSLOVAKIA

In the autumn of 1938, Hitler made his next move. He turned his attention to the German-speaking section of Czechoslovakia, the Sudetenland, where over three million Germans lived. The leader of Czechoslovakia, Eduard Benes, appealed to the other European powers for help and in September 1938 a conference was held at Munich to discuss the issues involved. Hitler, Mussolini, Deladier, the French leader, and Chamberlain, the British Prime Minister, were the main participants.

At this conference, Chamberlain continued Britain's policy of *appeasement* – he believed that by agreeing to German demands, Hitler would be satisfied and war in Europe would be prevented.

Appeasement was popular in Britain because many people felt that the Treaty of Versailles had been too harsh on Germany. Many people in Britain also dreaded a return to the trench warfare experienced in World War I, with its huge cost in numbers of dead and wounded. Britain and France therefore agreed at Munich that Hitler should take over the Sudetenland in return for a promise that he would make no further demands.

Hitler and Chamberlain at the Munich Conference in September 1938.

Neville Chamberlain showing his written agreement with Hitler on his return home from the Munich Conference.

WORKING WITH EVIDENCE: TWO VIEWS OF MUNICH

(a) Neville Chamberlain said on his return from Munich:

'My good friends, for the second time in our history, a British Prime Minister has returned bringing peace with honour . . . I believe it is peace for our time.'

(b) Winston Churchill commented on the Munich Agreement:

'We have suffered a total and unmitigated defeat. All is over . . . I think you will find that in a period of time Czechoslovakia will be engulfed in the Nazi regime. We have passed an awful milestone in our history, when the whole equilibrium of Europe has been deranged . . . And do not suppose that this is the end. This is only the beginning of the reckoning.'

1 *How did Churchill and Chamberlain differ over Munich?*
2 *Suggest reasons for their differences.*
3 *Why do you think Chamberlain's views were more popular in Britain at the time?*
4 *How do you think Czechoslovakia reacted to the Munich Agreement?*

Hitler soon showed his disregard for the agreement reached at Munich. In March 1939, Germany took over the rest of Czechoslovakia. For the first time, Hitler had taken control of a non-German-speaking people. It was only now that Britain fully realised the German threat. Chamberlain introduced conscription in Britain and promised to go to war if Germany invaded Poland.

TEST YOUR KNOWLEDGE

1 *Why did Hitler want to take over the Sudetenland?*

2 *Who was the Prime Minister of Britain in 1938?*

3 *What was meant by appeasement? With which country is this policy most associated?*

4 *What was decided at Munich in 1938?*

5 *How did Hitler show his disregard for the Munich Agreement?*

6 *How did Hitler's invasion of Czechoslovakia in March 1939 differ from his earlier moves?*

7 *How did Chamberlain respond to the German take-over of Czechoslovakia?*

THE INVASION OF POLAND

Poland was the next country in Hitler's plans for German expansion eastwards, a policy known as *Lebensraum* (living space). Realising this, Britain and France now tried to form an alliance with the Soviet Union in the face of the Nazi threat.

Stalin, concerned only for the security of the Soviet Union, no longer trusted them. In a desperate effort to keep Russia out of another war, Stalin came to an agreement with Hitler in August 1939 known as the *Nazi-Soviet Non-Aggression Pact*. Stalin agreed to stand aside while Germany invaded Poland, and both he and Hitler secretly agreed to divide Poland between them. On 1 September 1939, Germany invaded Poland. Two days later, Britain and France declared war on Germany. World War II had begun.

Following Hitler's invasion of Czechoslovakia, Britain prepares for war by building trenches in the middle of London as a protection against air raids.

Contemporary cartoon showing Hitler and Stalin at the time of the Nazi-Soviet Pact. What is the main message being conveyed?

Molotov and Ribbentrop, the Soviet and German foreign ministers, signing the Nazi-Soviet Non-Aggression Pact in August 1939. This pact ensured that, in the event of war, Hitler could concentrate on defeating Britain and France and avoid fighting on two fronts. Stalin desperately wanted to avoid Russian involvement in war. When he failed to persuade Britain and France to form an alliance with him against Hitler, he came to an agreement with the Nazi dictator in order to keep war from the USSR as long as possible.

Chapter 8: Review

- During the 1930s, Hitler built up Germany's armed forces and took the country out of the League of Nations. In 1936 he formed an alliance with Mussolini – the Rome-Berlin Axis – and later extended this to include Japan.

- In March 1936, Hitler's troops reoccupied the Rhineland. This was forbidden under the Treaty of Versailles but Great Britain and France took no action to stop it.

- In March 1938, Hitler again broke the Versailles Settlement when he marched into Austria and joined it to Germany – a policy known as the Anschluss.

- At the Munich Conference in September 1938, Britain and France agreed to allow Hitler to take over the Sudetenland area of Czechoslovakia. The British Prime Minister, Chamberlain, returned from the conference claiming that he had secured 'Peace for our time'.

- In March 1939, Hitler took control of a non-German people for the first time when he conquered the rest of Czechoslovakia. Britain now promised suppport to Poland if Hitler attacked that country.

- In August 1939, Hitler signed an agreement with the Russian Communist leader Stalin known as The Nazi-Soviet Non-Agression Pact. In a secret clause they agreed to divide Poland between them.

- On 1 September 1939, Hitler invaded Poland. Great Britain and France then declared war on Germany. World War II had begun.

ACTIVITIES

1 *Multiple Choice*
   (a) *In March 1936, Hitler's troops marched into: (i) Austria; (ii) Czechoslovakia; (iii) Poland; (iv) The Rhineland.*
   (b) *The Anschluss (1938) was Hitler's occupation of: (i) Denmark; (ii) Austria; (iii) Switzerland; (iv) Czechoslovakia.*
   (c) *The policy of appeasement was most assoicated with: (i) Winston Churchill; (ii) Benito Mussolini; (iii) Neville Chamberlain; (iv) Eduard Benes.*
   (d) *In March 1939, Great Britain threatened to go to war if Hitler attacked: (i) France; (ii) Russia; (iii) Czechoslovakia; (iv) Poland.*
   (e) *The Nazi-Soviet Pact was signed in: (i) 1939; (ii) 1934; (iii) 1937; (iv) 1940.*

2 *True or False?*
   (a) *Hitler took Germany out of the League of Nations in 1933.*
   (b) *Hitler opposed Mussolini's invasion of Abyssinia.*
   (c) *The Germans built the Maginot Line along the border with France.*
   (d) *There was a powerful Nazi Party in Austria.*
   (e) *Winston Churchill condemned the Munich Agreement (1938).*

3 *Draw up a Time Chart of the 1930s. On it, list at least four of Hitler's advances.*

4 *Write a letter to a friend either justifying or condemning the Munich Agreement. State your reasons for your point of view.*

THE WORLD
AT WAR

BLITZKRIEG: POLAND IS OVERRUN

On 1 September 1939, Germany invaded Poland. Hitler launched a new type of warfare – *blitzkrieg* or lightening war. This was a combination of rapid tank movements on the ground and heavy bombing from the air. Soon Poland was completely overrun by the might of the German war machine.

After Germany's conquest of Poland, there was a lull in fighting lasting for nearly six months during the winter of 1939-40. This was known as 'the Phoney War'. It was not until the spring of 1940 that war in Europe got fully underway.

German planes launch a blitzkrieg or 'lightning war' against Poland.

Newspaper headlines in London announcing the outbreak of World War II.

1940: GERMAN ATTACKS ON THE WEST

In April 1940, Hitler conquered Norway and Denmark. On 10 May, he launched a successful attack on Belgium and Holland. Hitler's armies then overran France in a matter of weeks, to the surprise of many people, and the French government surrendered on 24 June. Britain now stood alone to face the German attack.

A British Expeditionary Force (BEF) had arrived in France to assist the French in their fight against Hitler. With the rapid defeat of France, this force was trapped at the port of Dunkirk in northern France. A spectacular rescue attempt followed. Over a period of six days, a huge assortment of ships, including warships and pleasure boats, arrived from England and braved the German bombs to rescue over 300,000 soldiers.

60

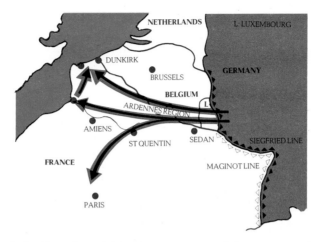

Hitler launched a lightning attack on the West in the Spring of 1940.

Read the British and German accounts of these events. What differences do you notice?

Source A *(BBC news bulletin, 31 May 1940)*

All night and all day, men of the undefeated British army have been coming home. From the many reports of their arrival and of interviews with the men, it is clear that if they have not come back in triumph, they have come back in glory; that their spirits are as high as ever; that they know that they did not meet their masters; and that they are anxious only to be back again soon – as they put it – 'to have a real crack at Jerry'.

Source B *(Official German bulletin, 4 June 1940)*

The full extent of our victory in Holland, in Belgium and in the north of France can be measured by enemy losses in men and material. The English, French, Dutch and Belgians have lost 1,200,000 as prisoners, plus dead and wounded. The arms and equipment of the whole Allied army, including tanks and vehicles of every type, have also been destroyed or captured.

Fighting in Dunkirk in May 1940.

British troops being evacuated from Dunkirk.

In the meantime, the British Prime Minister, Neville Chamberlain, had resigned and was replaced by Winston Churchill. Churchill was determined to lift the spirits of the British people and resist the German attack to the end. Here is what he told the House of Commons on 4 June 1940.

' . . . we shall defend our island, whatever the cost may be, we shall fight on the beaches, we shall fight on the landing grounds, we shall fight in the fields and in the streets, we shall fight in the hills; we shall never surrender.'

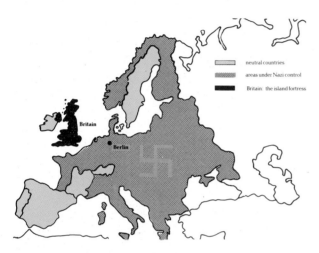

After the fall of France in June 1940, Britain stood alone agianst the power of Nazi Germany.

Winston Churchill, Great Britain's wartime Prime Minister.

TEST YOUR KNOWLEDGE
1 *What new method of warfare did Hitler use in his attack on Poland in September 1939?*
2 *What was the Phoney War? Why was it so named?*
3 *What new offensive did Hitler launch in the spring of 1940?*
4 *What happened at Dunkirk?*
5 *Who replaced Chamberlain as Prime Minister of Britain in 1940?*

THE BATTLE OF BRITAIN

After the defeat of France in June 1940, Hitler planned an invasion of Britain (*Operation Sealion*). Before he could attempt this, however, he first needed to control the air space. A huge battle took place in September 1940 between the German airforce, the *Luftwaffe*, and the British Royal Air Force (RAF). This air battle was known as the *Battle of Britain*. With the aid of radar, the RAF successfully repelled the German attack. Around a thousand British pilots of Fighter Command bore the brunt of the fighting and about 400 of these were killed in action. Churchill later paid tribute to the RAF when he commented:

'*Never in the field of human conflict was so much owed by so many to so few.*'

While Hitler postponed his plans to invade Britain, he continued to bomb London and extended the bombing campaign to other British cities. This marked the beginning of the 'Night Blitz'. Between 7 September and 13 November 1940, there was only one night when London escaped bombing, with an average of 163 German bombers flying over the city each night. The bombing of British cities, including London, Coventry, Southampton and Belfast, resulted in the deaths of 40,000 civilians and the injury of 46,000 others.

The Houses of Parliament at Westminster burning during the Blitz over London.

War in the air during the Battle of Britain.

Bomb damage in London during the Blitz.

Londoners spend the night in an underground shelter during a bombing raid.

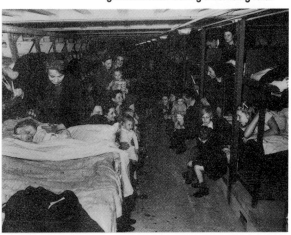

63

WORKING WITH EVIDENCE: ONE MAN'S BLITZ

Londoners got their first taste of 'the blitz' on the night of 7 September 1940, when 250 German bombers struck hard at the capital. For the rest of that year, and into the next, they were subjected to relentless pounding from the air.

'One evening after the sirens sounded their usual warning and nothing had happened, there was a sound like stones being thrown against the house or a number of slates falling off the roof. We ran to the front door and found an incendiary bomb burning brightly on the mat . . . I ran into the kitchen and snatched up a bowl of washing-up water. The suds doused the bomb, snuffing it like a candle.

From the doorway we could see that there were many other incendiaries, some burning out harmlessly in the road or basement area, some on houses, and one on the back seat of a car, having burned through the roof. Roland dumped his bucket of sand on that one and was pleased that it obediently went out. The bombs were about nine inches long and burned with a white light for three or four minutes, leaving only the tail fins . . . We were grabbed by a little old man in a white muffler who begged us to put out some incendiaries lodged in his attic. We got these out fairly quickly but he then pointed to a ladder and an open skylight, saying there were more on the roof . . . From up there we could see down into the street and over the rooftops. It was an extraordinary sight: all around the horizon fires glowed, searchlights slowly raked the dark sky, anti-aircraft guns flashed silently . . . High above us shells burst like fireworks. But the most insistent noise came from the street immediately beneath us. It was an excited sound of many people shouting as they scurried in and out of their houses . . .

The bombers, earlier in the evening, had dropped nothing but hundreds of incendiaries. But this wave, a couple of hours later, came back with instantaneous high-explosive bombs where the fires were brightest and most people were in the streets.

The explosions caused panic: people ran back into burning houses or threw themselves into basement areas. I heard screams above the explosions as I tried to dig myself into the slates of the roof.

The rain of bombs lasted only a few minutes but it was dawn before the fires were all out and the injured had been taken away. We sat in the kitchen of our house drinking cocoa with neighbours who had lived near each other for years but had never spoken. Now they were talking and gesticulating in a most un-English manner as they described the narrow escapes of the night. From the street shelters came the ones who had been down there during all the excitement. The rest of us looked at them sorrowfully, knit together by the experience we have shared.

(Contemporary account)

1 What types of bombs were dropped by the Germans in the first raid?
2 State two methods of extinguishing incendiary devices mentioned in the extract.
3 Describe the sight seen by the author from the roof of the building.
4 What form did the second wave of German bombing take?
5 What do you think the author means by the last sentence in the extract?

JUNE 1941: GERMANY ATTACKS RUSSIA

On 22 June 1941, Hitler broke the Nazi-Soviet Pact of 1939 by invading Russia. This was known as *Operation Barbarossa*. The Soviet Red Army was not prepared for this attack. It was poorly equipped and much of its aircraft and weaponry were outdated. Within a very short time, the German army had made rapid advances towards Leningrad and Moscow. By October, Moscow was almost a deserted city – only Stalin and his advisers remained on in the Kremlin, the Russian seat of government.

German tanks invading Russia in June 1941.

The German invasion of Russia (Operation Barbarossa), 1941. By December 1941 German troops had captured vast stretches of Russian territory, almost reaching Moscow, the capital city.

When the Russian winter set in, the German advance froze to a halt. This gave Stalin the breathing space he needed. The huge Russian army, under the command of Marshal Zhukov, was rebuilt and moved into action. The German advance was halted outside Moscow, but the great turning point came in the winter of 1942-43 at Stalingrad.

The German Sixth Army under General von Paulus began its attack on Stalingrad in September 1942. By the middle of November, most of the city had fallen to the Germans in street-by-street fighting. However, Marshal Zhukow now came to the aid of the city with an army of a million men which completely surrounded the Germans. Von Paulus asked Hitler for permission to surrender but this was refused.

'Surrender is forbidden. The army will hold their positions to the last man and the last round of ammunition.'

For over two months, the Russians attacked the starving, frozen Germans. When Von Paulus finally surrendered at the end of January 1943, out of a German army of 300,000 only 97,000 survived.

Hitler's invasion of Russia had been a serious error, resulting in massive casualties on both sides. The war in Russia had been fought with terrible savagery and brutality. Millions of Russians perished in the course of the campaign.

The German advance in Russia is blocked by the extreme cold.

German troops during the Battle of Stalingrad in 1942.

TEST YOUR KNOWLEDGE

1 *What was Operation Barbarossa?*
2 *Why do you think the Germans advanced rapidly through Russia?*
3 *What happened at Stalingrad? What was its outcome?*
4 *Do you think the Russian campaign was a serious error on Hitler's part? Give reasons for your answer.*

PEARL HARBOUR, DECEMBER 1941:
AMERICA ENTERS THE WAR

Throughout the 1930s, the heavily-populated Japanese Empire had looked greedily on American, British and French possessions in the Pacific. In 1936, the Japanese made an alliance with Hitler and Mussolini with a view to future expansion.

On the morning of Sunday, 7 December 1941, the Japanese air force launched a surprise attack on the US naval base at Pearl Harbour in Hawaii. When the Japanese finally departed, eight battleships were badly damaged, many aircraft were destroyed on the ground and 2403 Americans were dead. This attack brought the United States immediately into the war on the side of Great Britain and the USSR. Ever since the beginning, America had been sympathetic to the Allied side and had given equipment to Britain and France in a scheme known as *Lend-Lease*.

American ships burning after the Japanese attack on Pearl Harbour.

American propaganda posters following the attack on Pearl Harbour.

America's entry was a vital turning point in the war. From then on the American president, Franklin D. Roosevelt, co-operated closely with Churchill in planning the Allied military campaigns. The might of American manufacturing industry and finance was to play a key role in the eventual Allied victory.

TEST YOUR KNOWLEDGE
1 *What event brought America into the war?*
2 *Who was the president of America during World War II?*
3 *Why was America's entry into the war of such importance?*

1942-43: THE TIDE TURNS

In North Africa, the presence of the Afrika Corps of the German army under General Rommel was a serious threat to British interests in Egypt, especially the Suez Canal. The British Eighth Army, under General Montgomery, was strengthened by American aid and defeated Rommel's forces at the Battle of El Alamein in October 1942. In the following month, the American General Eisenhower led an army into Algeria and Morocco in North Africa (*Operation Torch*) and forced the remains of Rommel's Afrika Corps to surrender.

In July 1943, Eisenhower's forces combined with Montgomery's Eighth Army to invade Sicily. They proceeded from there to mainland Italy. Due to difficult countryside and fierce German resistance, their progress was slow – Rome did not fall to the Allies until June 1944. With the arrival of the Allies, some Italians rose against Mussolini and imprisoned him. However, he was rescued in a German parachute raid and brought north. In the meantime, a new pro-Allied government took over in Italy. Mussolini once again fell into the hands of his enemies. This time he was put to death and his body hanged in public. The Allied victories during 1942 and 1943 – in North Africa, Stalingrad and Italy – marked the beginning of the end of Nazi domination.

The tide turned for the Allies in 1942-43 as they conquered North Africa and advanced from there into Sicily and Italy.

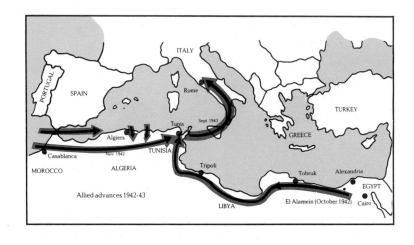

68

TEST YOUR KNOWLEDGE

1 *Name the commanders of the British and German forces in the Battle of El Alamein.*
2 *Who led the Allied forces in the invasion of North Africa?*
3 *What happened to Mussolini when the Allies entered Italy?*
4 *Name three Allied victories which showed that the tide was turning against Hitler.*

British forces in
action during the
Battle of
El Alamein.

Chapter 9: Review

- Hitler's new tactic, which he used against Poland, was known as blitzkrieg or lightening war. German troops soon conquered the country and after that there was a lull in the fighting until the following spring ('the Phoney War').

- In April and May 1940, Hitler attacked and conquered Norway, Denmark, Belgium and Holland. He also attacked France which, to the great surprise of many, surrendered to Germany on 24 June. Britain now stood alone against Hitler.

- In a dramatic rescue attempt, over 300,000 British soldiers were brought from Dunkirk to England in June 1940. The new British Prime Minister, Winston Churchill, was determined to resist the German attack to the bitter end.

- In a huge air battle in September 1940 between the British Royal Air Force and the German *Luftwaffe* (The Battle of Britain), the British successfully beat off the German attack.

- Following his failure to invade Britain, Hitler launched a blitz of night bombings on British cities throughout the following autumn and winter.

- On 22 June 1941, Hitler attacked Soviet Russia in an invasion known as Operation Barbarossa. The Germans made huge advances at first but were halted before reaching the three main cities at Moscow, Leningrad and Stalingrad.

- In the winter of 1942-43, World War II reached a major turning point when the German army surrendered to the Russians at Stalingrad. After that the Russians began to push the Germans back on the Eastern Front.

- The United States of America had entered the war in December 1941 when Germany's ally, Japan, attacked a navel base at Pearl Harbour. American entry was to eventually turn the tide in favour of the Allies.

- At the Battle of El Alamein in North Africa in October 1942, the British Eighth Army under General Montgomery defeated the German Afrika Corps of General Rommel. In the following month, the American General Eisenhower led an American army into Algeria and Morocco (Operation Torch).

- In July 1943, a combined force of British and American soldiers invaded Sicily and went on from there to Italy where they met with fierce German resistance – the city of Rome only fell to the Allies in June 1944.

ACTIVITIES

1 Complete the following sentences:
   (a) In September 1939, Hitler launched a new type of warfare known as _____.
   (b) In May 1940 over 300,000 British troops were evacuated from _____.
   (c) When the British Prime Minister Neville Chamberlain resigned, he was replaced by _____.
   (d) Operation Sealion was Hitler's codename for _____.
   (e) In June 1941, Hitler's forces began the invasion of _____.

2 Match an item in Column 1 with an item in Column 2.

COLUMN 1	COLUMN 2
Pearl Harbour	The Invasion of the USSR
Operation Barbarossa	The Battle of Stalingrad
General Rommel	America enters the war
Marshal Zhukov	Dunkirk
The British Expeditionary Force	The Afrika Corps

3 Draw a map of the world and mark in the main events in World War II between September 1939 and the end of 1943.

4 Pick out three sources in this chapter which reveal propaganda and write a short note on each of them.

5 Write a paragraph on two of the following:
   (a) Blitzkrieg
   (b) The Battle of Britain
   (c) The German Invasion of the USSR
   (d) American Entry to World War II

TOWARDS ALLIED VICTORY

D-DAY: ALLIED LANDINGS IN FRANCE

The generals who planned and directed Operation Overlord under the command of General Dwight D. Eisenhower, seen here in the centre.

For a long time, Stalin had been demanding that Britain and America open a second front in the west to relieve pressure on Russia. On 6 June 1944, the long-awaited *D-Day* (D for deliverance) occurred. A huge Allied force, under the command of General Eisenhower, crossed the English Channel and landed in Normandy in northern France. This invasion was known as *Operation Overload*. A bridgehead some 80 kilometres wide was specially built for the invasion. Despite fierce German resistance and heavy casualties, nearly a million Allied soldiers had landed in France by the end of June.

The headlines in an American newspaper after the D-Day landings.

Allied soldiers were also parachuted into France where they linked up with local resistance groups. These sabotaged transport and communications networks in an effort to disrupt the German forces. On 18 August, Paris was liberated from German control. The Allies now moved on towards Belgium.

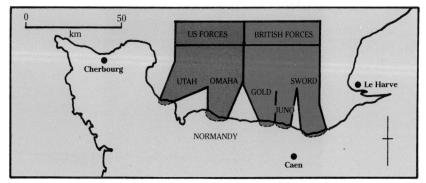

The Allied landings in Normandy, June 1944. Note the code names for the beaches (e.g. Utah).

Members of the French Underground or Resistance Movement planning an attack on German defences during the Allied invasion of France.

THE WAR IN EUROPE ENDS

By the end of 1944, both France and Belgium were freed from German control. The Allies now advanced towards Germany on two fronts. They continued to bomb German cities, which led to huge civilian casualties. One of these attacks was the bombing of Dresden in February 1945, which resulted in the loss of some 135,000 lives. From the east, the Red Army was making rapid progress, while British and American troops were closing in from the west. The Germans had not lost all hope, however. In December 1944, they tried to drive the Allies back into the Ardennes region of France and Belgium in a battle known as the Battle of the Bulge.

By 1945, Hitler's position was becoming desperate. His last hope rested in his newly-developed V1 and V2 rockets, but these failed to break the Allied advance. On 30 April 1945, with the Russian army entering Berlin, Hitler and his wife Eva Braun committed suicide in their underground bunker. On 7 May 1945 the Germans surrendered unconditionally. The war in Europe was over.

General Charles de Gaulle marching through Paris in triumph in August 1944 following the Allied liberation of the city from German control. De Gaulle had fled to London after the fall of France in June 1940. From there he played a key part in directing the French Resistance Movement.

Allied bombing of a German city.

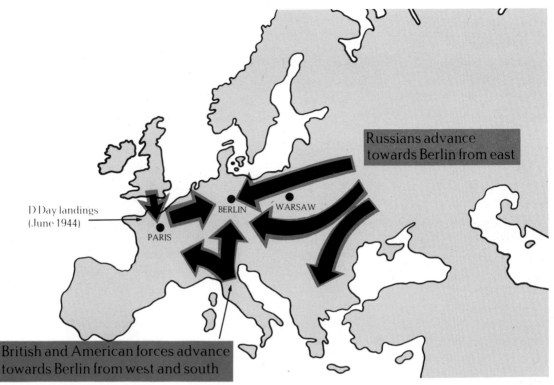

Russians advance towards Berlin from east

D Day landings (June 1944)

BERLIN

WARSAW

PARIS

British and American forces advance towards Berlin from west and south

Allied forces advancing towards Berlin

Members of the International Red Cross Movement clearing out concentration camps.

LIFE IN NAZI-OCCUPIED EUROPE

The war in Europe left a heavy toll of death and destruction in its wake. The full extent of the horrors of Nazi rule became clear as the Allies liberated German-occupied territory. In a plan known as 'the Final Solution' Hitler had exterminated some six million Jews in concentration camps throughout Europe such as Auschwitz, Dachau and Treblinka.

Joy on the faces of Jewish children as they are released from Dachau concentration camp on 12 May 1945.

The following is one survivor's account of life in Auschwitz.

'Total obedience, total humiliation. It was no use trying to predict logically what they would do. Yet at the same time you had to be somehow a step ahead. You had to develop special antennae . . . Above all keep away from those who said it wasn't worth trying to go on. Despair was contagious. There was one period when illness had almost the same awful effect on me. It started with a night when I couldn't sleep, tired as I was. I tossed and turned, hot and shivery, icy cold and then bathed in sweat. Was it typhus? Nearly everyone caught it sooner or later. It was as common a killer as the SS.

[Kitty Hart was then taken to the hospital block where her mother was working.] The block was full. I was put on to a single bunk which already had three occupants. One patient had diphtheria, another malaria and the third had typhus . . . I heard myself crying for water. Then I must have been unconscious for a long time. Then awake, or half awake, I thought I could see oranges, grapes and cool drinks at the foot of my bunk and screamed for them. Mother was there and I cursed her for being so cruel . . .

One day as I lay unconscious there was a selection. All those unable to get up were taken to be gassed. Mother saw what would surely happen to me. She pushed me inside a straw mattress and laid a corpse on top of me, praying I would keep still and not start raving and singing, as I had been doing some hours earlier. The SS doctor passed the bunk. The corpse was taken away. The incurably sick were taken also. I was still alive . . .

During my convalescence another selection was carried out. That day I was able to walk, but not very well. Mother was worried, too, about the sores and scratches on my body. And I was far too thin. One by one we had to parade naked outside. Mengele himself was there. He ordered us to run. Those who could not summon up the energy to run were sent to the left, the others to the right. I gathered all my strength, began to run and somehow made it. But Mengele was staring hard at my pimply body. He made me turn round, then round again, while he hesitated . . . and at last pointed to the right.'

Kitty Hart: Return to Auschwitz, *1981*

A scene of horror discovered by the Allies at Belsen concentration camp.

Millions of people in the occupied countries were sent to work as forced labour to Germany. Not everyone submitted peacefully to German domination. Resistance groups sprang up throughout Europe, most notably the French Resistance and Marshal Tito's Partisans in Yugoslavia.

The Allies were determined to bring the leading Nazi war criminals to justice. In a series of trials held in Nuremberg between November 1945 and September 1946, twelve leading Nazis were sentenced to death for crimes against humanity. Of these Goering, the leader of the *Luftwaffe*, committed suicide and the eleven others were hanged.

Leading Nazis on trial at Nuremberg in 1946.

TEST YOUR KNOWLEDGE
1 What happened on 6 June 1944?
2 Who was the commander of the D-Day landings?
3 Why was the German position in Europe becoming desperate by 1945?
4 What was the Final Solution?
5 What happened at Nuremberg between November 1945 and September 1946?

THE WAR IN THE PACIFIC

While the war in Europe had ended, the struggle in the Pacific between the Japanese and the Americans still raged. Soon after Pearl Harbour, the Japanese proceeded to attack the British and French empires in the Pacific. In June 1942, the Japanese and the American fleets confronted one another off the island of Midway. In the Battle of Midway, the Americans sank four Japanese carriers. The Japanese never really recovered from their defeat in this battle, which was a turning-point in the war in the Pacific.

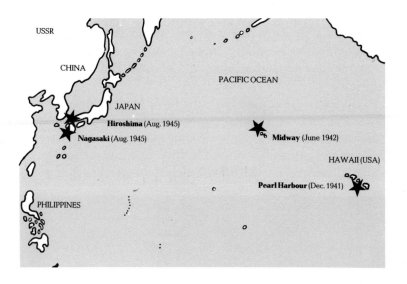

Warfare in the Pacific, 1941-45.

After this victory, the Americans began to retake the Pacific islands. By 1944, although the Japanese were effectively beaten, they refused to surrender. At this stage of the war, the casualties were huge as most Japanese soldiers chose to die rather than surrender.

THE ATOMIC BOMB IS DROPPED
WORLD WAR II ENDS

Throughout the war, American and British scientists had been developing the atomic bomb. Harry S. Truman who succeeded Roosevelt as president of the US in April 1945, decided to drop the atomic bomb on Japan.

On 6 August 1945 a single American plane, the *Enola Gay*, flew over the city of Hiroshima in southern Japan. It was carrying the most destructive bomb the world had ever seen. After the bomb was dropped, the city of Hiroshima was reduced to rubble. Some 80,000 people were burned to death on the first day and thousands died in agony in the weeks and months ahead. A second atomic bomb was dropped on the Japanese city of Nagasaki, killing a further 60,000 people.

The destruction of Hiroshima.

The after-effects of both bombs were horrific, with thousands suffering and dying from radiation in the years ahead. Read the following accounts, written by victims of the atomic bombs.

Source A

'Someone shouted "A parachute is coming down". I responded by turning in the direction she pointed. Just at that moment, the sky I was facing flashed. I don't know how to describe that light. I wondered if a fire had been set in my eyes. The next moment I was knocked down flat on the ground. Immediately things started falling down around me. I couldn't see anything. Soon I noticed that the air smelled terrible. Then I was shocked by the feeling that the skin on my face had come off. Then the hands and arms from the elbows to the fingernails, all the skin of my right hand had come off and hung grotesquely.

Source B

'I ran to the railway bridge. On the far side, crowds of maddened people were running like lemmings, trying to get across the river. In the middle of the bridge lay four or five bodies, unrecognisable as human beings, but still moving. Their skin hung from them like strands of seaweed! Instead of noses, holes. Their eyes and hands were so swollen as to be shapeless. There were still fifty or sixty clinging to red-hot rails. In their terror of dying, they clawed their way over one another, their eyes hanging from their sockets, pushing one another into the river, and screaming all the time.'

The Japanese, stunned by these events, surrendered on 10 August 1945, bringing World War II to an end.

The Japanese surrender to the American General MacArthur on board the *USS Missouri* in Tokyo Bay on 1 September 1945.

TEST YOUR KNOWLEDGE

1 *In what sense was the Battle of Midway a turning point in the war in the Pacific?*
2 *Who made the decision to drop the atomic bomb on Japan?*
3 *Describe the effects of the atomic explosions in Hiroshima and Nagasaki.*
4 *When did the war in the Pacific end?*

American troops arriving in Tokyo in 1945.

New York celebrates news of the surrender of Japan.

THE LEGACY OF WORLD WAR II

World War II had been the most destructive war in history. At its end, around forty million people lay dead. Millions of others were wounded or homeless, and cities and towns throughout Europe were almost totally destroyed. Unlike World War I, civilian populations were direct targets.

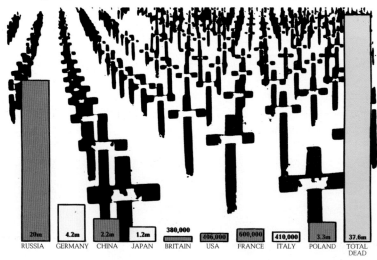

The vast numbers of casualties, civilian and military, in World War II.

RUSSIA	GERMANY	CHINA	JAPAN	BRITAIN	USA	FRANCE	ITALY	POLAND	TOTAL DEAD
20m	4.2m	2.2m	1.2m	380,000	406,000	600,000	410,000	3.3m	37.6m

Even before the end of the war, Allied leaders were drawing up plans for rebuilding Europe. Stalin, Roosevelt and Churchill had met at Tehran (October 1943) and at Yalta (February 1945) to plan a future shape of Europe after its liberation from Nazi occupation. The Allies met again at Potsdam in July 1945 to decide on the joint rule of Germany. However, while the Allies had won the war, they were to find it much harder to agree on the type of Europe they now wanted.

78

Churchill, Roosevelt and Stalin, the three wartime Allied leaders, at the Yalta Conference, February 1945.

CALENDAR
Important dates and events of World War II

1 September
1939
Germany invades Poland

3 September
1939
Britain and France declare war on Germany

April-May
1940
Germany overruns Norway, Denmark and the Low Countries

June
1940
The Fall of France

September
1940
The Battle of Britain

June
1941
The German invasion of Russia

December
1941
Pearl Harbour – America enters the war

June
1942
Japanese defeat at the Battle of Midway

October
1942
The Battle of El Alamein – German defeat in North Africa

January
1943
Russian victory at the Battle of Stalingrad

July
1943
Allied invasion of Italy

June
1944
D-Day: Allied landings in France

May
1945
The war ends in Europe

August
1945
Atomic bombs dropped on Japan. End of World War II

Chapter 10: Review

- On 6 June 1944 (D-Day) the Allies, Britain and America launched an attack on the coast of Normandy in France (Operation Overlord). On 18 August, Paris was liberated from German control and the French leader, General de Gaulle, set up his headquarters there.

- By the end of 1944, both France and Belgium were cleared of German troops. However, in December Hitler launched a last unsuccessful attack in the Ardennes region of France and Belgium (The Battle of the Bulge).

- On 30 April 1945, with Russian soldiers closing in on Berlin, Hitler committed suicide in an underground bunker in the centre of the city. A week later, Germany surrendered unconditionally to the Allies, bringing the war in Europe to an end.

- The war in the Pacific continued, however, and only ended when the Americans dropped atomic bombs on the Japanese cities of Hiroshima and Nagasaki in August 1945. As a result, the Japanese surrendered unconditionally and World War II finally came to an end.

- When the Allies liberated Europe, they discovered the full horrors of the Nazi concentration camps. As part of Hitler's Final Solution some six million Jews had been killed, along with other enemies of the Nazi regime.

- In the countries occupied by Germany during the war, resistance movements of local people had grown up. Two of the most famous were the French Resistance and the Partisans of Marshal Tito in Yugoslavia.

ACTIVITIES

1 *Multiple Choice*
  (a) *The Allied invasion of France in June 1944 was code-named Operation: (i) Sealion; (ii) Torch; (iii) Barbarossa; (iv) Overlord.*
  (b) *General Tito was a resistance leader in: (i) France; (ii) Czechoslovkia; (iii) Yugoslavia; (iv) Italy.*
  (c) *Trials of leading Nazis were held in the German town of: (i) Munich; (ii) Hamburg; (iii) Dresden; (iv) Nuremberg.*
  (d) *The decision to drop the atom bomb on Japan was taken by US President: (i) Eisenhower; (ii) Truman; (iii) Roosevelt; (iv) Hoover.*

2 *Complete the following sentences:*
  (a) *The Battle of Midway was fought between _____.*
  (b) *In August 1945, atomic bombs were dropped on the Japanese cities of _____ and _____.*
  (c) *Hitler's 'Final Solution' plan was _____.*
  (d) *The Allied commander of the invasion forces in France in 1944 was _____.*
  (e) *Hitler died on 30 April 1945 by _____.*

3 *Draw a map of the world. Mark in the main events of World War II between the start of 1944 and the war's conclusion in August 1945.*

4 *Write an account of Hitler's treatment of the Jews between 1933 and 1945.*

5 *List six points on the role of air power in World War II. You may include both fighter planes and bombers.*

6 *By the end of World War II Europe's position in the world had become much weaker. Which powers now took over a leading role? Using your knowledge of the war, explain this development.*

THE COLD WAR: 1945-53

THE AGE OF THE SUPERPOWERS

At the end of World War II, much of Europe lay in ruins, with millions dead, cities destroyed and economies shattered. Only the United States of America and the USSR emerged as Great Powers after 1945.

Of all the countries involved in World War II, the United States had suffered least. The American mainland had never been invaded or bombed. At the same time, American agriculture and industry enjoyed a boom period while providing food and equipment for the war effort. In 1945, the American economy was by far the strongest in the world.

The USSR or Soviet Union, on the other hand, had suffered huge casualties and massive destruction during the war. In 1945, however, the Soviet Union emerged with the largest army in the world which, in a short time, would control most of Eastern Europe.

With Europe weakened by the ravages of war, the United States and the Soviet Union dominated world affairs from 1945 onwards. Because of their size, power and influence, these two countries became known as the *Superpowers*. After the final defeat of Hitler's Germany, their friendship soon turned into bitter mistrust and rivalry. Before this happened, however, they worked together to set up a new world peace-keeping organisation – the *United Nations*.

THE UNITED NATIONS

Many lessons were to be learned from World War II. The Allied leaders realised that co-operation between the nations of the world was essential to ensure peace in the future. As the League of Nations had failed to prevent the outbreak of war, Roosevelt, Stalin and Churchill set about planning a new and stronger organisation which became known as the United Nations.

The UN Security Council in session in New York.

In April 1945, fifty countries signed the United Nations Charter in San Francisco. This international organisation aimed to preserve world peace through co-operation and joint action. New York was to be the headquarters of the United Nations. The organisation had three main parts:

The General Assembly: Each member country has a representative in this group which discusses world problems and the business of the UN.

The Security Council: This group is always in session to deal with any world crisis. It has eleven members, five of which are permanent (US, USSR, Britain, France and China).

The Secretariat: This is the civil service of the UN which is responsible for the day-to-day running of the organisation.

The most powerful figure in the UN is the Secretary General who is elected by the General Assembly. Since its foundation there have been five secretaries – General Trygve Lie (Norway); Dag Hammarskjold (Sweden); U Thant (Burma); Kurt Waldeim (Austria) and Javier Perez de Cuellar (Peru).

Unlike the League of Nations, the UN has its own peacekeeping force drawn from the armies of member nations. This force has served in various trouble spots around the world, including Cyprus, the Congo and Lebanon. The Irish army has played an important part in these peacekeeping operations.

Irish soldiers on United Nations peace-keeping duties in Lebanon.

The organisation of the United Nations.

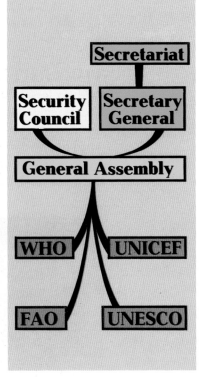

In addition to preserving the peace, the UN has become actively involved in attempts to improve social and economic conditions throughout the world. For this purpose it set up the following bodies:

The World Health Organisation (WHO): This organisation concerns itself with fighting disease and improving standards of health throughout the world.

United Nations International Children's Emergency Fund (UNICEF): It cares for children in the underdeveloped countries and assists children who are victims of war or natural disasters.

United Nations Educational, Scientific and Cultural Organisation (UNESCO): It aims to spread knowledge and understanding among people of different races, religions and cultures.

Food and Agricultural Organisation (FAO): This organisation attempts to improve world agriculture and food supplies.

The work of UNICEF: (a) a water project in Nigeria, Africa.

(b) Nigeria's children queue for vaccinations.

Despite the good work carried out by the United Nations since 1945, it was weakened from the start by the disagreements between the two Superpowers. These disagreements, which never led to an actual outbreak of fighting, became known as the *Cold War*.

TEST YOUR KNOWLEDGE

1 Describe the condition of European countries at the end of World War II.

2 Why did the United States emerge in a strong position after 1945?

3 How was the Soviet Union affected by World War II?

4 When was the United Nations organisation set up? What was its main aim?

5 Explain the role of the Security Council in the United Nations.

6 Who is the most important person in the UN?

7 Name two countries in which UN peacekeeping forces have served.

THE COLD WAR BEGINS

It was not surprising that the United States and the Soviet Union should quarrel once their common enemy had been defeated in 1945. As you can see from the chart, they had very different beliefs concerning how countries should be run.

USA	USSR
• A private enterprise Capitalist economy	• A state-controlled Communist economy
• Freedom of speech	• Strict government control over books, newspapers, radio
• Free multi-party elections	• Only one party, the Communist party, allowed to stand for election
• Free trade and Capitalism should spread throughout the world	• Worldwide spread of Communism

Eastern Europe during the Cold War.

Land gained by USSR during World War II.

Eastern European communist countries in the Soviet sphere of influence after 1945.

Because the Cold War was a disagreement over basic beliefs or ideologies, it was known as an *ideological conflict*. This ideological conflict between the Capitalist US and the Communist USSR added a strong extra element of bitterness to the ordinary rivalry which already existed between the Great Powers. It also helps to explain the bitter propaganda war carried out by both sides during the Cold War.

Stalin was determined to establish Russian control in the countries of Eastern Europe which the Red Army had liberated from Nazi control. Twice in the twentieth century, Russia had been invaded. As a result, Stalin declared that friendly governments in Eastern Europe were vital for Russian security. By 'friendly', the Russian leader meant Communist governments under his control.

American and British leaders saw matters differently. They believed that there should have been free elections in Eastern Europe to let the people decide on their own form of government. After all, the British claimed, had they not gone to war in 1939 to support Poland, one of the countries now under Russian control?

TRUMAN: A NEW PRESIDENT

President Franklin D. Roosevelt of the USA died suddenly in April 1945. He was succeeded by his vice-president, the strongly anti-Communist Harry S. Truman. At the Potsdam Conference in Germany in July 1945, Truman was determined not to make any concessions to the Soviet Union. Many people believed that his decision to drop the atomic bomb on two Japanese cities in August 1945 had another motive besides saving the lives of American soldiers who would have had to invade Japan. Truman's 'hidden motive' may have been that American possession of the atomic bomb would act as a warning to the Russians and remind them of how powerful the US was.

From then on, relations between the Superpowers went from bad to worse. By the start of 1946, the Cold War had well and truly begun.

Atlee, the new British Prime Minister, Truman and Stalin at the Potsdam Conference in July 1945.

WORKING WITH EVIDENCE

Read the following extracts and answer the questions which follow.

(a) Winston Churchill's 'Iron Curtain' Speech

In March 1946, Churchill spoke of the growing divisions in Europe in a speech at Fulton, Missouri in the USA. In it he coined the famous phrase 'the Iron Curtain'.

'From Stettin in the Baltic to Trieste in the Adriatic, an iron curtain has descended across the Continent. Behind that line lie all the capitals of the ancient states of central and eastern Europe. Warsaw, Berlin, Prague, Vienna, Budapest, Belgrade, Bucharest and Sofia, all these cities and the populations around them lie in the Soviet sphere, and are all subject, in one form or another, to a very high and increasing measure of control from Moscow. In other countries Communist parties or fifth columns constitute a growing challenge and peril to Christian civilisation.'

THE TRUMAN DOCTRINE AND THE MARSHALL PLAN

In 1947, President Truman of the US took two important steps which made it clear that he was determined to prevent the further spread of Communism in the world. In March, he proclaimed the *Truman Doctrine*. In June, his Secretary of State, George Marshall, announced the *Marshall Plan*.

The Truman Doctrine involved a foreign policy known as *containment*. By this, Truman meant that he would give help to any country trying to stop or 'contain' the spread of Communism, either in the form of attack from outside or revolution within. Truman said:

'I believe that it must be the policy of the US to support free people's who are resisting attempted subjugation by armed minorities or by outside pressures.'

At the time, the US was sending support to the governments of Greece and Turkey which were fighting against Communist rebels. However, Truman did not believe that military help was enough. He realised that people often supported Communists because they promised relief from poverty and hardship. On this subject, Truman commented:

> *'I believe that our help should be primarily through economic and financial aid which is essential to economic stability and orderly political processes. The seeds of totalitarian regimes are nurtured by misery and want. They spread and grow in the evil soil of poverty and strife. They reach their full growth when the hope of a people for a better life has died. We must keep that hope alive.'*

As Truman had hinted in his speech, the US government was planning to give economic aid to other countries. Europe in particular was singled out for assistance. If the countries of Western Europe could rebuild their shattered economies, they would not only be in a stronger position to resist Russian expansion; they would also provide markets for American exports. The American offer of economic aid was contained in the *Marshall Plan* of June 1947. European countries, including those behind 'the iron curtain', were offered Marshall Aid. After Stalin had forced the governments in Eastern Europe to reject the offer, only those in the West benefitted from it. (You will find a fuller account of Marshall Aid in Western Europe in Chapter 14.)

Within a year of the announcement of the Marshall Plan, one of the most serious crises of the Cold War developed in the very nerve-centre of East-West tension, the city of Berlin.

General George Marshall, the US Secretary of State, who announced the Marshall Plan.

TEST YOUR KNOWLEDGE
1 *Explain what is meant by an 'ideological conflict'?*
2 *Who became president of the USA in 1945?*
3 *What is meant by 'containment'?*
4 *State one weakness in the Truman Doctrine.*
5 *What was the Marshall Plan?*
6 *How did Stalin react to it?*

THE BERLIN BLOCKADE AND AIRLIFT

At the Yalta Conference in 1945, the Allied powers had decided to divide Germany into four occupation zones after the war. The US, Britain and France were to occupy zones in the west while the Russians would control the eastern part of Germany. This division was supposed to be a temporary measure, leading eventually to the reunification of Germany. Stalin, however, had other plans. He wanted Germany to remain permanently weak and divided.

In June 1948, a serious crisis developed between the Superpowers over the city of Berlin. Although inside the Russian zone, Berlin itself was divided into four zones, including an eastern section under Russian Communist rule and three western zones under the US, Britain and France. When the Western powers introduced currency reforms into West Berlin, Stalin tried to force them out of the city. On 23 June 1948, he cut off all road and rail links between West Berlin and the western

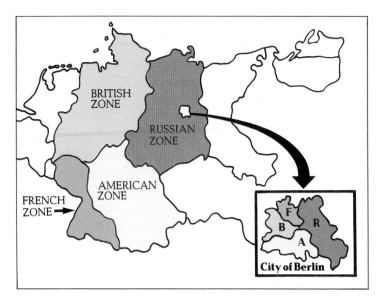

The Allied division of Germany and of the city of Berlin into four occupation zones after World War II.

zones of Germany. Electricity which came from the Russian sector of Berlin was also cut off.

The American, British and French governments responded by deciding to supply West Berlin with food, fuel and other essentials from the air. The *Berlin Airlift* was a huge achievement in terms of organisation. Over two million people were kept alive in West Berlin until the Russians admitted defeat and re-opened the transport routes in May 1949.

Although the Superpowers had avoided the outbreak of a third world war over Berlin, the incident led to increased tension between East and West. It also deepened the division of Germany into a Capitalist West and a Communist East. The Berlin Crisis had also shown the Western countries that Russian expansion was a constant threat.

Children from West Berlin look on as an American airplane arrives with essential supplies during the blockade.

THE NORTH ATLANTIC TREATY ORGANISATION (NATO)

In April 1949 the US, Canada, and ten Western European countries signed a defence pact known as the *North Atlantic Treaty Organisation* (NATO). An attack on any member of the alliance would be regarded as an attack upon them all. The US and Britain had nuclear weapons. In the year that NATO was established, the Soviet Union also produced its own atom bomb. As a result, tension between East and West reached an even higher level. The Cold War was now at its height. Each side confronted the other with the threat of nuclear weapons and a constant barrage of propaganda. Huge stockpiles of weapons were built up and large numbers of spies were active on both sides of the iron curtain.

TEST YOUR KNOWLEDGE
1 *What decision concerning the future of Germany was taken at the Yalta Conference in 1945?*
2 *What plans had Stalin for Germany?*
3 *Why did the Russians blockade West Berlin in June 1948?*
4 *Describe the response of the Western powers.*
5 *When was NATO founded? Which non-European powers were members?*
6 *Would you agree that the Cold War was at its height in 1949? Explain your answer.*

THE KOREAN WAR

In June 1950, war broke out in the Far Eastern country of Korea when the Communist North attacked its non-Communist neighbour to the South. This was a further incident in the Cold War because the Soviet Union supported and armed the North Koreans while the Americans assisted South Korea.

After the entire country had been freed from Japanese control at the end of World War II, the Russians had occupied the North where they set up a Communist government under Kim Il Sung. In the South, the Americans allowed free elections which resulted in a non-Communist government led by Syngman Rhee. As in Germany, it was originally hoped to unite both zones, but the Cold War divisions between the US and the Soviet Union prevented this.

It is unclear whether the Russians forced the North Koreans to attack the South in June 1950. It could well have been an effort by Stalin to compensate for his failure with the Berlin Blockade. However, it may have been the new Communist Chinese government of Mao Tse Tung, in power since 1949, which encouraged the North Koreans to start the war.

President Truman immediately went to the United Nations to get support for South Korea. As the Russians were boycotting the UN, they were not present to veto action against North Korea. It was decided to send United Nations forces to defend South Korea, although in practice most of the troops who went to Korea were Americans in UN uniforms. The American general, Douglas MacArthur, was placed in command.

Having expelled the North Koreans from the South, MacArthur's forces invaded North Korea. At this stage, the Chinese leader Mao Tse Tung ordered 300,000 soldiers to cross the Yalu River and go to the assistance of the North Koreans. The war which began between the two Koreas had now become a conflict between the US and China.

UN forces moving to the front line during the Korean War, in February 1951.

General MacArthur wished to attack bases in China and urged President Truman to use atomic weapons. Fearing Russian involvement and the possible outbreak of nuclear war, Truman sought to end the conflict and dismissed MacArthur in April 1951.

Although peace talks began in July 1951, they were to drag on for two years. Eventually, on 27 July 1953, peace terms were signed at the North Korean city of Panmunjom. As a result, the two Koreas returned to the pre-1950 position after a war which had cost many lives.

For the US, the settlement was a satisfactory solution to the Korean War. Containment as outlined in the Truman Doctrine had been put into action. Although relations with China were now at a low ebb, American relations with the USSR were about to improve slightly as new leaders came to power in both Washington and Moscow.

TEST YOUR KNOWLEDGE
1 *Explain how war broke out in Korea in June 1950.*
2 *Why was this an incident in the Cold War?*
3 *How did the situation in Korea resemble what had happened in Germany?*
4 *Name the Communist leader of China.*
5 *Explain the role of the United Nations in the Korean War.*
6 *Why did the Chinese become involved in the war?*
7 *Explain the outcome of the Korean War.*

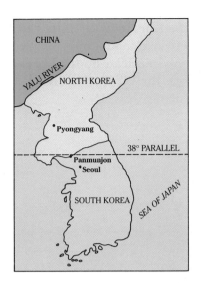

The Korean War, 1950-53

Mao-Tse-Tung, Communist leader of China for over twenty-five years

Chapter 11: Review

- At the end of World War II, much of Europe lay in ruins, and the US and the USSR emerged as the two Superpowers.

- In April 1945, the United Nations was set up in order to preserve world peace through international co-operation. The three main parts of the UN are the General Assembly, the Security Council and the Secretariat.

- The most powerful figure in the UN is the Secretary General. The UN has set up agencies such as UNICEF to improve social and economic conditions around the world.

- While the two Superpowers had been allies in the war against Hitler, there were fundamental differences between them. The US is Capitalist with a two-party democratic system of government, while the USSR is a one-party Communist state.

- By 1946 deep divisions had emerged between the USSR under Stalin and the US under Truman. While there was great rivalry between them it stopped short of open warfare. This state of affairs was known as the Cold War.

- In 1947 President Truman announced the Truman Doctrine. This involved a foreign policy known as containment. By this Truman meant that he would give help to any country trying to stop or 'contain' the spread of Communism.

- In June 1948, a crisis occurred over the city of Berlin which, along with Germany, had been divided into four occupation zones at the end of the war. The Russians tried to force the Western Allies out of the city by means of a blockade. This plan failed, however, when the Americans organised the Berlin Airlift to supply essential goods to West Berlin.

- In 1949, Western European countries joined the US and Canada to form a military alliance known as NATO.

- The Korean War started in June 1950, between communist North Korea and pro-American South Korea. Involving both the US and China, it ended with a truce in July 1953.

ACTIVITIES

1 Complete the following sentences.
  (a) After 1945, the two world Superpowers were _____.
  (b) In April 1945 at San Francisco, the representatives of fifty countries signed _____.
  (c) United Nations peace-keeping forces have served in trouble spots such as _____.
  (d) In April 1945, President Roosevelt of the US died and was succeeded by _____.
  (e) In March 1948, the famous 'Iron Curtain Speech' was made by _____.

2 Fill in the blanks with words from the box.

Truman	Communism	Plan	Containment
Doctrine	Stalin	Eastern	

After 1945, _____ was determined to extend _____ in _____ Europe. To counter the spread of Communism, President _____ of the United States decided on two policies. These were the Truman _____ and the Marshall _____. Another name for the first of these was _____.

3 Write a paragraph on the Korean War.

4 Write out an imaginary dialogue between a student who supported the West in the Cold War and a student who supported the East. You may use W for West and E for East.

5 Choose two pieces of primary evidence from this chapter and state how they helped your understanding of the Cold War.

PEACEFUL CO-EXISTENCE

FROM STALIN TO KHRUSHCHEV

During 1953, both Superpowers experienced changes of leadership. In January, Dwight D. Eisenhower, the former general who had led the Allied forces in World War II, succeeded Harry Truman as president of the United States. One of his main objectives was to bring about a quick end to the Korean War.

On 5 March, Joseph Stalin died in Moscow. For twenty-five years he had ruled the Soviet Union with his iron will. Since 1945 he had controlled all of Eastern Europe as well. It remained to be seen if his successors could maintain the same level of control.

For a few years there was a collective government in Moscow as a number of influential Communist party leaders shared power. Among these were Nikita Khrushchev, the First Secretary of the party, and Nikolai Bulganin, the Prime Minister. Under their leadership, the first thaw in the Cold War began to take place.

Nikita Khrushchev, who had emerged as leader of the Soviet Union by 1956.

A THAW IN THE COLD WAR

The first signs of the Russian desire to improve relations with the West were seen at the Korean Peace Settlement of July 1953 when the Soviet leaders encouraged the Chinese to agree to a settlement.

In 1955, the USSR and the western powers, the USA, Great Britain and France, agreed to end the occupation of Austria and to establish the country as an independent, neutral state.

Events at the United Nations in 1955 also showed a thaw in the Cold War. In that year, both Superpowers lifted their objections to a number of other countries joining the UN. Up to then, the US had prevented friends of the Soviet Union from joining, while the Russians had prevented the membership of pro-American countries. The Republic of Ireland, seen by the Russians as friendly to the US, was allowed to join the United Nations under this new arrangement.

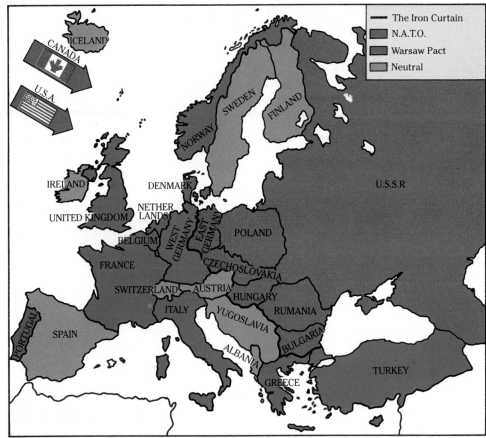

Europe in 1955, divided between NATO and Warsaw Pact countries

Legend:
- The Iron Curtain
- N.A.T.O.
- Warsaw Pact
- Neutral

THE WARSAW PACT: 1955

Despite this slight thaw in the Cold War, the Soviet leaders did not neglect the primary aim of Russian security. As a response to NATO, they set up a Communist defence pact in Eastern Europe in 1955. Because the agreement was signed at Warsaw, the Polish capital, it was known as the *Warsaw Pact*. Its members agreed to place their armed forces under the command of a Russian general.

From then on, two rival alliances, NATO and the Warsaw Pact, faced each other across the 'iron curtain' which ran down the middle of Europe.

TEST YOUR KNOWLEDGE
1 *Who became president of the US in 1953?*
2 *When did the Soviet leader, Joseph Stalin, die?*
3 *How was the Soviet Union ruled after Stalin's death?*
4 *Explain the Austrian settlement of 1955.*
5 *How did the thaw in the Cold War influence affairs at the United Nations?*
6 *What was the Warsaw Pact? When was it founded?*

PEACEFUL CO-EXISTENCE

Nikita Khrushchev and the other Soviet leaders who succeeded Stalin relaxed the control of the secret police in the Soviet Union. In a surprising speech to the Congress of the Communist party in February 1956, Khrushchev condemned Stalin as a tyrant and a dictator.

Khrushchev also began to change the way Soviet leaders spoke about the outside world. Lenin and Stalin had declared that Communism would eventually overthrow Capitalism throughout the world. While Khrushchev also believed this, he saw it as something which would happen in the distant future. In the meantime, the Soviet Union and her Communist allies should have friendly relations with Capitalist countries. This policy was known as *peaceful co-existence*.

UNREST IN EASTERN EUROPE

The policy of peaceful co-existence was put under strain in the countries of Eastern Europe. These Warsaw Pact countries were often known as Russian *satellites* because they were under the overall control of the Soviet government in Moscow. Only the presence of the Red Army kept the unpopular Communist governments in power in these countries If their peoples had been allowed to hold free elections, they would have turned the Communists out of government.

Harsh economic policies made many of these governments unpopular. Another cause of complaint was the persecution of people because of their religious beliefs. Practising Christians found it hard to get jobs. Even in largely Catholic countries like Poland and Hungary, bishops and priests were imprisoned, churches were closed and religious education was banned in the schools.

A few months after Stalin's death, people in East Germany rebelled against the Communist government in June 1953. The rising was crushed by the Red Army. Over 400 people died when unarmed workers found themselves helpless against tanks and machine guns.

In 1956, a rising in Poland led to a change by which the Communist leadership moved away from the previously hardline type of ruler. However, the country still remained under a Communist government and continued to be part of the Warsaw Pact.

The most serious of all the anti-Soviet rebellions in Eastern Europe, however, took place in Hungary in 1956.

TEST YOUR KNOWLEDGE
1 *What was surprising about Khrushchev's speech to the Communist Party Congress in 1956?*
2 *Explain the meaning of 'peaceful co-existence'.*
3 *Give one reason why this policy was followed.*
4 *What were the 'Russian satellite countries'?*
5 *State two reasons why Communist governments in Eastern Europe were unpopular.*

6 *What occurred in East Germany in June 1953?*
7 *What was the result of the rising in Poland in 1956?*

A RISING IN HUNGARY: 1956

Events in Poland influenced people in Hungary who longed to achieve complete freedom from the Soviet Union. In October 1956, a huge uprising against the Russians took place in the Hungarian capital, Budapest.

WORKING WITH EVIDENCE

The Uprising in Hungary: A Diary of Events

The following extracts are from newspapers written at the time of the Hungarian uprising. Read them and answer the questions which follow.

22 October
'The students of the Engineering University called a meeting in a big hall in the college. During it, one student jumped to the platform and shouted: "The truth is that the Russians exploit us worse than a colony". The 4000 students crammed in the hall howled their approval. When another student shouted "We want to be rid of the Russians", the roar of approval was deafening.'

23 October
'Demonstrators occupied the radio station and hung out Hungarian flags in front of the building.
Later a crowd stormed the office of the main Communist newspaper and another crowd attacked a Soviet bookstore.'

24 October
'Radio announcements condemned the rebels as fascists and counter-revolutionaries and declared that the government had invited in Soviet troops under the terms of the Warsaw Treaty.'

26 October
'Despite the presence of Soviet tanks on the streets, youths, pistols in hand, slink along the walls of buildings.'

29 October
'Soviet tanks and troops crunched out of the war-battered city of Budapest carrying their dead with them. They left a wrecked city where the stench of death rises from the smoking ruins.'

1 *What was the main message to come from the gathering of students?*
2 *Why do you think that demonstrators would have occupied the radio station?*
3 *Prove from the extract that the crowds in Budapest wished to prevent the spread of Communist propaganda.*
4 *Did the rebels succeed in capturing the main radio station by 24 October? Explain your answer.*
5 *What weapons had the Hungarians to use against Soviet troops in tanks?*

The statue of
Stalin was
knocked to the
ground during
the Hungarian
Uprising of 1956.

Soviet tanks on
the streets of
Budapest in 1956.

By the time the Hungarian Rising had been crushed on 7 November, 25,000 Hungarians and 3500 Russians lay dead in Budapest. The Hungarian leader, Imre Nagy, who wished to break away from Russian control, was executed and replaced by a pro-Russian Communist.

Although the Hungarians had appealed to the United States and other Western countries for help during the rising, they only received words of support. Any action by the West in their favour could have led to nuclear war.

Despite the improvements in relations between the Superpowers after Stalin's death, events in Hungary in 1956 proved that a vast gulf still existed between Communist-controlled states on the one hand and those in favour of free speech and free elections on the other.

THE BERLIN WALL

In January 1961, John F. Kennedy replaced Eisenhower as president of the US. When he and Khrushchev met for the first time in Vienna the following June, the sixty-seven year old Soviet leader was not impressed by the younger American president. Kennedy was forty-four at the time. Khrushchev mistakenly thought that Kennedy would turn out to be weak. Khrushchev was in difficulty at home because of the poor performance of the Russian economy. So he decided to attempt an aggressive policy towards the West. The first example of this was seen in Berlin.

The divided city had been free of major incidents since the East German uprising of 1953. In 1958, Khrushchev had tried and failed to get the Western powers to leave West Berlin. By 1961, vast numbers of East German citizens were moving to the more prosperous West Germany by travelling first to West Berlin. Indeed since 1945, the German Democratic Republic (East Germany) had lost over 3½ million citizens who had fled to the West.

On the morning of 13 August 1961, Berliners awoke to find a wall of barbed wire dividing Communist East Berlin from the rest of the city. Families were divided, homes bricked up, watch towers were built and border guards were told to shoot to kill.

The East German leader, Walter Ulbricht, declared that he was protecting his country from economic ruin by the Capitalist West. In non-Communist countries, however, people were horrified at the construction of the *Berlin Wall*. For them, it was a proof that Communism had failed if Communist governments had to imprison their peoples in this manner.

People made heroic attempts to escape across the Berlin Wall and many died in the attempt. In June 1963, President Kennedy visited West Berlin to express his solidarity with the people there.

As with the Berlin Blockade before it, the Berlin Wall added to the tension between the Superpowers and prolonged the bitterness of the Cold War.

President John F. Kennedy.

The visit of President Kennedy of the US to West Berlin and the Berlin Wall in June 1963.

THE CUBAN MISSILE CRISIS: 1962

Despite Khrushchev's belief in peaceful co-existence, both Superpowers continued to build up their supplies of weapons, especially nuclear missiles. Still believing that he could gain an advantage over President Kennedy, the Soviet leader decided to intervene in the island of Cuba in the Caribbean.

In 1959, a successful Communist revolution had taken place in Cuba under the leadership of Fidel Castro. As Cuba is only about 150 kilometres from the coast of Florida in the US, American leaders were greatly concerned. The US immediately banned all trade with Cuba. At the same time, the USSR came to the assistance of Castro. The Russians agreed to buy Cuba's entire sugar crop and to send economic aid to the island.

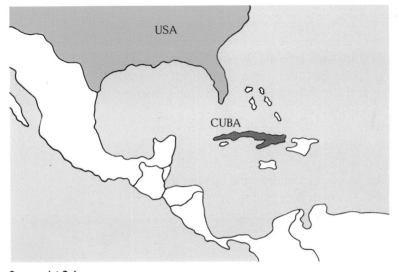

Fidel Castro, the Communist leader of Cuba.

Communist Cuba under Fidel Castro had close relations with the USSR.

Khrushchev went a step further, however. In 1962 he began to place secret missile sites in Cuba. When Kennedy demanded their removal, the crisis which followed became known as the *Cuban Missile Crisis*. It was one of the most serious developments of the Cold War and brought the world to the brink of a disastrous nuclear conflict between the Superpowers.

From aerial photographs, the Americans were able to observe the construction of the missile sites in Cuba. On 13 September 1962, Kennedy issued a strong warning:

'If at any time the Communist build-up in Cuba were to endanger or interfere with our military security in any way, or if Cuba should ever become an offensive military base for the Soviet Union, then this country will do whatever must be done to protect its own security and that of its allies.'

An American photograph of a Soviet missile base on the island of Cuba.

MISSILE SHELTER TENT

TRACKED PRIME MOVERS

OXIDIZER TANK TRAILERS

FUEL TANK TRAILERS

However, when Kennedy spoke to the Soviet foreign minister, Andrei Gromyko, he was assured that Khrushchev had no intention of sending nuclear missiles to Cuba. Kennedy now had three choices: give in to the Soviet Union; attack the missile sites in Cuba; or blockade the island and prevent Soviet ships from arriving there with weapons. He decided on a blockade, as an attack could start a nuclear war. Kennedy could not give in because, if the missiles were set up in Cuba, many American cities would be within their range.

When Russian ships were only half an hour's journey from the American fleet near Cuba, they suddenly stopped and turned back. Khrushchev had decided that his gamble could not succeed. To save face, he had promised that he would withdraw the missiles if the US agreed not to invade Cuba. Kennedy accepted these terms and the world was relieved that nuclear war was avoided.

The Cuban Missile Crisis was an important turning point in the Cold War. Although the Superpowers continued to be keen rivals, never again did they come so close to all-out nuclear war. Indeed a special telephone known as the *Hotline* was established between the US president's headquarters, the White House, and the headquarters of the Soviet leader, the Kremlin in Moscow. This was set up in order to make communication easier during a crisis. The Superpowers also began efforts to reduce the level of armaments in the wake of the Cuban Missile Crisis.

Castro with his ally, the Soviet leader Nikita Khrushchev.

A Russian ship bound for Cuba.

TEST YOUR KNOWLEDGE

1 Who became President of the US in 1961?

2 Why did Khrushchev decide on an aggressive policy against the West?

3 How many citizens fled from the German Democratic Republic (East Germany) between 1945 and 1961?

4 When was the Berlin Wall built and why?

5 Name the Communist leader who came to power in Cuba in 1959.

6 How did the Cuban Missile Crisis start?

7 Why did President Kennedy take action?

8 What did the two leaders agree to do in order to end the crisis?

THE SPACE RACE

During the 1960s, space exploration was another area in which keen rivalry existed between the Superpowers. Despite the harsh economic conditions which the people were experiencing, the Soviet leaders spent vast amounts of money on their space research programme. In 1957, this led to a sensational breakthrough when a Soviet rocket launched an artificial satellite, the *Sputnik*, into orbit around the earth.

Four years later, the Russians recorded another first in space exploration. In 1961, the Russian cosmonaut, Major Yuri Gagarin, became the first man to go into orbit around the earth.

The Americans were shocked by these early Soviet successes in space exploration. Up until then, they had believed that they were the world leaders in this area. The US government now stepped up its programme of space exploration. As rockets could also be used to launch weapons, space exploration became closely linked with the arms race.

Throughout the 1960s, both Russians and Americans conducted a 'space race' to place the first man on the moon. In 1969, the Americans won the race when Neil Armstrong and Edwin ('Buzz') Aldrin from the spaceship Apollo 11 became the first men to land on the moon.

Yuri Gagarin – the first man in space.

Edwin ('Buzz') Aldrin walking on the moon in July 1969.

From then on, American astronauts and Soviet cosmonauts have carried out longer and longer journeys of space exploration. At the same time, unmanned satellites have been sent vast distances from which they continue to transmit information back to earth.

The space race, which began as a contest between the Superpowers, has greatly increased people's knowledge of the vast universe of which the earth is just a small part.

The American space control centre (NASA).

THE BREZHNEV ERA

Although Khrushchev had led the USSR during the great early achievements in space exploration, his popularity as a leader suffered because of troubles in the Russian economy. Although most Russians were proud of their space exploration programme, they wondered why a government which could carry this out could not end food shortages and improve overall living conditions. In October 1964, Khrushchev was removed from the leadership by a majority of his colleagues. Unlike previous situations in the USSR, he was not executed or placed in prison but was allowed to retire quietly.

Khrushchev was replaced as leader by Leonid Brezhnev. Under Brezhnev and his colleagues, Khrushchev's policy of allowing criticism of Stalin was outlawed. Writers and others who criticised the government were placed in prisons or mental hospitals. This, in turn, worsened relations with the US and the rest of the world.

Leonid Brezhnev became leader of the Soviet Union in 1964.

102

THE BREZHNEV DOCTRINE

In 1968, Soviet troops intervened in Czechoslovakia to bring down the government of Alexander Dubcek, a reforming Communist leader. Although there was little bloodshed, unlike Hungary in 1956, the basic situation was the same. The Soviet Union would intervene to preserve hardline Communist regimes in the satellite states of Eastern Europe. Indeed this claim to the right of intervention became known as the *Brezhnev Doctrine*.

Despite the harshness of the government in the USSR during the Brezhnev period, there were some signs of a desire for peaceful co-operation. These were mainly found in the area of arms reduction which we shall read about in the next chapter.

Alexander Dubcek, the reforming leader of Czechoslovakia.

Soviet tanks rolling into Prague in August 1968.

TEST YOUR KNOWLEDGE

1 What was the Sputnik? When was it launched?
2 Name the first Russian cosmonaut in space.
3 Who were the first men to land on the moon?
4 Why was Khrushchev removed from power in 1964?
5 How did Brezhnev's policies differ from Khrushchev's?
6 What took place in Czechoslovakia in 1968?
7 Explain 'the Brezhnev Doctrine'.

Chapter 12: Review

- In the 1950s Eisenhower replaced Truman as American president. Within a few years of Stalin's death in 1953, Nikita Khrushchev emerged as leader in the USSR. Khrushchev believed in a policy known as peaceful co-existence.

- The USSR continued to maintain strict control over Eastern Europe. A rising took place in Hungary in 1956 against Soviet control. However, it was ruthlessly put down by the USSR.

- In January 1961, John F. Kennedy replaced Eisenhower as president of the US. Khrushchev decided to attempt an aggressive policy towards the West. The first example of this was seen in the erection of the Berlin Wall, cutting off contact between the East and the West.

- The Cuban Missile Crisis of 1962 was probably the most serious episode of the Cold War. A nuclear war was avoided when Kennedy forced Khrushchev into withdrawing Soviet missiles from the island of Cuba.

- During the 1960s, space exploration was another area of keen rivalry between the Superpowers.

- In 1964, Leonid Brezhnev became the new leader of the Soviet Union. Despite the harshness of his government in the USSR, there were some signs of a desire for peaceful co-operation with the West.

ACTIVITIES

1 *Multiple Choice*
   (a) *In 1953, a new president came to power in the US. His name was:*
      (i) George Marshall; (ii) Franklin Roosevelt; (iii) John Kennedy (iv) Dwight Eisenhower.
   (b) *In July 1953, agreement was reached concerning: (i) the Korean War; (ii) the Berlin Blockade; (iii) Arms Reduction (iv) the Borders of Poland.*
   (c) *In 1955, a Communist defence pact was signed at: (i) Moscow; (ii) East Berlin; (iii) Warsaw; (iv) Prague.*
   (d) *Peaceful co-existence is associated with the following Soviet leader: (i) Bulganin; (ii) Khrushchev; (iii) Molotov; (iv) Stalin.*
   (e) *Imre Nagy was executed for leading a rising in: (i) East Germany; (ii) Poland; (iii) Chechoslovakia; (iv) Hungary.*

2 *Match an item in Column 1 with an item in Column 2.*

COLUMN 1	COLUMN 2
Dubcek	East Germany
Castro	Yugoslavia
Gromyko	Cuba
Ulbricht	USSR
Tito	Czechoslovakia

3 *Write a paragraph on Khrushchev as leader of the USSR.*

4 *Choose one crisis described in the chapter and answer the following questions about it:*
   (a) *Its origins*
   (b) *The events of the crisis itself*
   (c) *How it fitted into the Cold War as a whole.*

5 *Write a newspaper article on the Cuban Missile Crisis.*

THE AGE OF DETENTE

During the 1960s, the policy of peaceful co-existence between the Superpowers was taken a step further. They began to move towards more friendly relations. This movement was known as *detente*, which means an easing of the strained relations which had existed up to then. The area in which detente was most in evidence was the attempt to limit the spread of nuclear weapons.

ARMS LIMITATION

In 1963, the first step was taken along the road to arms reduction between the Superpowers. In October of that year, a *Test Ban Treaty* was signed in Moscow between the US and the USSR. This outlawed nuclear testing in the air, in space and underwater. Many other countries added their names to the treaty.

One serious problem facing the Superpowers was the possibility that smaller states would develop nuclear weapons. To prevent this they signed a *Non-Proliferation Treaty* in 1968. Under this agreement, existing nuclear powers agreed not to help non-nuclear states to develop nuclear weapons.

In 1972, the *Strategic Arms Limitation Talks* (SALT) began between the Superpowers. The agreement, known as SALT 1, limited the number of nuclear missiles held by the US and the USSR. In 1979, SALT 2 placed further limits on the number of these missiles.

President Richard Nixon of the US and the Soviet Leader, Leonid Brezhnev, sign a SALT Agreement in Moscow in 1972.

During the 1980s, arms limitation talks between Washington and Moscow proceeded further. However, the Soviet leaders insisted on a halt to an American research project known as *Star Wars*. Star Wars involved the development of weapons which could shoot down enemy missiles in space. It was a favourite project of Ronald Reagan, president of the United States from 1981 to 1988.

Despite disagreement concerning Star Wars, the Superpowers continued with negotiations on arms reductions. Along with other benefits, it would help their economies if they could spend less on weapons.

HUMAN RIGHTS AND THE HELSINKI CONFERENCE (1975)

Throughout the 1970s and 1980s, people in Western Europe and America expressed grave concern over the treatment of people who criticised the governments in Communist countries. These critics were known as *dissidents* because they expressed dissent or disagreement with the policies of their Communist rulers. In the USSR and other Communist countries, they were frequently placed in prisons or mental hospitals. Prominent Russian dissidents included the famous novelist, Alexander Solzhenitsyn, and the brilliant scientist, Andrei Sahkarov. Solzhenitsyn was persecuted because he exposed the conditions in Soviet labour camps and Sahkarov because he criticised the nuclear weapons programme.

Alexander Solzhenitsyn, the Soviet author and dissident. His first great novel, *A day in the life of Ivan Denisovich*, exposed the conditions in a Siberian labour camp.

Dr Andrei Sakharov, the Soviet scientist and dissident and winner of the Nobel Peace prize.

Many people in the West argued that any future military or economic co-operation with Communist countries should include commitments from them that the human rights of all citizens in these states would be respected. In 1975, a conference took place at Helsinki in Finland in which these human rights issues were discussed. It resulted in the *Helsinki Declaration on Human Rights*, which was signed by all the states which took part. In Europe, every state except Albania signed the agreement.

Despite the Helsinki Agreement, there were repeated cases of the denial of human rights in the Soviet Union and Eastern Europe. Human rights in the USSR and in Eastern Europe, however, improved greatly when a new Soviet leader came to power in 1985. His name was Mikhail Gorbachev.

TEST YOUR KNOWLEDGE
1 *Explain what is meant by* detente.
2 *What was agreed under the Test Ban Treaty (1963)?*
3 *Why did the Superpowers sign the Non-Proliferation Treaty in 1968?*
4 *What do the initials SALT stand for?*
5 *Who were the dissidents?*
6 *Name two famous Russian dissidents.*
7 *What was agreed at Helsinki in 1975?*

PRESIDENT GORBACHEV IN POWER
GLASNOST AND PERESTROIKA

From the outset, President Gorbachev made it clear that he wanted to introduce reforms in the Soviet Union. In order to improve living conditions at home, he needed the assistance of the US and other Western states. He also genuinely wished to end the Cold War and to improve relations between East and West.

Mikhail Gorbachev.

A visit of President and Mrs Reagan to Moscow in May 1988. As part of the spirit of glasnost, visits between American and Soviet leaders became more frequent.

Gorbachev's two main approaches to reforming the Soviet Union were *glasnost* and *perestroika*. *Glasnost* is a Russian word for 'openness'. Gorbachev believed that criticism of mistakes made by Soviet governments should be allowed. He believed that such openness or *glasnost* would lead to reforms and improvements in the Soviet economy and in society generally. As part of his policy of *glasnost*, Gorbachev extended the hand of friendship to many leading dissidents. He allowed freedom of speech in television, radio, books and newspapers. This restoration of human rights to Soviet citizens greatly pleased people in the West and led to improved relations with the Soviet Union.

By *perestroika*, Gorbachev meant a restructuring of the Soviet economy which would reduce the level of state control and allow a certain amount of private enterprise. He did this in order to improve living conditions for the Soviet people.

Gorbachev did not restrict his reforms to the Soviet Union alone. He allowed Russia's 'satellites' in Eastern Europe to press ahead with reforms themselves. In these countries this decision was to have startling results.

THE COLLAPSE OF COMMUNISM IN EASTERN EUROPE

With the death of Leonid Brezhnev came the end of the Brezhnev Doctrine. Instead Mikhail Gorbachev decided that the Soviet army would not intervene to keep unpopular Communist regimes in power. As a result, these governments collapsed one after another and were replaced by democratically elected rulers.

In Poland, there was a powerful trade union movement. Known as *Solidarity*, it was under the leadership of Lech Walesa. While the Communists held power in Poland, Solidarity members were harassed by the police. However, in 1989, Solidarity provided many of the members of Poland's first democratically elected government in over fifty years.

Like Poland, the Communist regimes in Hungary and Czechoslovakia came under pressure from the ordinary people and were replaced by freely elected governments. In Czechoslovakia, the new president, Vaclav Havel, was a playwright and former dissident who had been imprisoned many times for his beliefs by the Communist rulers.

Bulgaria, Yugoslavia and Rumania also witnessed the collapse of Communist regimes. In Rumania, the revolution only came about with a great deal of bloodshed. In December 1989, the Communist dictator, Nicolai Ceaucescu, a ruthless tyrant, was overthrown by a popular revolution. As the world looked on, people could see the events unfold on their television screens. Pictures of the fighting were broadcast and the new government even released scenes from the trial and execution of Ceaucescu and his wife.

A Solidarity march in Poland led by the movement's leader, Lech Walesa, who is seen here in the centre. In 1990, he was elected President of Poland.

The US greatly welcomed the changes in Eastern Europe. Here we see the American President George Bush (right) on a visit to Czechoslovakia where he met Vaclav Havel, the Czech president.

By far the most exciting changes, however, took place in East Germany. Berlin, the scene of many conflicts during the Cold War, was to be at the centre of its last act in the autumn of 1989.

TEST YOUR KNOWLEDGE
1 *Did President Gorbachev wish to introduce changes in the Soviet Union? Explain your answer.*
2 *Explain the meaning of: (a) glasnost; (b) perestroika.*

People take to the streets in Bucharest to demonstrate against the government of Nicolai Ceaucescu.

Nicolai Ceaucescu and his wife, Elena, pictured during their trial.

The fall of Communism in Eastern Europe

EAST GERMANY

POLAND

U.S.S.R.

CZECHOSLOVAKIA

HUNGARY

RUMANIA

BULGARIA

countries where popular revolutions against communist rule took place

109

3 *How did the condition of dissidents in the USSR improve under Gorbachev?*

4 *What was Gorbachev's attitude to the 'satellite' states in Eastern Europe?*

5 *What is Solidarity? Who was its leader?*

6 *Who was Vaclav Havel?*

7 *Name the Rumanian dictator who was overthrown in December 1989.*

GERMANY REUNITED

In the summer of 1989, the government of Hungary opened up its border with Austria. Thousands of East Germans travelled immediately to Hungary in order to reach West Germany through Austria. For nearly thirty years, the Berlin Wall had closed off the last exit in the Iron Curtain. Now, once again, East Germans availed of any opportunity to flee to the more prosperous Capitalist West Germany.

The East German Communist leader, Erich Honecker, called on the Hungarians to seal their borders, but his request was refused. Throughout the autumn of 1989, people began to protest publicly against the Communist government on the streets of East German towns such as Leipzig, Dresden and East Berlin. On 18 October, Honecker was replaced as leader by a reforming Communist, Egon Krenz. Events were now moving at a fast pace. On 9 November, Krenz's government agreed to open the Berlin Wall.

Jubilant crowds make their way over the Berlin Wall on the night of 9-10 November 1989.

WORKING WITH EVIDENCE

On hearing the news about the Berlin Wall, thousands of people gathered to celebrate and to cross into West Berlin. To avoid injury, the border guards had to stop checking people's passports and to let everybody through. The rejoicing went on until dawn. Read the following newspaper account and answer the questions which follow.

A Dream of Freedom

'Some of the West Germans who on Thursday night (9 November) climbed over the wall at the Brandenburg gate were scarcely making sense. "It's madness! madness!", a young woman screamed as she pushed between unresisting East German border guards to step into West Berlin. The Easterners were possessed by a quieter, more mysterious joy.

In the early hours of Friday morning, a few minutes away from the party going on at the Brandenberg gate, Easterners who had gone into the Western part of the city were slipping home again through Checkpoint Charlie. Three men turned out to be bakers, hurrying back to bake their morning's bread. The oldest, genial and quite toothless, had not set foot in the West since Erich Honecker built the wall 28 years ago. "What was it like?", one of his younger colleagues shook his head and smiled. "It was just like a dream," "a fairytale", someone else said.'

From The Sunday Observer, 12 November 1989

1 How does the reporter convey the excitement displayed by the West Germans in Berlin?
2 What approach was taken by the East German border guards?
3 How did the behaviour of the East Germans encountered by the reporter differ from that of the West Germans at the Brandenburg gate?
4 How did some East Germans describe their first experience of the West?

Demolishing the
Berlin Wall.

People from East Berlin receive a great
welcome as they cross over to the West.

It was now obvious that, given free elections, most East Germans would vote for unity with West Germany. On 18 March 1990, the first free elections since 1933 were held in East Germany. There was a clear majority in favour of unity with the West. On 1 July, the two German economies were united with a single currency in operation. Finally, on 3 October 1990, Germany became a united country once again under the government of the former West German Chancellor, Helmut Kohl.

Before German unity could come about, the four former World War II Allied powers – the US, the USSR, Britain and France – had to agree. Cold War divisions had kept Germany divided. The ending of this division was a sign that the Cold War was coming to an end. President Gorbachev of the USSR even agreed that the united Germany could become a member of NATO. Many people, however, wondered if NATO would last indefinitely if Cold War divisions were ended.

THE SUPERPOWERS IN AGREEMENT

By 1990, it was clear that the Superpowers were in agreement on many issues. Nowhere was this more evident than in the United Nations. We have seen already how both the United States and the Soviet Union had often used their power of veto in the UN Security Council during the Cold War. This prevented the United Nations from taking decisive action in various trouble spots throughout the world.

By the late 1980s, however, it became clear that the two Superpowers were willing to co-operate in the United Nations in the cause of world peace. They agreed on united action in areas such as South Africa and the Middle East. When the ruler of Iraq, Saddam Hussein, invaded neighbouring Kuwait in August 1990, the US and USSR agreed at the United Nations to send a peace-keeping force to the area. Such agreement was unthinkable even a few years previously.

Saddam Hussein (seated), the Iraqi President whose takeover of Kuwait in August 1990 led to the Gulf War.

A US paratrooper, on patrol in the Saudi-Arabian desert during the Gulf War.

With the Cold War drawing to a close, many people hoped that the two Superpowers were entering on a new age of co-operation. It was hoped that reduced spending on armies and weapons would pave the way for a more determined attack on the real enemies of the human race such as ignorance, poverty and starvation in the Third World and elsewhere.

Presidents of the USA and Soviet Leaders since 1945	
PRESIDENTS OF USA	**SOVIET LEADERS**
Harry Truman 1945-52	Joseph Stalin 1928-53
Dwight Eisenhower 1953-60	Nikita Khrushchev 1953-64
John Kennedy 1961-63	Leonid Brezhnev 1964-82
Lyndon Johnson 1963-68	Yuri Andropov 1982-84
Richard Nixon 1969-75	Konstantin Cernenko 1984-85
Gerald Ford 1975-76	Mikhail Gorbachev 1985-
Jimmy Carter 1977-80	
Ronald Reagan 1981-88	
George Bush 1989-	

Chapter 13: Review

- During the late 1960s, the two Superpowers began to move towards friendly relations. This movement was known as detente. It was most evident in the attempt to limit the spread of nuclear weapons.

- The cause of arms limitation was advanced in the following agreements: Test Ban Treaty; Non-Proliferation Treaty; SALT 1; and SALT 2.

- There was also some advance in the area of human rights. Many people in the West were very concerned over the treatment of those who criticised the governments in Communist countries.

- In 1985, Mikhail Gorbachev became leader of the Soviet Union. He had two new approaches to reforming the Soviet Union: glasnost and perestroika. By glasnost, he meant a new openness. Perestroika meant a restructuring of the Soviet economy in order to reduce the amount of state control.

- A new wave of reforms also took place in the countries of Eastern Europe. In countries like Poland, Hungary and Czechoslovakia, Communist regimes came under pressure from the ordinary people and were replaced by freely-elected governments.

- The most exciting changes took place in East Germany. On 9 November 1989, the new Eastern German leader, Egon Krenz, agreed to open the Berlin Wall. On 3 October 1990, Germany became a united country once again under the government of the former West German chancellor, Helmut Kohl.

ACTIVITIES

1 *Fact of Opinion?*
   State whether each of the following statements is a fact or an opinion.
   (a) *During the 1960s, there was an improvement in relations between the Superpowers in the area of arms control.*
   (b) *During the 1970s, Communist leaders did their best to improve human rights.*
   (c) *President Gorbachev ought to have introduced reforms at a faster pace.*
   (d) *Gorbachev's two main approaches to change in the Soviet Union were known as glasnost and perestroika.*
   (e) *In Poland, there was a popular trade union movement known as Solidarity.*

2 *Complete each of the following sentences.*
   (a) *In the autumn of 1989, exciting changes took place in East _____.*
   (b) *In October 1963, a Test Ban Treaty was signed between _____.*
   (c) *The initials S.A.L.T. stand for _____.*
   (d) *The Helsinki Conference (1975) was very concerned about the area of human _____.*
   (e) *In December 1989, the ruthless dictator of Rumania was overthrown and executed. His name was _____.*

3 *List four steps which the Superpowers took to limit the spread of nuclear arms from 1963 onwards.*

4 *Write a paragraph on President Mikhail Gorbachev of the USSR.*

5 *Describe the collapse of Communism in Eastern Europe in the late 1980s.*

THE SEARCH FOR EUROPEAN UNITY: 1945-57

A CONTINENT IN RUINS

In 1900, Europe was the most powerful area in the world. Some of the European Great Powers such as Britain and France ruled over vast overseas empires, while Europeans lent money to other parts of the world such as the United States. In 1945, however, much of the continent of Europe lay in ruins.

The devastated condition of the German city of Berlin in 1945. Conditions such as this were to be found throughout Europe as a result of bomb damage during World War II.

The decline of Europe which began with World War I was definitely completed by World War II. Weak and divided Europeans were overshadowed by the power of the United States in the West and by the Soviet Union in the East. Even countries which were on the winning side in the war such as Britain and France were heavily in debt and greatly in need of economic recovery.

In this situation, two parallel movements were required. First, a vision of a new Europe was needed in order to inspire people to work for the recovery of the continent. Secondly, a practical programme of economic assistance and organisation was essential if Europe was to be prosperous once again. In the years after 1945, both developments took place. They contributed enormously to the spectacular recovery of the continent.

THE IDEAL OF A UNITED EUROPE

As early as 1930, the French Foreign Minister, Aristide Briand, had called for a United States of Europe both as a means of tackling the Great Depression and a way of helping Germany play a peaceful role in Europe. When Hitler and the Nazis came to power in Germany, such ideas became impossible.

115

With the final defeat of Nazi Germany amid the destruction of much of Europe in 1945, the idea of European unity was revived. Some people saw it as a means of healing the centuries-old hostility between France and Germany. With Stalin's Soviet Union in control of Eastern Europe, people in Western Europe began to consider unity as a possible means of protection against further Soviet expansion.

The United States encouraged this idea for security reasons, as did the former British prime minister, Winston Churchill. In a famous speech at Zurich on 19 September 1946, he called for the establishment of a United States of Europe. Churchill declared that the first step in the creation of the European family must be a partnership between France and Germany. As a mark of his commitment to European unity, Churchill became the first president of the newly founded United Europe Movement in 1947.

On the continent of Europe at this time, three great statesmen led the way in proposing European unity – Jean Monnet and Robert Schuman in France and Alcide de Gasperi in Italy.

The strong feeling for unity and co-operation in Europe after 1945 was not sufficient in itself. Economic recovery was also required. This gained a great impetus in 1947 when the United States produced a plan for assisting the slowly recovering economies of Europe.

Alcide de Gasperi (1881-1954), an Italian statesman who worked hard to bring Europeans of different nations closer together from 1945 onwards.

TEST YOUR KNOWLEDGE

1 Describe the condition of Europe in 1945.
2 Why was the idea of European unity revived after 1945?
3 What was the attitude of the US to European unity?
4 Who made a famous speech at Zurich in September 1946 calling for European unity?
5 Name two European statesmen who favoured a united Europe.

THE MARSHALL PLAN

Speaking at Harvard University on 5 June 1947, the American Secretary of State, General George Marshall, announced his government's plan to help European states along the road to economic recovery.

Marshall Aid made possible the re-cultivation of these fruit crops in Germany.

WORKING WITH EVIDENCE

Read the following extracts from Marshall's famous speech and answer the questions which follow.

'In considering the requirements for the rehabilitation of Europe, the physical loss of life, the visible destruction of cities, factories, mines and railroads was correctly estimated, but it has become obvious during recent months that this visible destruction was probably less serious than the dislocation of the entire fabric of the European economy . . .

The rehabilitation of the economic structure of Europe will require a much longer time and a greater effort than had been foreseen . . .

The initiative, I think, must come from Europe. The role of this country should consist of friendly aid in the drafting of a European program and of later support of such a program so far as it may be practical for us to do so . . .

The plan's purpose should be the revival of a working economy in the world so as to permit the emergence of political and social conditions in which free institutions can exist . . .

Before the US government can proceed much further in its efforts to alleviate the situation and help start the European world on its way to recovery, there must be some agreement among the countries of Europe as to the requirements of the situation and the part those countries themselves will take in order to give proper effect to whatever might be undertaken by the government.'

1 *List some of the causes of Europe's economic crisis.*
2 *According to Marshall, what was the most serious economic difficulty in Europe?*
3 *From where did he believe that the initiative for recovery should come?*
4 *What would be the role of the US government?*
5 *What political link did Marshall connect with economic recovery?*
6 *What first steps had to be taken by European countries?*

Although economic assistance under the Marshall Plan was offered to all of the countries of Europe, Stalin rejected it on behalf of the USSR and forced the Communist countries in Eastern Europe to reject the offer as well. Western European countries eagerly welcomed the plan, however, and in April 1948 the Organisation for European Economic Co-Operation (OEEC) was set up to administer Marshall Aid.

THE OEEC

Ireland was among the fourteen countries which participated in the OEEC. The organisation drew up a report and sent it to America's President Truman. In the first two and a half years, over twelve million dollars of Marshall Aid was provided. However, each country receiving Marshall Aid had to contribute an equal amount itself towards projects of economic recovery.

The US also gained from the Marshall Plan. Improved economies in Europe provided markets for American goods. More prosperous countries would be less likely to support Communism. In this way, the Marshall Plan fitted in with President Truman's containment policy against the spread of Communism.

Although the OEEC declined in importance with the formal ending of Marshall Aid in 1952, it continued to draw up reports and to advise governments on ways to improve their economies. By encouraging European countries to co-operate and work together, the Marshall Plan was an important stage in the movement towards greater economic unity in Europe.

A meeting of the Council of Europe in 1949.

Konrad Adenauer became the first chancellor or prime minister of the Federal Republic of West Germany in 1949. He remained in power until 1963 and was a strong supporter of closer co-operation between European states.

THE COUNCIL OF EUROPE

While the Marshall Plan was forwarding economic unity in Europe, there was also a movement to bring about closer political union on the continent. We have seen already the first steps taken by Winston Churchill and others in 1946.

In 1948, those in favour of political unity in Europe came together in a great conference at the Hague in the Netherlands. Churchill, Adenauer, Schuman and de Gasperi were among the politicians in attendance. The conference drafted the following 'Message to Europeans'.

Although the Hague Conference rejected the idea of a European Assembly directly elected by the people, the delegates agreed that a Council of Europe should be formed consisting of members of national parliaments.

In May 1949, the Council of Europe was established at Strasbourg in eastern France. It put into practice the plans agreed at the Hague Conference. It contained a consultative assembly of members of various national parliaments and a Committee of Ministers from the various member states.

The powers of the Council of Europe were very limited. It was mainly a forum where politicians of different countries, including Ireland, could exchange ideas. However in two areas it had a deeper influence:

- It drew up the European Convention on Human Rights which was signed by all the member states.
- It set up a Court and Commission of Human Rights to enforce the Convention.

CO-OPERATION ON COAL AND STEEL

In May 1950, the pro-European French foreign minister, Robert Schuman, put forward proposals for the establishment of joint institutions in Europe to take charge of the coal and steel industries. This proposal became known as the *Schuman Plan* and it was eagerly welcomed by the West German chancellor, Konrad Adenauer. Schuman and his adviser, the economist Jean Monnet who drew up the plan,

Robert Schuman announcing the Schuman Plan in Paris on 9 May 1950.

hoped that their *Coal and Steel Plan* would be the first step towards eventual economic unity throughout Europe. Along with Adenauer, the Italian prime minister, de Gasperi, warmly welcomed the plan as did the US government of President Truman.

Eventually six countries decided to join a European Coal and Steel Community: France, West Germany, Italy, the Netherlands, Belgium and Luxembourg. These countries signed a treaty setting up the community in Paris in April 1951.

From the start, the European Coal and Steel Community was a great success. It contributed enormously to the stunning economic recovery which took place in Western Europe during the 1950s.

Success on the economic front further encouraged European governments to attempt co-operation in military matters.

Robert Schuman, the French statesman, was a leading supporter of European union. His *Schuman Plan* laid the foundations for the European Economic Community.

Jean Monnet, the French economist and supporter of European unity.

TEST YOUR KNOWLEDGE
1 *When was the Council of Europe established?*
2 *In what city was its headquarters?*
3 *Name the two greatest achievements of the Council of Europe.*
4 *What was the Schuman Plan (1950)?*
5 *Name two government leaders who welcomed the Schuman Plan.*
6 *List the six countries which formed the European Coal and Steel Community in 1951.*

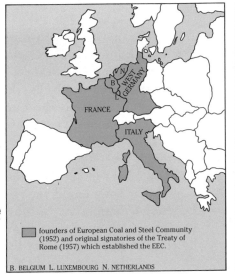

founders of European Coal and Steel Community (1952) and original signatories of the Treaty of Rome (1957) which established the EEC.

B. BELGIUM L. LUXEMBOURG N. NETHERLANDS

Members of the European Coal and Steel Community.

European consumers enjoyed increasing prosperity due to the economic recovery of the 1950s. This led to an increased demand for labour-saving devices or 'modern conveniences'.

THE DEFENCE OF EUROPE

Most Western European countries joined the North Atlantic Treaty Organisation (NATO) which was established in 1949. Since non-European powers such as the US and Canada were members of NATO, some Europeans hoped that they could set up a purely *European defence community* (EDC) in which soldiers from different European countries would serve alongside one another.

In October 1950, the French prime minister, René Plevin, drew up a plan for a European army which would include West Germans, although West Germany could not have a national army of its own. A treaty based on these lines was drawn up and signed by the six members of the European Coal and Steel Community in May 1952.

Great Britain, however, refused to participate in the European Defence Community, as she preferred close friendship rather than unity with the rest of Europe. However, Britain did promise 'all support, short of membership'.

The US government supported the EDC enthusiastically, seeing it as a defence against Communist expansion. After Britain's refusal to join, however, other countries became less enthusiastic. They were unwilling to shoulder the burden of European defence without British assistance. The proposed European Defence Community finally came to an end in 1954 when it was rejected by the French parliament. This decision greatly annoyed the Americans while their rival Superpower, the USSR, rejoiced at the news.

The rejection of the European Defence Community was a setback for those in favour of European unity. In the years ahead, however, they continued to put forward plans for closer co-operation in military matters.

While defence co-operation faltered, economic union was proceeding rapidly in the 1950s. The high point of this movement was reached in 1957 with the establishment of the *European Economic Community*.

121

Chapter 14: Review

- At the end of World War II, many European statesmen believed that the answer to the continent's difficulties lay in some form of European unity. Three men led the way – Jean Monnet and Robert Schuman in France and Alcide de Gasperi in Italy.

- In 1947, the US provided Marshall Aid with the aim of promoting European economic recovery. The European countries formed the Organisation for European Economic Co-operation (OEEC) as a condition of receiving this aid.

- In 1949, a new type of international assembly known as the Council of Europe was set up. In 1951 France, Italy, West Germany, Belgium, the Netherlands and Luxembourg formed the European Coal and Steel Community (ECSC).

- Although most West European countries were members of NATO, some Europeans hoped that they could set up a European Defence Community. In May 1952, this idea was supported in the form of a treaty by the six members of the ECSC. However, the proposed EDC came to an end in 1954 when it was rejected by the French parliament.

ACTIVITIES

1 *True or false?*
   (a) *In May 1949, the Council of Europe was established at Strasbourg in France.*
   (b) *In 1950, Konrad Adenauer, the French foreign minister, put forward a plan for co-operation in the coal and steel industries.*
   (c) *The proposed European Defence Community came to an end when it was rejected by the French parliament in 1954.*
   (d) *In a speech at Zurich in 1946, Winston Churchill spoke in favour of European unity.*
   (e) *Great Britain agreed to join the European Coal and Steel Community in 1951.*

2 *Match an item in Column 1 with an item in Column 2.*

COLUMN 1	COLUMN 2
Monnet	West German Chancellor
OEEC	Coal and Steel Plan
Plevin	a pro-European economist
Adenauer	Marshall Aid
Schuman	A plan for a European Defence Union

3 *List the arguments made in favour of closer European union after 1945.*

4 *Explain the origin and structures of the Council of Europe.*

5 *Outline the attempts made to set up a European Defence Union. Show why they had failed by 1954.*

THE EUROPEAN ECONOMIC COMMUNITY

THE TREATY OF ROME, 1957

On 25 March 1957, an historic event affecting the lives of millions of Europeans took place in Rome. On that day, representatives of the six member states of the European Coal and Steel Community signed the *Treaty of Rome*. Under this treaty, a new organisation known as the *European Economic Community* (EEC) or the *Common Market* was to come into being on 1 January 1958.

The signing of the Treaty of Rome on 25 March 1957 established the European Economic Community.

This was a major step along the road to European union, and the two founding fathers of this union, Jean Monnet and Robert Schuman, were very active in bringing it about. There were 248 Articles in the Treaty of Rome setting up the EEC. The most important were:

- Abolition of all tariffs and restrictions on trade among the six member states
- A common tariff and trade policy towards other countries
- Free movement of people, capital and services among member states
- A common agricultural policy
- A common transport policy
- Fair and free competition within the EEC

To help poorer and more backward regions, a *European Social Fund* was established. At the same time, the six countries signed a *Euratom Treaty* under which they agreed to co-operate in the development of peaceful atomic energy projects.

Take a look at the chart to see the main institutions of the EEC.

In March 1958, Robert Schuman was elected first president of the European Assembly which later became known as the European Parliament. From the outset, the Common Market was to show that free trade could lead to high levels of economic growth. European countries outside the EEC then decided to form a free trade area of their own.

THE EUROPEAN FREE TRADE ASSOCIATION (EFTA)

The failure of Britain to join the EEC in 1957 brought about closer links with five other European countries which were also outside the Common Market. Together with Britain, these five – Denmark, Sweden, Norway, Switzerland and Austria – began talks in 1958 about setting up a free trade area. Portugal later joined in and the seven countries set up the *European Free Trade Association (EFTA)* in July 1959. Finland joined the group in 1961.

Tariffs were gradually reduced on industrial goods entering member states. As a result, trade between EFTA countries almost doubled between 1959 and 1965.

Although British trade within EFTA increased by 72 per cent between 1958 and 1964, her trade with the EEC rose by 98 per cent. As

The institutions of the EEC

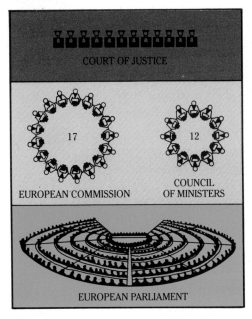

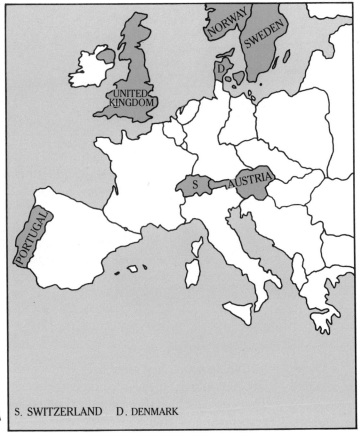

Members of EFTA S. SWITZERLAND   D. DENMARK

well as this, EFTA contained a market of 38 million outside Britain, as four times as large. It was not surprising, therefore, that the British government under their prime minister, Harold Macmillan, decided to apply for membership of the EEC.

TEST YOUR KNOWLEDGE
1 *When was the Treaty of Rome signed?*
2 *List the provisions in the treaty concerning free trade.*
3 *How were poorer regions to be assisted in the EEC?*
4 *What was the Euratom Treaty?*
5 *Who was elected first president of the European Assembly in 1958?*
6 *What was the European Free Trade Association (EFTA)?*
7 *Why did Great Britain apply for membership of the EEC?*

GENERAL DE GAULLE BLOCKS BRITISH ENTRY TO THE EEC

On 29 January 1963, the president of France, General Charles de Gaulle, announced that he would block British entry to the EEC. De Gaulle had been president of France since 1958 and had built up a close relationship with the West German Chancellor, Konrad Adenauer. Despite Adenauer's pleas, de Gaulle would not change his mind regarding Great Britain. He believed that the British were too closely linked with the members of the Commonwealth. He felt that they would try to have the best of both worlds by being members of the EEC while still maintaining close economic links with Commonwealth countries like Canada and Australia.

The president of France, General Charles de Gaulle, blocks British entry to the EEC in January 1963.

De Gaulle's decision was a setback for closer European union. However, he himself was not concerned at this. He did not really believe in complete European union. Instead, he favoured a close partnership between European nation states. Many people believed that another reason why de Gaulle blocked British entry to the EEC was that it would inevitably reduce French influence in the community. With the failure of the British application, the Irish application to enter the EEC was also dropped. It would be almost another ten years before both countries succeeded in joining the Community.

125

AGRICULTURE IN THE EEC

Throughout the 1960s, agriculture was a difficult and divisive area of policy in the EEC. It was obvious that any moves towards closer European union and any sound economic growth would have to involve a healthy farming sector.

The Treaty of Rome had committed the member states to a Common Agricultural Policy, but left it up to institutions in the community to draw up such a policy. Under the Common Agricultural Policy, three main results were hoped for:

- A fair standard of living for farmers
- Reasonable prices to be charged to consumers
- A steady guaranteed market

The Council of Ministers adopted the Common Agricultural Policy in January 1962 following lengthy negotiations. A common market for agricultural produce was to be set up gradually between then and 1970. After 1970, foodstuffs were to circulate freely throughout the EEC at a common price.

In June 1965, difficulties over agriculture led to a walk-out by the French representatives in the EEC. These were only resolved in January 1966 at a special meeting in Luxembourg. The agreement, known as the Luxembourg Compromise, stated that where the vital interests of any member state were involved, decisions could not be reached in the Council of Ministers until all the member states came to an agreement.

Despite difficulties such as this, the EEC continued to prosper. On 1 July 1968, full customs union was achieved when all duties on goods travelling between member states were abolished and a common tariff was established for trade with non-member countries.

With the growing prosperity of the EEC, it is not surprising that Great Britain, Ireland, Norway and Denmark renewed their applications to join the community in 1967.

TEST YOUR KNOWLEDGE
1 *Why did President de Gaulle block British entry to the EEC in 1963?*
2 *Did de Gaulle believe in European union? Explain your answer.*
3 *How did de Gaulle's action affect the Irish application to join the Common Market?*
4 *What is the Common Agricultural Policy?*
5 *When was it first adopted by the Council of Ministers of the EEC?*
6 *List three aims of the Common Agricultural Policy.*
7 *Explain the Luxembourg Compromise (1966).*

THE FIRST ENLARGEMENT OF THE EEC: 1973

With the retirement of General de Gaulle in 1969, the major obstacle to the enlargement of the EEC was removed. Negotiations began between the governments of Great Britain, Ireland, Norway, Denmark and the EEC on terms of entry to the community. These were successfully concluded and on 22 January 1972, an Act of Accession or entry to the EEC was signed by these countries' representatives at the community's headquarters in Brussels.

The people of Ireland and Denmark voted in favour of entry, as did the British parliament. In Norway, however, the people rejected membership of the EEC by a slight majority.

On 1 January 1973, the membership of the EEC increased from six to nine with the entry of Great Britain, Ireland and Denmark. The first Irish person chosen to be a member of the EEC Commission was Dr Patrick Hillery who had negotiated the terms of entry while he was foreign minister in the Fianna Fáil government of Jack Lynch.

Dr Patrick Hillery who as foreign minister negotiated Ireland's entry to the EEC and then became the first Irish member of the EEC Commission.

Soon after its enlargement, however, the European Economic Community was to face serious difficulties when the economic climate took a serious turn for the worst.

The headquarters of the EEC in Brussels, Belgium.

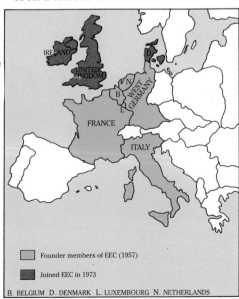

Founder members of EEC (1957)

Joined EEC in 1973

B. BELGIUM D. DENMARK L. LUXEMBOURG N. NETHERLANDS

Members of the EEC in 1973

127

Chapter 15: Review

- On 25 March 1957, the six members of the ESCS signed the Treaty of Rome which set up the European Economic Community (EEC) or Common Market.

- The EEC stood for the abolition of all tariffs and restrictions on trade among the six member countries, a common agricultural and transport policy, and fair and free competition within the EEC.

- In 1959, the European Free Trade Association (EFTA) was set up. This brought about closer links between six countries which were not members of the EEC.

- Throughout the 1960s, agriculture was a difficult and divisive area of policy. The Common Agricultural Policy hoped to achieve a fair standard of living for farmers, reasonable prices and a steady guaranteed market.

- In 1973, three new members joined the EEC – Britain, Denmark and Ireland. The first Irish person chosen to be a member of the European Commission was Dr Patrick Hillery.

ACTIVITIES

1 Complete the following sentences.
   (a) In March 1957, the EEC was founded at the signing of _____ .
   (b) In the EEC, all tariffs and restrictions on trade between member states were _____.
   (c) In March 1958 Robert Schuman was elected _____.
   (d) European countries outside the EEC decided to set up _____.
   (e) The British government of Harold Macmillan applied to _____.

2 True or false?
   (a) The EEC failed to set up a Common Agricultural Policy.
   (b) The Scandinavian countries were prominent members of the European Free Trade Association.
   (c) In January 1963 the West German leader, Konrad Adenauer, blocked British entry to the EEC.
   (d) In 1973, the EEC gained three new member states.
   (e) The first Irish representative on the EEC Commission was the former foreign minister, Dr Patrick Hillery.

3 List the most important provisions of the Treaty of Rome (1957).

4 Write a paragraph on agriculture in the EEC.

THE IMPACT OF THE OIL CRISIS

Hardly had the EEC been enlarged to include nine members, when a serious economic crisis faced its member countries. In October 1973, war between Israel and the Arab countries in the Middle East led to a serious oil shortage and a huge rise in prices. As the community imported over 60 per cent of its energy requirements from abroad, mostly from the Middle East, the economies of member states were seriously damaged.

An Israeli soldier during the Arab-Israeli War of 1973. This war, which led to dearer oil, also brought about closer co-operation between the member states of the EEC.

The crisis helped the process of closer European union, however. First, it encouraged member states to move towards a common energy policy. It also brought about closer co-operation in foreign policy. The foreign ministers of the member states issued a joint statement on the Middle East in November 1973. In the following July, discussions began between the EEC and representatives of twenty Arab states.

During the mid 1970s, the rise in unemployment throughout the community acted as a spur to the leaders to work out a common programme of social action to alleviate poverty and unemployment.

This spirit of closer co-operation was clearly seen at a summit meeting of EEC heads of government which was held in Paris in December 1974.

THE EUROPEAN COUNCIL

At the Paris summit, the EEC leaders agreed to the suggestion of President Giscard d'Estaing of France that they should meet three times a year in future. This new arrangement was to be known as the *European Council*. Not only would the government leaders in the European Council debate community affairs: they would also discuss foreign policy in order to reach a common approach towards countries outside the EEC.

Heads of government at a meeting of the EEC states. From 1974 onwards, these meetings became known as the European Council.

However, the most important decision taken at the Paris summit concerned the European parliament. Up until then, the parliament was made up of MEPs (Members of the European Parliament) sent by each national parliament. It was now decided that, in future, MEPs should be directly elected by citizens in the various member states.

TEST YOUR KNOWLEDGE
1 *What event triggered off an oil crisis in October 1973?*
2 *Why was the EEC so badly affected?*
3 *How did the oil crisis bring EEC member states closer together?*
4 *What was the response of the EEC to unemployment and poverty in the 1970s?*
5 *Explain the formation of the European Council.*
6 *What was decided at the Paris summit of December 1974 concerning the European Parliament?*

A DIRECTLY-ELECTED EUROPEAN PARLIAMENT

In June 1979, voters throughout the EEC went to the polls to elect members to the European parliament. Although such direct elections had been called for in the Treaty of Rome, it was only now that they came into being.

A meeting of the
European Parliament
at Strasbourg.

The European
Parliament flag.

The first directly-elected European parliament contained 410 MEPs. Each member state was allocated a certain number of MEPs, according to the size of its population. The Republic of Ireland elected fifteen MEPs, while Northern Ireland was allocated three out of the United Kingdom's total.

Each country was allowed to use its own system of election. However, when the MEPs went to the European parliament at Strasbourg, they joined fellow MEPs from other countries in larger groups. The main political groupings in the European parliament included:

- The Socialists
- The European People's Party or Christian Democrats
- The European Democratic Group
- The Communists
- The Liberals
- The European Progressive Democrats

Although the power of the European parliament was limited, members expected their influence to grow now that they were directly elected by the people.

MONETARY UNION

One of the aims of the founders of the EEC was to bring about closer financial unity in Europe. In 1979, steps were taken at last to reduce the upward and downward movement of different European currencies against one another.

On 13 March 1979, the *European Monetary System (EMS)* was established. It had two main elements:
- The European Currency Unit (ECU)
- The Exchange Rate Mechanism (ERM)

The ECU is a special European type of currency which depends for its value on the value of the various EEC currencies. The Exchange Rate Mechanism drastically reduced the movement of the different currencies against each other. The EMS brought about an improvement in the financial affairs of the community. Although Ireland joined the system from the beginning, Great Britain did not become a full member until 1990.

Some people like the British prime minister, Mrs Margaret Thatcher, were very suspicious of monetary union, believing that it would reduce the powers of national governments. Others, however, longed for greater monetary union as a step towards political union. Enthusiastic pro-Europeans looked forward to the day when the different national currencies would be no more and the ECU would be in use from the northern tip of Scotland to the isles of Greece.

Mrs Margaret Thatcher, Prime Minister of Great Britain from 1979 to 1990, was very suspicious of moves towards closer European unity.

TEST YOUR KNOWLEDGE
1 *When did the first direct elections to the European parliament take place?*
2 *How many MEPs were elected throughout the community?*
3 *Name two political groupings in the European parliament.*
4 *What do the initials EMS stand for?*
5 *Explain the European Currency Unit (the ECU).*
6 *When did Ireland join the EMS?*
7 *What hopes had pro-Europeans concerning future monetary union?*

THE COMMUNITY EXPANDS

In 1981, Greece became the tenth member state of the EEC. The addition of 9 million Greeks increased the population of the community to 269 million. As Greece was the birthplace of democracy, the country's entry to the EEC had great historic significance. It also meant that the community was less of a northern or western European institution.

The next accession of member states further broadened the area of the EEC by the addition of two southern European states. On 1 January 1986, Spain and Portugal became members. These two countries had only recently become democracies. Their entry to the community strengthened democracy within them and brought Europe further along the road to union. Except for Eastern Communist countries and strictly neutral states, almost all of Europe now belongs to the EEC.

By 1990, the community of twelve had a population of 321 million, over 80 million more than the United States and around 50 million more than the Soviet Union.

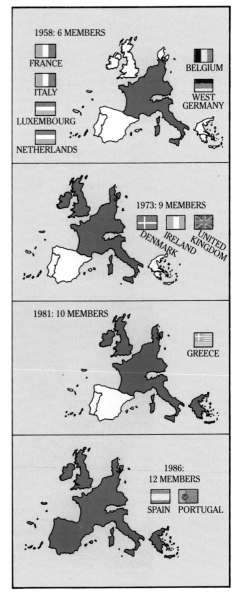

The growth of the European Community

THE SINGLE EUROPEAN ACT

Not only were the member states of the EEC committed to enlarging the community: they also desired closer union among themselves.

In February 1986, representatives of the twelve member states of the EEC signed the Single European Act. This was an amendment of the original Treaty of Rome and an attempt to bring about even closer union. Under this measure, all remaining restrictions on free trade in the community are to be removed by the end of 1992. By then, a Single Market will be created throughout the community. Freedom of movement will be total for people, goods and capital.

Under the Single European Act, there are also reforms in the way in which the EEC conducts its business. In place of unanimous decisions, a qualified type of majority voting is to be used in the Council of Ministers.

The EEC is also committed to move towards greater union in foreign policy and security issues. When trouble arose in areas such as South Africa or the Middle East, foreign ministers of the EEC met and decided on a joint policy.

The Single European Act also covers co-operation in scientific and technological research and a joint approach to protection of the environment. It also sets common standards concerning health and safety in the workplace throughout the member states.

Thus the Single European Act has been built on the foundations established thirty years previously by the Treaty of Rome. It is clear that the year 1992 will have an important impact on the lives of ordinary people throughout the community and form a landmark on the road to closer European union.

A press conference following an EC meeting in Dublin Castle in 1990.

TEST YOUR KNOWLEDGE
1 When did Greece join the EEC?
2 Why was Greek entry of such historic importance?
3 Name the two countries which joined the EEC in 1986.
4 How did the population of the community compare with those of the US and the USSR in 1986?
5 What was the main aim of the Single European Act (1986)?

WESTERN EUROPE OR EUROPE?

Ever since 1945, plans for European union could only be applied to Western European countries because Eastern Europe remained under the control of the USSR. While Stalin and Khrushchev tended to see these movements as anti-Soviet and a threat, later Soviet leaders took a different view.

Mikhail Gorbachev, who became leader of the Soviet Union in 1985, expressed his belief in a single European homeland from the Atlantic to the Urals. Such a vision had been held in earlier years by Churchill and de Gaulle. In his famous Iron Curtain speech in 1946, Churchill had listed the various Eastern European capitals which were then behind the Iron Curtain. Many citizens of these capitals such as Prague and Warsaw longed for closer links with the rest of Europe. Indeed there were always cultural and historic links uniting people in Eastern and Western Europe.

For over forty years, hopes for a European union involving all of Europe remained dreams concerning a distant future. However, the break-up of the Berlin Wall and the end of the iron curtain dividing East from West in 1989 led to a new optimism that all of Europe might be included in future plans for European union.

As the Warsaw Pact begins to break up in the East, it is expected that, eventually, NATO will soon have no useful role in the West. Ultimately, the dream of the founding fathers of the European Movement might be realised: a Europe whose peoples are united, not against any enemy, but among themselves in order to preserve their rich cultural heritage handed down by past generations, providing a better life for themselves and their children.

Chapter 16: Review

- During the 1970s, the economies of EEC countries were seriously damaged when war between Israel and the Arab countries in the Middle East led to an oil shortage and a huge increase in prices.

- The crisis helped the process of European unity by encouraging member states to move towards a common energy policy and by also bringing about closer co-operation in foreign policy.

- In 1974, EEC leaders decided that the European parliament would, from then on, consist of MEPs elected directly by the citizens of the various member countries. The first election to the European parliament took place in June 1979. The Republic of Ireland elected 15 MEPs.

- In 1979, the European Monetary System was set up with the aim of establishing a European Currency Unit and an Exchange Rate Mechanism.

- In 1981, the community expanded when Greece became its tenth member. In 1986, Spain and Portugal became members.

- In 1986, the twelve members of the EEC signed the Single European Act. This was an attempt to bring about closer union by removing all remaining restrictions on free trade in the community by 1992.

ACTIVITIES

1 Complete the following sentences:
   (a) In October 1973, a war in the Middle East led to a shortage of _____.
   (b) At the meeting of heads of government of the EEC in Paris in December 1974, it was decided _____.
   (c) In June 1979, voters throughout the EEC went to the polls to elect the first _____.
   (d) The European Monetary System established in 1979 had two main elements. These were _____.
   (e) In 1986, the EEC was enlarged by the addition of _____.

2 Write a paragraph on the Single European Act.

3 Draw a map of Europe in 1990 and shade in the members of the European Community and the cities which housed its headquarters.

POLITICAL DEVELOPMENTS IN IRELAND IN THE TWENTIETH CENTURY

A DIVIDED LAND

IRELAND UNDER THE UNION

If you were growing up in Ireland over a hundred years ago, you would have seen reminders everywhere of the connection with Great Britain. Each letter box was painted red and decorated with the letters V.R. (*Victoria Regina*), in honour of Queen Victoria. The British flag, the Union Jack, flew from the top of important buildings and British soldiers in their red uniforms were a regular sight on the streets of towns and cities. In maps on the schoolroom wall, Ireland was coloured red, along with the rest of the British Empire.

King Edward VII on a visit to Dublin in 1903

At this time, Ireland was part of a United Kingdom which also included England, Scotland and Wales. Since the abolition of the old Irish parliament in 1800, all Irish MPs attended the British parliament at Westminster in London. Ireland was ruled directly by the British government.

The Houses of Parliament at Westminster in London where Irish lords and MPs attended the British parliament from 1801 onwards.

RULE FROM DUBLIN CASTLE

Dublin Castle was the headquarters of British rule in Ireland. The queen of England was represented by a nobleman known as the Viceroy. His office was in Dublin Castle, but he lived in style at the Viceregal Lodge in the Phoenix Park.

The Viceregal Lodge, Phoenix Park, Dublin where the queen's representative, the Viceroy, lived. Today it is Aras an Uachtarain, the residence of the President of Ireland.

Although the Viceroy represented the queen in Ireland, most of the important business was carried out by the Chief Secretary who was an MP and a member of the British government in London.

When the Chief Secretary was in London attending parliament, he left the Under-Secretary in charge in Dublin Castle. The Under-Secretary was not a politician, but held a permanent post as head of the British civil service in Ireland.

Visiting British monarchs sat on these thrones in Dublin Castle

Soldiers on duty in the courtyard of Dublin Castle

Dublin Castle was also the headquarters of the police force, the *Royal Irish Constabulary* (RIC). Although they usually did their best to act in a fair manner, the members of the RIC were unpopular because they assisted at evictions and passed on information concerning the local

An eviction scene in Co. Donegal in 1880 with members of the Royal Irish Constabulary (RIC) in attendance.

people to police headquarters at Dublin Castle. They were especially required to report on the activities of any people suspected of being against the rule of the British government in Ireland.

Members of the R.IC.

TEST YOUR KNOWLEDGE
1 *Give two signs of British rule in Ireland around 1880.*
2 *What was meant by the term 'United Kingdom'?*
3 *Where did Irish MPs attend parliament?*
4 *Explain the role of the Viceroy.*
5 *Where was the headquarters of the British government in Ireland?*
6 *What did the letters RIC stand for?*

THE UNIONISTS

Around 1880, about a quarter of the people living in Ireland were quite happy to be ruled by the British government. Because they supported the full union between Great Britain and Ireland, they were known as *Unionists*. Although some better-off Catholics supported the Union, the vast majority of Unionists were Protestants, mainly members of the Church of Ireland or the Presbyterian Church. Most of them

Belfast in 1882. The majority of people living in Belfast were Protestants and Unionists.

lived in Ulster where around a million Protestants, from the poorest workers to rich lords and businessmen, supported the Union. In the rest of Ireland, Unionists were usually landlords or businessmen who formed a small minority of the local population.

Because of their deep loyalty to the queen of England and the belief that British governments protected them, the Unionists' great fear was that the Catholic majority in Ireland would one day succeed in setting up some form of government which was independent of Great Britain.

IRISH NATIONALISTS

While the Unionist minority in Ireland was content with the connection with Great Britain, over three-quarters of the population of Ireland had a different political outlook. The people who formed this majority were known as *Irish Nationalists* because they believed that the Irish nation should be ruled by the Irish people. While they shared a belief in self-government, Irish Nationalists were deeply divided over the means of achieving their aims. Some groups were in favour of using violence against Britain, but others relied on peaceful methods. Because of this, two main types of Irish Nationalist can be identified.

- *Constitutional Nationalists*: They worked through the British parliament and used arguments and the support of the people to achieve their aims. Realising that British governments would never give Ireland complete independence without war and bloodshed, they agreed to struggle for Irish self-government inside the British Empire. Daniel O'Connell was the leading example followed by Constitutional Nationalists.

- *Physical Force Republicans*: They followed Wolfe Tone's belief in complete separation from Great Britain and hoped to achieve this by an armed uprising. While Constitutional Nationalists often enjoyed widespread public support, physical force movements were usually secret societies supported by small minorities.

After the passing of the Act of Union (1800), Irish Nationalist movements of both types grew from time to time. After the death of Daniel O'Connell (1847) and the Great Famine, Nationalists were weak and divided for a number of years. In 1856, however, a new movement was founded which had a lasting influence on Irish Nationalists in the years ahead. This was the *Fenian Movement*.

TEST YOUR KNOWLEDGE
1 *Explain the term 'Unionist'.*
2 *To which religious denominations did most Unionists belong?*
3 *How was the position of Unionists in Ulster different from their position in the rest of Ireland?*
4 *What was the great fear of Unionists?*
5 *Who were the Irish Nationalists?*
6 *List the two main types of Irish Nationalists.*

THE FENIAN MOVEMENT

The *Fenian Movement* or *Irish Republican Brotherhood* (IRB) was set up with the aim of organising a rebellion against British rule in Ireland. The leading organiser of this secret society was James Stephens who travelled throughout Ireland swearing in new members. Within a few years, the secret society had many members in Ireland, as well as among Irish emigrants in England and in the United States of America. Catholic bishops strongly condemned the movement because it was a secret oath-bound society which supported violence.

After a number of delays, a Fenian rising eventually took place in March 1867. Small risings broke out in different parts of the country. These were easily put down by the British government, which was well prepared because of its successful use of spies within the IRB.

Although the rebellion of 1867 was a total failure, the IRB did not die, but lived on to plan future attacks against the British government in Ireland. After the execution of a group of Fenians known as the Manchester Martyrs in November 1867, many people in Ireland began to sympathise with them.

The Irish in America continued to support the Irish Republican Brotherhood. Even British politicians were influenced by the Fenians; by highlighting Irish problems, they forced leading politicians in London to improve conditions for the Irish people.

After the defeat of the Fenian rebellion, Constitutional Nationalists made another attempt to secure self-government for Ireland. They were to be guided by Isaac Butt, a barrister who had first come to the attention of the public when he defended Fenian prisoners at their trials.

ISSAC BUTT AND THE HOME RULE PARTY

In 1870 Issac Butt, the son of a Church of Ireland clergyman, founded the Home Rule Party. Butt was not satisfied that either of the two main British parties, the Conservatives and the Liberals, gave proper attention to Irish problems.

Butt not only believed that Irish MPs should form their own party. He also wanted the return of an Irish parliament in Dublin which would have control over Irish affairs. He was willing to allow the British parliament to continue to run matters like foreign affairs, defence, customs, and the post office, with Ireland remaining part of the British Empire under the queen. This belief in limited self-government was known as *Home Rule*. For the next fifty years, this new political party was to enjoy the support of the vast majority of the people of Ireland.

In the general election of 1874, against all odds, Butt's Home Rule Party won fifty-nine seats at Westminster. This success was partly due to the Secret Ballot Act (1872) which finally gave tenants the freedom to vote without interference from their landlords.

Despite their gains in the general election of 1874, the Home Rule MPs made little or no headway in the British parliament. Neither the Conservative government under Prime Minister Disraeli, nor the opposition Liberal Party, had any intention of granting Home Rule to Ireland. At the same time, the Home Rule Party was weak and divided. Many of its members had only pretended to be in favour of Home Rule to get elected. Butt himself was not a strong leader and he was often absent from parliament because of ill health and financial worries.

Some Home Rule MPs became tired of Butt's lack of progress and decided to hold up the work of the British parliament in order to get attention for Irish grievances. Led by Joseph Biggar of Belfast, they disrupted the work of the House of Commons with lengthy speeches. This new tactic, known as *parliamentary obstruction*, greatly annoyed British MPs. Butt himself did not approve of it because it was ungentlemanly and unparliamentary.

Isaac Butt, the founder of the Home Rule Party.

Irish MPs creating a disruption in the House of Commons during the obstruction campaign.

Butt's greatest achievement lay in the foundation and sudden rise of the Home Rule Party. By the time of Butt's death in 1879, an up-and-coming young MP for Co. Meath who had taken part in the obstruction campaign, was ready and willing to lead the party. His name was Charles Stewart Parnell.

TEST YOUR KNOWLEDGE

1 What was the main aim of the Fenian Movement?
2 Was the movement limited to Ireland?
  Explain your answer.
3 Why did the Catholic Church condemn the Fenians?
4 Who were the 'Manchester Martyrs'?
5 Why did Isaac Butt found a new political party in 1870?
6 Explain the meaning of 'Home Rule'.
7 How did Butt's party perform in the 1874 general election?
8 What was 'parliamentary obstruction'?

Chapter 17: Review

- In 1800, the old Irish parliament was abolished and Ireland was governed directly by the British government. Three officials looked after the government of Ireland: the Viceroy, the Chief Secretary and the Under-Secretary.

- About a quarter of Irish people supported the full union between Britain and Ireland. They were called Unionists and lived mainly in Ulster.

- The majority of Irish people were Nationalists. They believed that the Irish nation should be ruled by Irish people themselves. Constitutional Nationalists aimed for Irish self-government within the British Empire by peaceful means. Physical force republicans wanted to gain full independence from Britain by means of armed rebellion.

- The Fenian Movement was the nineteenth century's most famous example of physical force Republicanism. Although the Fenian Rebellion of 1867 was a total failure, the IRB did not die out but lived on to plan future attacks against the British government in Ireland.

- Isaac Butt founded the Home Rule Party in 1870. He wanted Ireland to have its own parliament again, while still remaining part of the British Empire. Although fifty-nine Home Rule MPs were elected in the general election of 1874, the party was weak and divided and made little or no headway in the British parliament.

ACTIVITIES

1 *Multiple Choice*
   (a) *The nobleman who represented the queen of England in Ireland was known as: (i) the Chief Secretary; (ii) the Lord Chancellor; (iii) the Viceroy; (iv) the Under-Secretary.*
   (b) *Constitutional Nationalists followed the example of: (i) Robert Emmet; (ii) Daniel O'Connell; (iii) Wolfe Tone; (iv) Benjamin Disraeli.*
   (c) *The leading Fenian organiser in Ireland was: (i) James Stephens; (ii) Isaac Butt; (iii) Wolfe Tone; (iv) Joseph Biggar.*
   (d) *The obstruction campaign in the British parliament was led by: (i) Isaac Butt; (ii) Charles Stewart Parnell; (iii) James Stephens; (iv) Joseph Biggar.*

2 *True or false?*
   (a) *The vast majority of Unionists around 1880 were members of the Catholic Church.*
   (b) *The Chief Secretary was the leading British civil servant in Ireland.*
   (c) *After the death of Daniel O'Connell in 1847, Irish Nationalists were weak and divided for a number of years.*
   (d) *The Fenian rising was defeated by the British forces in 1877.*
   (e) *Fifty-nine Home Rule MPs were elected in the general election of 1874.*

3 *Write a paragraph on Isaac Butt and the Home Rule Party.*

THE AGE OF PARNELL

CHARLES STEWART PARNELL (1846-91)

In 1846, Charles Stewart Parnell was born at Avondale, Co. Wicklow, into a family of Protestant landowners. He was educated in England where he attended Cambridge University. While there he developed a hatred of British rule in Ireland. He may have been influenced by his American mother who held strong anti-British views.

Charles Stewart Parnell (1846-91).

Although distant and shy in company, Parnell was a very ambitious man. Soon after his entry to the British parliament in 1875 as an MP for Co. Meath, he began to make a name for himself. He praised the Fenian Manchester Martyrs and took an active part in the obstruction campaign in parliament.

Parnell being removed from the British House of Commons because of his part in the obstruction campaign.

When Parnell became leader of the Home Rule Movement in 1880, most Irish people hardly knew what Home Rule meant and had little interest in it. Survival on the land was the main issue affecting their everyday lives. A terrible crisis had hit the Irish countryside around 1878. Before Parnell could even begin to campaign for Home Rule, he first had to tackle the problems facing the people on the land.

THE CRISIS ON THE LAND

Most tenant farmers in Ireland were very insecure on the land. They could be evicted from their cottages and farms whenever it suited the landlord. By the 1870s, however, evictions usually took place only when tenants failed to pay their rents. Around 1878, a serious crisis hit the Irish countryside.

- There were a number of bad harvests.
- Prices for Irish farm products fell as cheaper grain was imported from America.
- In British markets, Irish meat could not compete with cheaper imports from Argentina, New Zealand and Australia.

Eviction and starvation on a scale not experienced since the Great Famine of the 1840s now faced thousands of farmers and their families throughout the country, especially in the West of Ireland. At this stage, a remarkable man named Michael Davitt, a former Fenian prisoner on parole from jail in England, set up the *Land League* so that tenants could organise themselves to resist evictions.

Founded by Davitt in Co. Mayo in 1879, the Land League had the following aims:

- To stop evictions and to get reductions in rent for tenants.
- In the longer term, to ensure that tenant farmers replaced landlords as owners of the land.

Michael Davitt (1846-1906), the founder of the Land League, was evicted with his family from a farm in Mayo when he was only five years of age. After emigrating to England, he lost his right arm in an accident while working in a cotton mill. In 1870, he was jailed for fifteen years for Fenian activities in England. It was on his release in 1877 that he witnessed the horrific conditions of people in the West of Ireland. As a result, he established the Land League to help tenant farmers to work together to seek a reduction in rents and to prevent evictions.

As Irish landlords had the powerful backing of the British government, Davitt decided to step down as leader and allow Parnell to unite the Home Rule party and the Land League in the struggle for the rights of tenant farmers.

For three years, from 1879 to 1882, a widespread upheaval known as the *Land War* took place throughout Ireland. Although the movement was meant to be a peaceful one, violence often broke out as landlords, their agents, and people taking over the land of evicted tenants were attacked and sometimes murdered.

An attack on unsuspecting landlords during the 'Land War'.

William Gladstone, the British Prime Minister.

In parliament, Parnell led the struggle against the British government which was headed by the prime minister, William Gladstone. In response to the widespread unrest in Ireland, Gladstone decided on two main approaches: harsh laws to impose order, and a Land Act bringing about improvements in the conditions of tenants.

When the Land Act was passed in 1881, Parnell condemned the act because it did not help the tenants as much as he had wished. As a result of his continuing campaign against the British government, Parnell was arrested and spent the winter of 1881-82 in Kilmainham Jail, Dublin. He now became an even more popular hero than ever.

While Parnell and other leaders were in prison, they instructed the tenants not to pay any rent. As a result, violence increased on a huge scale throughout the countryside. Gladstone realised that if he reached an understanding with Parnell, the Irish leader would control the more extreme members of the Land League. In April 1882 an agreement was reached known as the *Kilmainham Treaty*. Gladstone released Parnell and his followers and promised to further improve the 1881 Land Act. In return, Parnell agreed to call off the rent strike and to accept Gladstone's Land Act.

Later British governments went further than Gladstone by advancing loans to tenants to help them buy out their farms from the landlords. As a result, from around 1900 onwards, most Irish farmers owned their own farms and there were very few landlords left in the country. The main leaders in the movement which led to this important change were undoubtedly Michael Davitt and Charles Stewart Parnell.

The Kilmainham Treaty of 1882 was a major turning point in Parnell's career. From then on he gave less and less attention to the land problem and concentrated on winning Home Rule for Ireland.

TEST YOUR KNOWLEDGE
1 *When and where was Parnell born?*
2 *How did he come to the attention of the public after entering the British parliament?*
3 *Who founded the Land League?*
4 *Explain what is meant by the 'Land War'.*
5 *What was William Gladstone's response to the Land War.*
6 *Explain the agreement known as the 'Kilmainham Treaty'.*
7 *How was this a turning point in Parnell's career?*

THE PHOENIX PARK MURDERS

A week after Parnell's release from Kilmainham Jail, a terrible event took place in Dublin which would create difficulties for him in the future. On the evening of 6 May 1882, the new Chief Secretary, Lord Frederick Cavendish and the Under-Secretary, Thomas R. Burke, were brutally murdered as they walked in the Phoenix Park. The murder was carried out with surgical knives by a violent secret society known as 'the Invincibles'. Most of those responsible were later tried and hanged for the murders.

The Phoenix Park Murders, May 1882.

People in England and Ireland were horrified by the Phoenix Park murders. They left a terrible impression on Parnell, who wanted to give up politics as a result. Gladstone, equally horrified at the murders, managed to persuade Parnell to remain on as leader of the Home Rule Party. The years ahead were to truly test the ability of the Irish leader.

THE ORGANISATION OF THE HOME RULE PARTY

When the Land League was banned by the government in October 1881, Parnell replaced it by a new organisation called the *National League*. He had very strong control over this and he used it in his campaign for Home Rule. The National League:

- Chose Home Rule candidates in general elections;
- Collected money for the party;
- Organised support on a local level throughout the length and breadth of the country.

As well as improving party organisation at home, Parnell also tightened his control over Home Rule MPs at Westminster. All Home Rule candidates agreed that, if elected, they would always vote together as a group at Westminster. This was known as a *party pledge* and any MP breaking it was expected to resign his seat in parliament. This gave Parnell a united party which could exert great influence in Westminster.

A great opportunity arose when a general election was called in November 1885. In this election, eighty-six Home Rule MPs were elected. These MPs found themselves in a powerful position, as neither the Conservatives nor the Liberals had enough seats to form a government on their own.

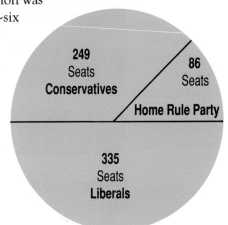

Parnell first of all decided to support the Conservatives with Lord Salisbury as prime minster. However, despite the new powerful position of the Home Rule party, both British parties were still against Home Rule. All of this was to change dramatically in the months ahead.

The number of seats held by each party after the 1885 election.

TEST YOUR KNOWLEDGE

1 *Why were both the Liberals and Conservatives against Home Rule for Ireland?*
2 *What were the Phoenix Park Murders?*
3 *State two ways in which Parnell improved the organisation of the Home Rule party.*
4 *In what way did Parnell's party find itself in a powerful position after the 1885 election?*

GLADSTONE SUPPORTS HOME RULE

In December 1885, Gladstone, leader of the opposition Liberal party, made the dramatic announcement of his support for Home Rule. In January 1886, the Conservative government fell from power when the Home Rule party joined the Liberals to defeat it.

Gladstone and the Liberal party, with the help of the Home Rule MPs, formed a government which for the first time ever supported Home Rule in Ireland. At the earliest opportunity, Gladstone brought the first Home Rule Bill into parliament. However, groups within Gladstone's own Liberal Party refused to support the bill and joined the Conservatives to defeat it in June 1886.

Although the first Home Rule Bill was defeated, it was the beginning of the Liberal Alliance in which Parnell and the Irish Party continued to support the Liberals in return for a promise to continue to support Home Rule.

The Liberal Prime Minister, William Gladstone, introducing the first Home Rule Bill in the British House of Commons in 1886.

THE CONSERVATIVES IN POWER
'KILLING HOME RULE WITH KINDNESS'

After the failure of the first Home Rule Bill, Gladstone's Liberal government fell from power. In the general election which followed, the Conservatives won a huge majority and returned to power with Lord Salisbury as prime minister. They remained in power until 1892.

The Conservatives continued to oppose Home Rule. However, they hoped to lessen support in Ireland for Home Rule by bringing about other improvements in the country. Under the Ashbourne and Balfour Land Acts, the government made loans available to tenant farmers to buy their farms from the landlords. In 1891, a *Congested Districts Board* was set up to help the poorer areas of the West of Ireland by promoting local schemes of road, rail and pier building.

These various improvements were part of a policy known as *Killing Home Rule with Kindness*. However, they failed to lessen support for Home Rule in Ireland.

THE PIGOTT FORGERIES

In the meantime, the Conservatives and other enemies of Parnell set out to discredit the Irish leader.

In the spring of 1886, the powerful London newspaper, *The Times*, published a series of articles known as 'Parnellism and Crime'. *The Times* claimed that Parnell supported the Phoenix Park Murders in 1882! To prove this, the paper printed letters which were supposedly written by Parnell. When these claims were investigated by a special commission set up by parliament, it was discovered that the letters had been forged by a journalist called Richard Pigott who eventually fled to Spain where he committed suicide. Parnell was found to be innocent and his fame increased even more. He was now at the height of his power.

TEST YOUR KNOWLEDGE
1 What important change of policy did Gladstone make towards the end of 1885?
2 What happened to Gladstone's first Home Rule Bill in June 1886?
3 What is meant by 'Killing Home Rule with Kindness'?
4 What were the Pigott Forgeries? How did they affect Parnell's career?

THE FALL OF PARNELL

In November 1890, the news of Parnell's involvement in a divorce case in London shocked people throughout Britain and Ireland. Parnell had been having a love affair for many years with a married woman, Katharine O'Shea. When her husband, Captain William O'Shea, sued for divorce, the 'scandal' became public knowledge.

Katharine O'Shea, who married Parnell in 1891 after her marriage to Captain William O'Shea ended in divorce.

There was an immediate outcry in Ireland and Britain. Some people said that Parnell should resign, while others said his private life was his own business. Matters came to a head when Gladstone declared that he could not continue to support Home Rule if Parnell remained as leader of the Irish Parliamentary Party. The Irish Catholic bishops also believed that Parnell should resign.

The Irish Party itself met to consider the whole question in Committee Room 15 of the House of Commons at Westminster in early December 1890. Parnell used his position as chairman to delay the taking of a vote on his leadership. Eventually, a majority of the MPs present left the room and elected Justin McCarthy as their leader. The Irish Party, so noted for its unity during the 1880s, was now bitterly split into two groups – for, and against, Parnell. Rejected by a majority of his parliamentary colleagues, Parnell now decided to look for the support of the Irish people.

THE DEATH OF PARNELL

Throughout 1891, Parnell put his own candidates forward in three by-elections in Ireland and suffered three successive defeats. During the campaigns, he had to put up with much personal abuse, including mud-slinging and stone-throwing. He finally married Katharine O'Shea in June 1891.

Parnell addressing a hostile crowd in Kilkenny during a by-election campaign in 1891.

Although Katharine begged him to retire from public life, Parnell continued with the struggle. Worn out from exhaustion and disappointment, Parnell died at Brighton on 6 October 1891 at the early age of forty-five.

His funeral at Glasnevin cemetery in Dublin was one of the biggest ever seen in the city. The death of the 'Uncrowned King of Ireland' was deeply mourned. Those who lined the streets to see the funeral procession realised that they were witnessing the end of an era in Irish history. Things would never be quite the same again.

TEST YOUR KNOWLEDGE
1 Who was Katharine O'Shea?
2 What news broke in November 1890?
3 Describe the public reaction to this news.
4 How did Gladstone react?
5 What happened in Committee Room 15 in December 1890?
6 How did Parnell's fall from power affect the Home Rule party?

The funeral of Parnell passing by the old Irish Parliament buildings at College Green, Dublin.

Chapter 18: Review

- In 1875, Charles Stewart Parnell was elected Home Rule MP for Meath. However, during the 1870s most Irish people were far more concerned with making a living on the land than with political issues like Home Rule.

- In the late 1870s, a serious crisis hit the Irish countryside. Many families faced hunger and eviction on a scale not witnessed since the Famine.

- In 1879, Michael Davitt set up the Land League with the aim of protecting tenant farmers from eviction. Parnell became leader of the Land League and the Home Rule party.

- Between 1879 and 1882, the Irish countryside was in a state of crisis. This was known as the Land War. In 1881 William Gladstone, the British prime minster, introduced a Land Act which improved the conditions of Irish tenants.

- When Parnell condemned the Land Act for not helping tenants as much as he wished, he was imprisoned in Kilmainham Jail.

- In April 1882, Parnell reached an agreement with Gladstone known as the Kilmainham Treaty. From then on, Parnell gave less attention to the land question and devoted his time to gaining Home Rule for Ireland.

- The Phoenix Park Murders of 6 May 1882 horrified most people in Britain and Ireland. The Chief Secretary and the Under-Secretary were murdered by a group called the Invincibles.

- From 1882, Parnell concentrated on building up a strong Home Rule party in Westminster. In the general election of 1885, his party won eighty-six seats. He was in a very strong bargaining position as neither of the two British parties could form a government without his help.

- Towards the end of 1885 Gladstone, leader of the Liberal party, agreed to support the cause of Home Rule. He became prime minister, with Parnell's help, in February 1886. The following April, Gladstone introduced the first Home Rule bill, but it was defeated in the House of Commons.

- The Conservatives continued to oppose Home Rule. They had a policy called 'Killing Home Rule with Kindness'. This involved bringing in improvements on the land in the hope that the Irish would then forget about Home Rule.

- In November 1890, news broke of Parnell's involvement in a divorce case between Captain William O'Shea and his wife Katharine. Gladstone and the Irish Catholic bishops called for Parnell's resignation. At a meeting of the Irish Home Rule party, Parnell was deposed as leader.

- Parnell refused to accept this verdict and decided to look for supporters in Ireland. He lost three by-elections and died on 6 October 1891. His fall from power and death left the Irish Home Rule party deeply divided into two groups.

ACTIVITIES

1 *Match an item in Column 1 with an item in Column 2.*

COLUMN 1	COLUMN 2
The 1881 Land Act	Davitt
The Land League	Salisbury
Avondale	Pigott
The Times	Gladstone
'Killing Home Rule with Kindness'	Parnell

2 *Complete the following sentences.*
  (a) Before Parnell could begin to campaign for Home Rule, _____.
  (b) Under the 'Kilmainham Treaty' (1882), _____.
  (c) The Phoenix Park Murders were carried out by _____.
  (d) The Conservatives hoped to lessen support for Home Rule in Ireland by means of a policy known as _____.
  (e) In November 1890, people in Britain and Ireland were shocked to hear _____.

3 *Draw a chart on the Land War and make entries under the headings Causes, Course and Consequences.*

4 *Write a short paragraph on two of the following: (a) Gladstone and Home Rule; (b) 'Killing Home Rule with Kindness'; (c) Parnell and the Pigott Forgeries.*

5 *Write a by-election speech either for or against Parnell which you would have written in the spring of 1891.*

THE GAELIC REVIVAL

IRELAND'S IDENTITY

By the time of Parnell's death in 1891, small groups of people throughout Ireland were beginning to wonder if Home Rule was the answer to all of the country's problems. More and more Irish people were turning away from their native customs and pastimes in favour of English ones. If this trend continued, it was feared that Ireland would lose its cultural identity and become like an English province. To prevent this from happening, a number of important organisations were set up to preserve Ireland's cultural heritage. They were founded by small groups of people but grew and developed into a powerful movement catering for a wide variety of activities including sport, language, literature, drama and politics.

The first such movement to be founded was the *Gaelic Athletic Association* (GAA).

THE GAELIC ATHLETIC ASSOCIATION (GAA)

On 1 November 1884, a group of seven men met in Hayes' Hotel, Thurles, Co. Tipperary. They were brought together by a common concern for the future of the traditional Irish games of hurling and football. These traditional pastimes were under increasing threat from the spread of English sports; soccer, for example, had become especially popular after the formation of the Irish Football Association in 1880. From the 1860s, rugby football had spread among the upper classes and the Irish Football Union was founded in 1874. Alarmed by these developments, the seven men who met in Thurles in November 1884 founded the Gaelic Athletic Association (GAA).

Hurling Then and Now.

(a) The Tipperary hurling team which won the first All-Ireland championship in 1887.

(b) A modern scene at the GAA headquarters, Croke Park, Dublin – the hurlers of Cork and Kilkenny in competition.

The aim of the new movement was to promote traditional Gaelic games and, above all, to give them official rules and standards. Up to this time, hurling had no rules, and hurling matches frequently developed into brutal events resulting in numerous injuries.

Michael Cusack (1847-1906), a teacher from Co. Clare, was the leading figure in the new organisation and became its first secretary. A Tipperary athlete named Maurice Davin became the first president of the association. Archbishop Croke of Cashel, Charles Stewart Parnell and Michael Davitt were among the GAA's patrons.

Michael Cusack, the founder of the Gaelic Athletic Association (GAA).

Archbishop Thomas Croke of Cashel, one of the first patrons of the GAA, helped to prevent the young organisation from falling under the control of the Fenians. He was a life-long supporter of Gaelic games and other forms of Irish culture.

From its foundation, many IRB men were involved in the GAA and used it as a recruiting ground for new members. It was, therefore, strongly anti-British and imposed on its members a 'ban' on the playing or viewing of foreign sports. This 'ban' remained in operation until the 1970s.

GAA clubs sprang up throughout the country and had a major impact, especially in rural areas where they provided much needed leisure activities. Competitions were organised between clubs and Sunday became the traditional day for matches. The first All-Ireland finals were held in 1887.

TEST YOUR KNOWLEDGE
1 *Why do you think traditional Irish games and pastimes were under threat in the late nineteenth century?*
2 *Where and when was the GAA founded?*
3 *What was the aim of the new organisation?*
4 *Name two of the founders of the GAA. State what position each held within the organisation.*
5 *Who became the first patrons of the GAA?*
6 *'From its foundation, the GAA was very anti-British'.*
  Give two examples to show this.
7 *When were the first All-Ireland finals held?*

THE GAELIC LEAGUE

By the closing years of the nineteenth century, the Irish language, like Gaelic games, had been under increasing threat from the spread of English influence. While no single cause may be given for this great decline in the use of Irish, the following points taken together help us to explain what happened.

- The Great Famine (1845-49) resulted in death and emigration, especially in the West of Ireland where Irish was mostly spoken.
- Children were taught in the national schools through English. Parents co-operated with teachers in discouraging children from talking in Irish.
- English was associated with progress; Irish became identified with poverty and backwardness.
- English was also the language of politics, and all leading Irish politicians, from O'Connell to Parnell, spoke English.

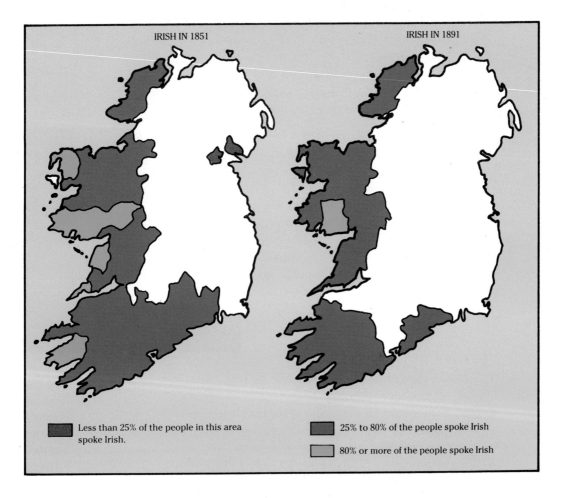

IRISH IN 1851   IRISH IN 1891

Less than 25% of the people in this area spoke Irish.

25% to 80% of the people spoke Irish

80% or more of the people spoke Irish

The decline of the Irish language. Between 1851 and 1891 the areas where nearly everyone spoke Irish had become much smaller.

Concerned about the poor state of the Irish language and culture, Douglas Hyde, the son of a Church of Ireland rector from Co. Roscommon, founded the *Gaelic League* in 1893. He had a great love for the Irish language and became the first president of the League. Eoin MacNeill, an Irish scholar from Co. Antrim, became its first secretary. The League had three main aims:

1 to restore Irish as the spoken language of the country;
2 to encourage the writing and publication of Gaelic literature;
3 to remove English cultural influence from Ireland (Hyde called this the 'de-anglicisation of Ireland').

The Gaelic League hoped to achieve these aims by:

- The organisation of Irish classes throughout the country run by travelling teachers known as *timirí* (these travelled around the country using the newly-invented bicycle).
- The publication of its own newspaper, *An Claidheamh Soluis* (Sword of Light).
- The publication of books in the Irish language.
- The holding of *feiseanna* and *ceilis*.

Douglas Hyde, the Gaelic scholar and writer who was first president of the Gaelic League.

The Gaelic League gave its members a greater sense of their Irish identity. Douglas Hyde hoped to keep the movement totally separate from politics, but in this he failed. For many people, such as Patrick Pearse, the Gaelic League formed a stepping stone on the road to open involvement in violent Republican organisations.

TEST YOUR KNOWLEDGE
1 *Why was there cause for concern about the Irish language in the closing years of the nineteenth century?*
2 *State three reasons for the decline of the Irish language.*
3 *Who founded the Gaelic League? What were the aims of this organisation?*
4 *Who were the timirí?*
5 *What newspaper was founded by the Gaelic League?*
6 *Why do you think the organisation provided a stepping stone for some towards involvement in violent Republican movements?*

Eamon de Valera, a member of the Gaelic League, giving an Irish class in 1912

THE ABBEY THEATRE

While members of the Gaelic League were trying to promote new stories, plays and poems in the Irish language, there was also a new and exciting movement based on writings about Ireland in the English language. These writings are known as *Anglo-Irish literature*.

The most brilliant Anglo-Irish writer at this time was a young poet called William Butler Yeats (1865-1939). He believed that Ireland could and should have writers who could be as good as any in the world. Instead of writing in the fashion of Britain, Europe or America, Yeats believed that Irish writers should explore Irish topics in their works. Therefore in 1899, along with Lady Augusta Gregory and Edward Martyn, Yeats founded the *Irish Literary Theatre* with the aim of writing and producing plays on Irish topics. In 1904, the Abbey Theatre in Dublin became the company's new headquarters where all their most famous plays were produced.

William Butler Yeats (1865-1939).

Lady Augusta Gregory, one of the founders of the Abbey Theatre.

Many of these plays concerned Irish history or folklore and they encouraged resistance to British rule in Ireland. For the opening of the Abbey Theatre in 1904, Yeats wrote *Cathleen Ni Houlihan* with the beautiful Maud Gonne, whom he greatly admired, in the title role. This play was set in Mayo during the rebellion of 1798 and Cathleen Ni Houlihan

The Abbey Theatre, which was opened in 1904.

was the representation of Ireland as an old woman calling on her sons to fight. At the end of the play, she calls a young man away from his wedding in order to fight and die in the rebellion. The play ends with the lines:

'Did you see an old woman going down the path?'
'I did not; but I saw a young girl, and she had the walk of a queen.'

Those who were at the play said that these lines caused great excitement. After the Easter Rising of 1916, Yeats wondered if he had encouraged people to join in the fighting:

'Did that play of mine send out
Certain men the English shot?'

As well as patriotic plays, there were also plays about life in the countryside. One of these, *The Playboy of the Western World* by John Millington Synge, caused riots in the Abbey in 1907 when young Nationalists believed that ordinary Irish country people were being mocked.

By 1910, the Abbey Theatre had gained a reputation as one of the finest in the world. Along with the GAA and the Gaelic League, it emphasised Ireland's special cultural identity which was separate and distinct from Britain's.

TEST YOUR KNOWLEDGE
1 *Who founded the Irish Literary Theatre?*
2 *What is meant by Anglo-Irish literature?*
3 *What theatre became the headquarters of the Literary Theatre in 1904?*
4 *What was the main idea in Yeats's play, Cathleen Ni Houlihan?*
5 *Who was John Millington Synge? What was his most famous work?*
6 *In what way do you think the Abbey emphasised Ireland's unique cultural identity?*

ARTHUR GRIFFITH AND SINN FÉIN

Not all the movements founded at this time were concerned with cultural activities. One new organisation emphasised the need for Ireland to industrialise and to become above all self-sufficient in economic terms. This was *Sinn Féin*, founded by Arthur Griffith in 1905.

Born in Dublin in 1871, Griffith was a printer by trade. After spending some years in South Africa he returned to Ireland in 1898 and founded his own newspaper, the *United Irishman*. Although he favoured Ireland's total separation from Britain, he realised the difficulty of attaining this. He proposed instead for Ireland the Austro-Hungarian system of government known as *dual monarchy*. This would involve a separate parliament in Dublin under the British crown. Griffith said that Irish MPs, when elected, should refuse to take their seats in the Westminster parliament (*abstention*) and should instead set up their own parliament in Ireland.

In economic matters, Sinn Féin called for industrial growth to be achieved by means of tariff protection. It wanted Ireland to become self-sufficient and self-reliant – the words Sinn Féin mean 'we ourselves' or 'ourselves alone'. However, this organisation did not play an important part in Irish affairs until after 1916.

Arthur Griffith (1871-1922), the founder of Sinn Féin.

TEST YOUR KNOWLEDGE
1 *Who founded Sinn Féin and when?*
2 *What was meant by dual monarchy?*
3 *Sinn Féin favoured a policy of parliamentary abstention. What was meant by this?*
4 *What did Sinn Féin mean by tariff protection?*
5 *Sinn Féin wanted Ireland to become self-sufficient and self-reliant. Explain these terms.*

Chapter 19: Review

- **The Gaelic Athletic Association (GAA) was founded at Thurles, Co. Tipperary on 1 November 1884. Its aims were to promote Gaelic games and to give them official rules and standards. Michael Cusack, a Clare man, was its first secretary and Maurice Davin of Tipperary became its first president.**

Archbishop Croke of Cashel, Charles Stewart Parnell and Michael Davitt were its first patrons.

- **The Gaelic League was founded in Dublin in July 1893 with the aim of reviving the Irish Language. Douglas Hyde was the league's first president,** while Eoin MacNeill was its first secretary. The organisation founded its own newspaper *An Claidheamh Soluis* and sent travelling teachers (*timirí*) around the country to run classes in Irish.

- In 1899, the Irish Literary Theatre was founded by W.B. Yeats, Lady Gregory and Edward Martyn with the aim of writing and producing plays on Irish topics. In 1904 the Abbey Theatre in Dublin became its new headquarters and its most famous playwright was John Millington Synge whose *Playboy of the Western World* caused riots in the Abbey in 1907.

- Arthur Griffith founded Sinn Féin in 1905. This organisation wanted Ireland to become self-sufficient, that is supplying its own people with adequate food and employment. Griffith believed in a dual monarchy for Ireland and Britain, which meant that the king of England would also be king of Ireland, but that Ireland would have its own parliament.

ACTIVITIES

1 Match an item in Column 1 with an item in Column 2.

COLUMN 1	COLUMN 2
The Gaelic Athletic Association	John Millington Synge
The Gaelic League	Arthur Griffith
The Abbey Theatre	Michael Cusack
Sinn Féin	Douglas Hyde

2 Fill in the blanks with words or phrases from the box.

reviving	The Gaelic League
Eoin McNeill	An Claidheamh Soluis
Douglas Hyde	Patrick Pearse
timirí	

In 1893, _____ was founded with the aim of _____ the Irish language. _____ became its first secretary. The league published a newspaper called _____. This was edited for a time by _____ . Travelling teachers known as _____ went around the country teaching Irish. In 1915, the Gaelic League's president, _____ resigned because he believed that the movement was becoming involved in politics.

3 Write a paragraph on two of the following: (a) the Abbey Theatre; (b) the Gaelic League; (c) Arthur Griffith and Sinn Féin.

4 If there is a Gaelic Athletic Association club in your local area, find out when it was established. Write a short account of its early days.

WORKERS IN REVOLT – DUBLIN 1913

DUBLIN 1913 – A CITY IN CRISIS

In 1913, twenty per cent of Dublin's population – about 87,000 people – lived in tenements. Each tenement housed a large number of families. About 20,000 Dublin families lived in one-room tenements, while a further 5,000 had only two rooms. The head of the family, if lucky enough to have work, earned about £1 per week. Most of this wage went on basic necessities like food and rent. However, many people in Dublin at the time were out of work or could only find casual (occasional) work.

Poor children in Dublin in 1913. Notice their cast-off clothing and bare feet, in contrast to the better-off people in the background.

There were no unemployment benefits to reduce the hardships experienced by families in this position. In such times, many women had to rely on the pawnshops as their only means of income. Because of the squalor and the poor diet, disease was rampant in the tenements and infant mortality was especially high.

Poor diet, lack of sanitation and damp conditions resulted in the spread of disease, especially among children. Despite the desperate conditions endured by tenement dwellers, they were noted for their spirit of friendliness towards those neighbours in greater difficulty than themselves.

Two men in particular devoted their energies to improving these desperate conditions: James Connolly and James Larkin.

The proportion of people living in tenements in Dublin in 1913.

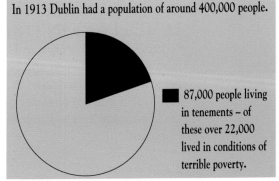

In 1913 Dublin had a population of around 400,000 people.

■ 87,000 people living in tenements – of these over 22,000 lived in conditions of terrible poverty.

JAMES CONNOLLY (1868-1916)

James Connolly was born in 1868 of Irish parents in the slums of Edinburgh. His father worked as a carter and the family lived in a constant state of poverty. James left school at an early age and later spent some time in the British army. He read widely and was indeed largely self-educated.

James Connolly became deeply concerned with the plight of ordinary workers. He came to Ireland in 1896 to become the organiser of a socialist society. In 1898, he set up Ireland's first socialist newspaper called *The Workers' Republic*, which had a very small circulation.

James Connolly (1868-1916).

He later spent some time in America and returned to Ireland in 1910 as a trade union organiser in Belfast. While there, he stood up for the rights of dockers and the women in the linen mills. In 1911 he started a second newspaper, *The Irish Worker*.

As well as being a socialist, Connolly was also an Irish republican. In his view, equality for Irish workers could only be achieved in an Ireland which was free from British rule. Connolly was therefore to play an important part in the Easter Rising of 1916.

TEST YOUR KNOWLEDGE
1 *When and where was James Connolly born?*
2 *Describe Connolly's family background.*
3 *Why did he come to Ireland in 1896?*
4 *What work did he do in Belfast?*
5 *Name the newspapers founded by James Connolly in 1898 and 1911.*
6 *Why did James Connolly become an Irish republican?*

JAMES LARKIN (1876-1947)

James Larkin was born in Liverpool in 1876. Like Connolly, he came from a very poor family and began work before he was twelve years of age. He worked as a docker in Liverpool where he experienced at first hand the hardships of working-class people. He became a leader of the dockers' union and was sent to Ireland in 1907 to organise the dockers in Belfast.

From Belfast, Larkin moved to Dublin and Cork where he also stirred up the workers and persuaded them to stand up for their rights against their employers. Larkin was a powerful speaker and a gifted leader. He soon earned the name of 'Big Jim Larkin'. In January 1909, he founded the *Irish Transport and General Workers Union* (ITGWU) with the aim of securing better working conditions and higher wages for unskilled workers. The union grew quickly and soon had over 10,000 members. Larkin and Connolly together founded the *Irish Labour Party* in 1912.

TEST YOUR KNOWLEDGE

1 Where and when was James Larkin born?
2 What type of work did James Larkin do in Liverpool?
   How did it help to form his views?
3 Why did Larkin come to Ireland in 1907?
4 What trade union did he found?
5 What political party did Larkin and Connolly found in 1912?

THE EMPLOYERS BECOME ALARMED

By 1913, employers throughout the country were alarmed at the success of Larkin's ITGWU. Dublin businessmen became so concerned that they started their own employers' organisation. The leader of this group was William Martin Murphy – a highly successful Catholic businessman. He was chairman of the Dublin United Tramways Company and owned the *Irish Independent* newspapers. In 1913, Murphy and other employers ordered their workers either to resign from the ITGWU or to sign a statement promising not to join it. Everything was now pointing towards a clash between the employers led by Murphy and the workers led by Larkin.

William Martin Murphy, the leader of the employers in the Dublin strike and lockout of 1913-14.

James Larkin (1876-1947) addressing a group of workers.

THE GENERAL STRIKE AND LOCKOUT

James Larkin ordered all members of his union to come out in a general strike rather than give in to Murphy's demands. The strike began on Tuesday 26 August 1913, when some 700 Dublin tramworkers left their trams wherever they happened to be. The stoppage occurred at a time when the trams were in most demand – it was Horse Show Week in Dublin. Murphy and the other employers immediately 'locked out' all members of Larkin's union – the ITGWU. Soon, about 25,000 workers were out of work.

Two opposing views of events in Dublin in 1913. State which newspapers supported the employers and which supported the workers. Give reasons for your answer in each case.

EVENING HERALD

TELEGRAMS: "HERALD." DUBLIN
EDITORIAL TELEPHONE: 104

CERTIFIED NET SALES EXCEED THOSE OF ANY OTHER DUBLIN EVENING PAPER.

VOL. 22. NO. 205.   DUBLIN, TUESDAY, AUGUST 26, 1913.   PRICE ONE

ATTEMPT TO CAUSE A TRAM STRIKE IN DUBLIN

Some of the Men Leave Work and Wear Red Hand Badge

THEIR EXAMPLE NOT FOLLOWED BY VAST BODY OF MEN

No Dislocation of Traffic and Cars Running as Usual

At a quarter to ten o'clock precisely this morning an attempt was made to rush a strike on the Dublin Tramways.

Up to that hour cars were running as usual, and there was not the slightest sign that developments were so near.

The whole thing was organised evidently with a view to taking the public by surprise, but it was a manifest failure.

At a quarter to 10 o'c. a about a dozen or a score of tram cars stopped at Nelson's Pillar, and some of the men left them and placed the sign of the Red Hand on the lapels of their coats.

This was evidently to be the signal for the strike.

One hot-headed young conductor on a city bound car stopped in the centre of the street and told the passengers to get out, that there would be no more cars run.

The passengers quietly left the car, but there was no excitement.

Soon, however, order came out of the little

gathered in the vicinity of the Pillar, but there was little to reward their curiosity.

Policemen, both D.M.P. and R.I.C., were on duty and kept the people who were not travelling by the cars on the move in the centre of the street, but the pathways on both sides of the street were crowded.

Several mounted D.M.P. men were also on duty.

ALONG THE COAST.

Some anxiety was felt along the coast this morning, when a report reached Blackrock, Kingstown, and Dalkey that the tram men had struck.

So far as the coast line was concerned, there was no cessation of the running of the trams, but for less than half an hour the trams did not run as regularly as usual.

DUBLIN UNITED TRAMWAYS COMPANY (1896), LTD.

OFFICIAL STATEMENT.

Shortly before 10 o'clock this morning some of the Company's cars were deserted by the men in charge of them, and left standing in the streets. These cars were promptly cleared off, and the traffic was continued with a slightly reduced service.

The Company regrets the inconvenience to the public, which will be of short duration.

The cars will not, however, be run after dark this evening.

26th August, 1913.

temporary chaos, and it was possible to estimate the amount of dislocation that could be caused.

However, from 11 o'clock they were dispatched every 8 minutes from Dalkey in the normal way.

TRAMS WORKING AS USUAL

SNAPSHOT SHOWING TRAMS WORKING AS USUAL THIS EVENING.
"Herald" Photo.

hands, already trained in the driving and handling of cars, were ready to take the places of the men who had gone out.

No sooner did a conductor arrive in the office and the bag in which he carried his tickets and money handed over to the officials than another driver and conductor set off for the derelict car. With extraordinary rapidity the streets were cleared. A service of trams was run over almost every line, and to the delight and surprise of the general public it was soon seen that the tramway strike was a fiasco. Out of 224 cars which started from the various depots that morning something like 70 only had been stopped, involving but an insignificant number of the com-

tened voice to point out to the conductor the evil of his ways in not responding to "the command."

The latter gazed abstractedly at the little man for a few minutes, and then with the roar of a giant shouted, "Get away out of that you miserable little worm."

Larkin's emissary was so terrified by the outburst that he fell off the steps of the car, and picking himself up quickly ran down Henry street, leaving his "Red Hand" behind him.

The incident caused no little amusement amongst the passengers.

A manifesto issued by Liberty Hall and displayed on a number of hoardings, contains the usual vile tirade against Mr

LATEST NEWS

TRAMWAY TROUBLE IN DUBLIN.

SOLDIERS IN READINESS.

About half a dozen labourers in the Tramways Co.'s power-house at Ringsend ceased work about noon. Their places were immediately filled. The military are being held in readiness to cope with any serious disturbance which may take place to-night, and a large body of the R.I.C. Reserve at the Depot are in readiness under arms.

TRAMWAY TROUBLE.

NUMBER OF MEN OUT.

In spite of some alarmist statements as to the number of men out we are informed that the number is approximately about 150, and that the exaggerated statements appearing in contemporaries are quite baseless.

LATEST CRICKET.

Worcester—185 for 3.
Northants—219 for 3.
Yorks—181 for 6.

SEVEN STRIKERS

FRONT PAGE OF "THE DAILY MIRROR," SEPTEMBER 4, 1913;
AT BOTTOM CENTRE JAMES KEIR HARDIE, M.P. AT THE FUNERAL OF
JAMES NOLAN ON WEDNESDAY, SEPTEMBER 3, 1913.

During the strike, Larkin spoke to huge crowds of workers in the city.
He often had to appear in disguise in order to avoid arrest. On one
occasion, he arrived up the Liffey in a boat, from which he addressed
the excited crowds.

WORKING WITH EVIDENCE

On Sunday 31 August 1913, Larkin tried to address a crowd in O'Connell Street from one of the windows of the Imperial Hotel – owned by William Martin Murphy. As he was wanted by the police at the time, Larkin entered the hotel in disguise and went to an upstairs window. He was promptly arrested. The police then carried out baton charges on the crowd. Read the following account by Ernie O'Malley who witnessed the events.

'*I was in O'Connell Street when Jim Larkin, to keep a promise, appeared on the balcony of the hotel, wearing a beard as a disguise. He spoke amidst cheers, and hoots for the employers. Police swept down from many quarters, hemmed in the crowd, and used their heavy batons on anyone who came in their way. I saw women knocked down and kicked – I scurried up a side street; at the other end the police struck people, and as they lay injured on the ground, struck them again and again. I could hear the crunch as the heavy sticks struck unprotected skulls. I was in favour of the strikers.*'

from Ernie O'Malley, *On Another Man's Wounds*

1 *What was the reaction of the crowd when Larkin appeared?*

2 *Describe the reaction of the police.*

3 *How did the author reach safety?*

4 *What was his attitude to the events which he witnessed?*

There followed several months of extreme hardship for the Dublin workers and their families. Thousands were forced to depend on charity in order to live.

Larkin rallied support for the strike among British workers. As a result, ships arrived up the Liffey carrying food for the locked-out workers. By Christmas, however, much of this support had dried up. A soup kitchen was opened at Liberty Hall in an attempt to lessen the hardships experienced by the striking workers and their families.

Major clashes resulted when Larkin tried to send the children of those who were locked out to live with British families. Many Catholic priests led people to the docks to prevent the children from going to Protestant homes in England.

A food ship arriving from England at the Dublin docks during the strike and lockout.

Violent clashes occurred between the workers and police. By early 1914, after a severe winter, the workers of Dublin had been brought to their knees. In February 1914, the lockout ended when the workers returned to work on the employers' terms.

Police baton-charging a crowd of workers in O'Connell Street, Dublin.

Countess Constance Markievicz helped to run food kitchens for the hungry in Dublin during the strike. She was also one of the leading members of the Irish Citizen Army.

THE IRISH CITIZEN ARMY

The *Irish Citizen Army* was founded by Jack White and James Connolly in November 1913 to protect the workers in their clashes with the police. Sean O'Casey and Countess Markievicz were other well-known members of this group.

The Citizen Army remained in existence after the end of the lockout. It was to be used by Connolly for another purpose in the years ahead.

TEST YOUR KNOWLEDGE
1 Who was the leader of the Dublin employers in 1913?
2 What order did the employers issue to the workers in the summer of 1913?
3 How did James Larkin respond to the employers' demands?
4 When did the Dublin strike begin? What group of workers came out first?
5 How did the general strike and lockout end?
6 Who set up the Irish Citizen Army? Why was it founded?

Chapter 20: Review

- In 1913, twenty per cent of the people of Dublin lived in tenements; each tenement house contained a large number of families. About 20,000 Dublin families lived in one-room tenements while a further 5,000 had only two rooms.

- James Connolly, who was born in Edinburgh in 1868, came from a poor family and was largely self-educated. He was a socialist and came to Ireland to campaign for the rights of Irish workers. He was also a republican. He became an organiser in the Irish Transport and

General Workers' Union (ITGWU) and founded the Irish Citizen Army in 1913.

- James Larkin was born in Liverpool in 1876. He came to Ireland in 1907 to organise the dockers into trade unions. In 1909 he founded the Irish Transport and General Workers Union (ITGWU) with the aim of gaining better working conditions and higher wages for unskilled workers.

- The employers were worried by the rapid growth of Larkin's union. William Martin Murphy, a rich businessman, set up an employers' organisation to stand up to the ITGWU. In 1913 Murphy and the other employers ordered their workers to resign from the ITGWU and to sign a statement promising not to join it.

- Larkin ordered the workers to come out in a general strike rather than give in to Murphy's demands. On 26 August 1913, Dublin tramworkers came out on strike. Murphy and other employers immediately locked out members of Larkin's union. The Strike and Lockout lasted until February 1914 when the workers were forced to return to work on the employers' terms.

- The Irish Citizen Army was founded by James Connolly and Jack White in November 1913 to protect the workers in their clashes with the police.

ACTIVITIES

1 *Multiple choice*
   (a) *In 1913, the proportion of Dublin people who lived in tenements was: (i) 50%; (ii) 5%; (iii) 10%; (iv) 20%.*
   (b) *James Connolly was born of Irish parents in 1868 in: (i) Edinburgh; (ii) Liverpool; (iii) Manchester; (iv) Glasgow.*
   (c) *James Larkin was sent to Ireland in 1907 to organise the dockers in the city of: (i) Cork; (ii) Limerick; (iii) Dublin; (iv) Belfast.*
   (d) *In 1913, William Martin Murphy provoked a strike in Dublin by: (i) reducing wages; (ii) demanding that his workers leave trade unions; (iii) increasing working hours; (iv) reducing the number of workers in his companies.*

2 *Complete the following sentences.*
   (a) *In Dublin around 1913, most of the wages of the poor were spent on _____.*
   (b) *James Connolly returned from America to Ireland in 1910 to work as _____.*
   (c) *In 1909 James Larkin founded his own trade union, _____.*
   (d) *The Irish Citizen Army was founded in November 1913 by _____.*
   (e) *The Citizen Army was founded in order to _____.*

3 *Write a paragraph on each of the following:*
   (a) *James Larkin and the events of 1913-14 in Dublin;* (b) *The life of James Connolly up to 1914.*

THE HOME RULE CRISIS: 1912-14

HOME RULE ON THE WAY

While the people of Dublin and other towns were experiencing strikes and lockouts, and while Irish workers became more organised, the Irish Parliamentary Party at Westminster was enjoying a period of good fortune.

After Parnell's death in 1891 and the bitter split in the party, many people lost respect for its members and believed that Home Rule would not be passed for a very long time. In 1893, Gladstone had succeeded in getting his Second Home Rule Bill passed by the House of Commons, but it was decisively rejected by the House of Lords. The opponents of Home Rule, the Conservatives, were then in power continuously from 1895 until 1906.

Although the Irish Home Rule Party was reunited in 1900 under the leadership of the Parnell supporter, John Redmond, few people in Ireland believed that Home Rule was on the way. Indeed many young people preferred to become involved in the GAA, the Gaelic League and other cultural movements, rather than in the Irish Parliamentary Party.

In 1910, however, John Redmond and his party became very influential in London when the Conservatives and Liberals were almost evenly balanced in the British House of Commons. The eighty-two Irish MPs now held the balance of power. Not since Parnell's time in 1885 had the Irish party enjoyed this position.

John Redmond, who became leader of the re-united Irish Parliamentary Party in 1900.

The Liberal Prime Minister, H.H. Asquith, who needed the support of the Irish Parliamentary Party in order to stay in power after 1910.

The Liberal government of H.H. Asquith was dependent on the Irish MPs to stay in power. As a condition of his support, Redmond insisted that a Home Rule Bill be introduced. The hopes of the Irish nationalists were high. As a result of the Parliament Act (1911), the House of Lords could no longer completely reject a law. They could only delay it for two years. When the Third Home Rule Bill was passed in the House of Commons in 1912, it appeared that nothing could prevent it from becoming law by 1914.

Although under the bill the powers of an Irish parliament would be quite limited, Redmond and his followers were prepared to accept it as a big improvement on direct rule from London.

However, neither the British Liberal party nor their Irish supporters fully realised the strength of resistance to Home Rule among Irish Unionists and British Conservatives.

ULSTER SAYS 'NO' TO HOME RULE

Ulster Protestants were determined to block the Third Home Rule Bill. They began to organise an anti-Home Rule campaign throughout Ulster. They opposed Home Rule for three main reasons:

- *Religious*: They feared that, in a Home Rule parliament with a Catholic majority, Protestants would be treated unfairly. This belief was summed up in the slogan *Home Rule is Rome Rule*.
- *Political*: They were loyal to the king of England and wished to remain under the direct rule of the British government.
- *Economic*: Ulster had prospered under the Union since 1800. Unionisits feared that a Home Rule parliament in Dublin would pass laws which would damage trade and industry in the province.

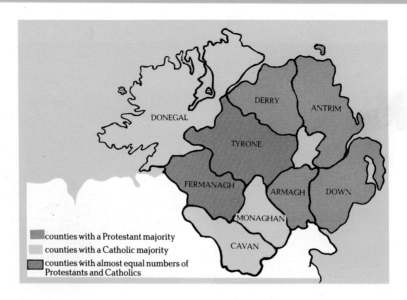

Catholic and
Protestant
divisions in Ulster
about 1910

Edward Carson addressing an anti-Home Rule meeting in 1912.

Edward Carson, a Unionist MP for Trinity College, and James Craig, an MP for Down since 1906 and a millionaire businessman, were the leaders of the Unionist campaign. In September 1912, they drew up the *Ulster Solemn League and Covenant*. This pledged resistance to Home Rule and was signed by over 250,000 Protestant men throughout Ulster. The following is an extract from the Solemn League and Covenant.

WORKING WITH EVIDENCE

The Solemn League and Covenant

'Being convinced in our conscience that Home Rule would be disastrous to the material well-being of Ulster as well as the whole of Ireland, subversive of our civil and religious freedom, destructive of our citizenship and perilous to the unity of the Empire, we, whose names are underwritten, men of Ulster, loyal subjects to His Gracious Majesty King George V, humbly relying on the God whom our fathers in days of stress and trial confidently trusted do hereby pledge ourselves in solemn Covenant throughout this time of threatened calamity to stand by one another in defending for ourselves and our children our cherished position of equal citizenship in the United Kingdom and in using all means which may be found necessary to defeat the present conspiracy to set up a Home Rule Parliament in Ireland. And in the event of such a Parliament being forced upon us, we further solemnly and mutually pledge ourselves to refuse to recognise its authority. In sure confidence that God will defend the right we hereto subscribe our names. And further, we individually declare that we have not already signed this Covenant.

The above was signed by me at _____ Ulster Day, Saturday 28th September 1912.'

God Save The King

1 State three reasons given by the Unionists why 'Home Rule would be disastrous'.
2 What did they mean by 'our cherished position of equal citizenship in the United Kingdom'?
3 Would you agree with the phrase 'the present conspiracy to set up a Home Rule Parliament in Ireland'? Explain your answer.
4 What did those who signed the Covenant propose to do if a Home Rule Parliament was established?

Carson and Craig signing the Solemn League and Convenent in Belfast City Hall.

THE ULSTER VOLUNTEERS

The Ulster Unionists, supported by the Conservatives under their leader Andrew Bonar Law, were prepared to resist Home Rule by force if necessary. To this end they set up the *Ulster Volunteers* early in 1913. They were a force of loyal Ulstermen determined to go to any lengths to block Home Rule. The Ulster Volunteers, under the leadership of Carson and Craig, grew steadily in numbers throughout 1913. They drilled and took part in military manoeuvres and prepared to seize control of the province in the event of Home Rule becoming law.

Eoin MacNeill, one of the founders of the Gaelic League, whose newspaper article, 'The North Began', prepared the way for the foundation of the Irish Volunteers in November 1913.

THE IRISH VOLUNTEERS

Meanwhile, Irish Nationalists paid close attention to events in the North. Eoin MacNeill, a founder member of the Gaelic League, wrote an article called 'The North Began'. In this article, he called for the setting up a similar volunteer force in the South in order to defend Ireland's right to Home Rule. In response to this article, a meeting of Irish Nationalists took place at the Rotunda in Dublin on 25 November 1913. It was at this meeting that the *Irish Volunteers* were formed. Many members of the Irish Republican Brotherhood (IRB) joined this new force. They hoped to use it when the time was right to stage a rebellion. By the summer of 1914, more than 100,000 men had joined the Irish Volunteers.

TEST YOUR KNOWLEDGE
1 Who were the Ulster Volunteers? Why were they set up?
2 Who led this group of Ulstermen?
3 Who wrote the article 'The North Began'? What was its immediate outcome?
4 When were the Irish Volunteers set up? What was the purpose of this organisation?
5 Why did many IRB men join this force?

1914: IRELAND ON THE VERGE OF WAR

In the early months of 1914, many people believed that Ireland was on the brink of civil war. In this year, the Ulster Volunteers and the Irish Volunteers illegally imported arms and ammunition. The stage now seemed set for a war between North and South.

THE LARNE GUN-RUNNING

On 24 April 1914, the Ulster Volunteers illegally imported arms from Germany. Most of these arrived safely ashore at the Co. Antrim port of Larne. The cargo numbered some 24,000 rifles and three million rounds of ammunition.

The Larne gun-running.

Although the British government knew what was going on, no effort was made to seize the arms or to arrest those involved. This was an important triumph for the Ulster Volunteers. They could now back up their campaign against Home Rule with force of arms.

THE HOWTH GUN-RUNNING

The Irish Volunteers smuggled arms into the country at Howth, Co. Dublin, on 26 July 1914. The ship used was Erskine Childers' yacht, the *Asgard*. Hundreds of Volunteers helped to unload the arms and to take them safely away. On their way back to Dublin, the Volunteers were challenged by the army and police but managed to get the weapons away safely. Later that day, when British soldiers were marching along Bachelor's Walk, they were jeered by local onlookers. The soldiers opened fire on the crowd, killing three and injuring thirty-eight.

The Howth gun-running.

WORLD WAR I BEGINS
HOME RULE IS SHELVED

The Third Home Rule Bill, passed in 1912, was due to become law in the autumn of 1914. John Redmond and his followers were about to see their hopes come true. These hopes were dashed when World War I broke out in August 1914. The British government now decided to postpone Home Rule until after the war. As soon as the war broke out, the Ulster Volunteers showed their loyalty by joining the British army and marching off to fight for the empire.

THE IRISH VOLUNTEERS SPLIT

World War I was not so simple an issue for the Irish Volunteers. In September 1914, in a speech at Woodenbridge, Co. Wicklow, John Redmond strongly urged the Volunteers to fight for Britain in the war. He hoped that, in return, Britain would grant Home Rule at an early date.

This speech brought about a split in the Irish Volunteers. The vast majority followed Redmond's call and changed their names to the *National Volunteers*. A minority of 10,000, under the leadership of MacNeill, refused to fight for Britain and retained the name Irish Volunteers.

An Irish recruiting
poster during
World War I

TEST YOUR KNOWLEDGE
1 What happened at the port of Larne on 24 April 1914?
2 What was the reaction of the British government to this event?
3 What event occurred at Howth on 26 July 1914?
4 What ship was used? Who assisted in unloading its cargo?
5 What happened at Bachelors Walk, Dublin, later the same day?
6 Ireland seemed to be on the brink of civil war in 1914. Explain why.
7 What led to a split among the Irish Volunteers?

Chapter 21: Review

- From 1910 onwards, the British Liberal government under H.H. Asquith needed the support of the Irish Home Rule Party under John Redmond in order to stay in power. In return for this support, Asquith promised to bring in a Home Rule Bill for Ireland at the earliest possible opportunity.

- The Third Home Rule Bill was passed by the British House of Commons in 1912 but was immediately rejected by the House of Lords. However, as the House of Lords could only delay a bill for two years, it was due to become law in 1914.

- Ulster Unionists and British Conservatives were bitterly against Home Rule. Edward Carson and James Craig drew up the *Solemn League and Covenant* (1912) which was signed by over 250,000 Ulster Protestants opposed to Home Rule. In 1913 they set up the Ulster Volunteers which was a force of loyal Ulstermen determined to block Home Rule at all costs.

- On 25 November 1913, the Irish Volunteers were set up in Dublin under the leadership of Eoin MacNeill. Their aim was to defend Ireland's right to Home Rule. Many IRB men joined the Irish Volunteers and hoped to use them to organise a rebellion against British rule in Ireland.

- On 24 April 1914, the Ulster Volunteers landed arms illegally at Larne, Co. Antrim. On 26 July, the Irish Volunteers landed guns at Howth, Co. Dublin.

- When World War I broke out in August 1914, the British government decided to put off Home Rule until the war was over.

- The Ulster Volunteers immediately responded to the war by joining the British army. However, when John Redmond advised the Irish Volunteers to do the same, a split occurred in the organisation. The majority, known as the National Volunteers, followed Redmond's call, while the minority under Eoin MacNeill refused to fight for Britain and kept the name Irish Volunteers.

ACTIVITIES

1 Match an item in Column 1 with an item in Column 2.

COLUMN 1	COLUMN 2
A Northern Unionist	Asquith
Leader of the Irish Volunteers	Craig
A Dublin-born Unionist	Redmond
A Home Rule leader	MacNeill
A Liberal statesman	Carson

2 Complete the following sentences.
(a) The Irish Parliamentary Party was re-united in 1900 under the leadership of _____.
(b) As a result of the Parliament Act (1911), _____.
(c) The Ulster Solemn League and Covenant (1912) was _____.
(d) The Irish Volunteers were founded in _____.
(e) Guns were landed at Howth, Co. Dublin, in July 1914 on board _____.

3 Choose three illustrations from this chapter and state what each tells you about the events of the Home Rule Crisis.

4 Imagine that you were a Unionist present at the signing of the Solemn League and Covenant (1912). Describe the event and outline your feelings on the political events of the time.

5 Write a paragraph on two of the following. (a) The founding of the Irish Volunteers; (b) The Larne Gun-running; (c) The Howth Gun-running.

REBELLION IN IRELAND: 1914-18

A REVIVED IRB

As we have seen, the IRB was a secret illegal organisation waiting for the right opportunity to stage a rebellion against British rule in Ireland. They were also members of the Irish Volunteers and hoped to use that organisation when the time came to stage a rebellion. When the split came in the Volunteers, the IRB members were among those who refused to answer Redmond's call to join the British army.

By this time several young men, including Sean Mac Diarmada and Patrick Pearse, had been recruited into this secret organisation. Both they and older Fenians like Thomas Clarke welcomed Britain's involvement in World War I. They saw this as Ireland's great opportunity to strike another blow for freedom. This view was summed up in the phrase: 'England's difficulty is Ireland's opportunity'.

PATRICK PEARSE (1879-1916)

Born in Dublin in 1879, Patrick Pearse was the son of an English stone cutter and an Irish mother. He received his early education in the Christian Brothers' school, Westland Row, and later trained as a barrister. From an early age, Patrick showed an interest in the Irish language and became a member of the Gaelic League. In 1903 he became editor of the League's newspaper, *An Claidheamh Soluis*.

Thomas Clarke, the elderly Fenian whose tobacco shop in the centre of Dublin was used by the IRB for secret meetings in the years before 1916.

Patrick H. Pearse (1879-1916).

Pearse spend his summers in a cottage he built at Rosmuc in the Connemara Gaeltacht. He was very interested in education and opened a bilingual school, St. Enda's, at Cullenswood House, Ranelagh, in Dublin. In 1910, 'The Hermitage', Rathfarnham, Dublin, became the new home for Pearse's school. Subjects taught included the Irish language, history, legends and nature study. He inspired his students with a love of Ireland.

Patrick Pearse was committed to the cause of Irish freedom and he joined the Irish Volunteers and the IRB. He became convinced that freedom could only be achieved by the spilling of Irish blood. He made this clear in 1915 when he spoke at the graveside of the old Fenian, O'Donovan Rossa. He ended this graveside oration with the words: 'Ireland unfree shall never be at peace'. From then on, Pearse and other IRB leaders plotted an early rebellion.

TEST YOUR KNOWLEDGE
1 Why did many IRB members join the Irish Volunteers?
2 How did the IRB view Britain's involvement in World War I?
3 How did Patrick Pearse show his interest in the Irish language?
4 What do you think was unusual about Pearse's school at St Enda's?
5 In what way did Pearse believe that Irish freedom could be achieved?
6 What famous speech did he make in 1915?

PREPARATIONS FOR A RISING

In January 1916, the Supreme Council of the IRB decided to hold a rising around Easter. Those involved in this decision included Thomas Clarke, Patrick Pearse, Sean Mac Diarmada, Eamonn Ceannt and Joseph Plunkett. Meanwhile, James Connolly and the Irish Citizen Army were planning their own rebellion. When the leaders of the IRB learned of this, they persuaded Connolly to join forces with them.

Both the Irish Volunteers and the Citizen Army marched through the centre of Dublin on St Patrick's Day 1916, while Eoin MacNeill, the Volunteer leader, looked on. The IRB had chosen Easter Sunday, 23 April 1916, as the date of the rising.

Patrick Pearse (in uniform) addressing a meeting in 1916.

PLANS GO WRONG
A DIARY OF EVENTS, HOLY WEEK 1916

Holy Thursday, 20 April 1916

The IRB had kept their plans for the Easter Rising top secret. It was not until as late as this that Eoin MacNeill, commander of the Volunteers but not himself a member of the IRB, discovered these plans. MacNeill believed that a rising could not succeed because of lack of arms.

As the IRB needed MacNeill's support, they forged a document known as *The Castle Document* which stated that the government was about to suppress the Volunteers and arrest its leaders. The IRB also told MacNeill of the expected arrival of arms from Germany.

Good Friday, 21 April 1916

A German boat, the *Aud*, full of arms and ammunition, arrived off the Kerry coast.

Sir Roger Casement, a former British diplomat who had organised this arms supply, arrived on board a German submarine. He shaved off his beard in an effort to hide his identity and arrived ashore at Banna Strand, Co. Kerry. Despite his precautions, however, he was almost immediately arrested. The *Aud* was also captured.

Sir Roger Casement, the former British diplomat who travelled to Germany for the IRB to seek German support for a rising against Great Britain.

Holy Saturday, 22 April 1916

The *Aud*, while being escorted into Cork harbour, was scuttled by her crew. MacNeill learned of this and also discovered that the so-called 'Castle Document' had been a forgery. He immediately set about cancelling all Volunteer activities for the following day.

Easter Sunday, 23 April 1916

MacNeill's order forbidding all Volunteer movements for that day was published in the *Sunday Independent*. Because of this, the Rising could not take place on Easter Sunday. However, the IRB leaders decided to have a rising on the following day, Easter Monday.

THE RISING BEGINS

The centre of Dublin was deserted and peaceful on this bank holiday Monday. Ordinary Dubliners were completely taken by surprise when they saw groups of armed Volunteers capturing important buildings throughout the city – the Rising had begun.

The rebels chose the General Post Office as their headquarters. From its steps, Patrick Pearse read the *Proclamation of the Irish Republic* to a small and bewildered group of onlookers. The tricolour was raised on the roof of the building. Other centres manned by the rebels included St Stephen's Green, the Four Courts, Boland's Mill, Jacobs, and the South Dublin Union in James' Street. However, they failed to capture Dublin Castle, the headquarters of the British government in Ireland.

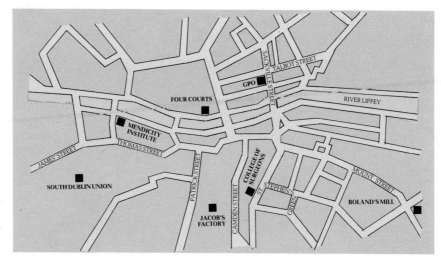

Buildings in Dublin occupied by the rebels during Easter Week, 1916.

THE RISING FAILS

The outbreak of the Rising in Dublin took the British authorities completely by surprise. There were only 2500 troops based in the city and many of them had gone off to the Fairyhouse Races on that bank holiday Monday. However, by Tuesday, troops and artillery were pouring into Kingstown harbour. Some 12,000 British soldiers had arrived by Thursday.

The only real resistance which the incoming soldiers faced was at Mount Street bridge where a group of about seventeen rebels from Eamon de Valera's garrison at Boland's Mill fired on the soldiers from nearby houses. Many British soldiers were killed before the army eventually stormed the doorways with hand grenades. Another rebel garrison which offered strong resistance was the South Dublin Union in James' Street.

By midweek, however, it was becoming increasingly obvious that the rebels were fighting a losing battle. On Wednesday, a gunboat, the *Helga,* sailed up the Liffey and began to shell Liberty Hall and other buildings. During the next few days, the sounds of gunfire could be heard throughout the city and many buildings, including the GPO, were burning. Looting of shops was widespread as people from nearby tenements took advantage of the confusion. Women could be seen wearing stolen fur coats and wheeling prams which were full of stolen goods.

The British forces gradually closed in on the rebels, whose situation was hopeless by the end of the week. At 3 pm on Saturday, 29 April, Pearse, shocked by the number of civilian casualties, surrendered unconditionally to General Maxwell, the British commander. The Easter Rising had ended in failure.

Artists' views of the fighting in Dublin during Easter Week 1916.

In all, owing to confusion before the Rising, only about 2000 rebels had fought, and there was little activity in the rest of the country. Casualties had been very high – about 450 people were killed and another 2600 wounded, most of them civilians. The damage to property had also been considerable, amounting to about £2½ million. Therefore, for most Dubliners, the Rising had been a major inconvenience, resulting in a costly loss of life and destruction of their city.

The centre of Dublin in ruins after the Easter Rising:
(a) O'Connell Street

(b) The shell of Liberty Hall, the headquarters of the Irish Transport and General Workers' Union.

TEST YOUR KNOWLEDGE

1 *What did the IRB decide to do in January 1916?*
2 *Why did MacNeill disapprove when he heard of the IRB plans to hold a rising?*
3 *What part did Sir Roger Casement play in the events leading up to the 1916 Rising?*
4 *Why did the IRB change the date of the Rising?*
5 *What buildings did the rebels occupy?*
6 *What steps did the British authorities take to deal with the Rising?*
7 *How had ordinary Dubliners regarded the Rising?*

AFTER THE RISING

Prisoners being marched along the streets of Dublin after the defeat of the Easter Rising.

Huge numbers were arrested after the Rising and brought to Richmond Barracks for questioning. As the arrested leaders of the Rising were marching through Dublin, they were jeered and taunted by onlookers. The military was now in charge of the city, the streets were cleared and a curfew was enforced.

Eamon de Valera, the Commandant of the Bolands' Mills Garrison, under arrest after surrendering at the end of the Rising.

Military courts were set up to try the rebels. Fifteen men were shot between 3 and 12 May, including the seven signatories of the Easter Proclamation – Clarke, Pearse, Connolly, Ceannt, Mac Diarmada, Plunkett and MacDonagh. Roger Casement was hanged in August. Some of those sentenced to death, including Eamon de Valera and Countess Markievicz, had their sentences changed to life imprisonment. The vast majority of those who took part in the Rising were sent to internment camps in Britain.

The following account clearly shows the effect which the harsh treatment of the rebels had on many Irish people.

'The executions, which followed the defeat of the Volunteers, horrified the nation . . . The first open manifestation of the deep public feeling aroused by the executions was at the Month's Mind for the dead leaders. A Month's Mind is the Mass celebrated for the soul of a relative or friend a month after his death. It was the first opportunity that sympathisers of the rebels had to come out in the open. I went with my father to the first of the Month's Minds, which was for the brothers Pearse, at Rathfarnham. We arrived well in time for Mass but could not get into the church and the forecourt was packed right out to the road. I was surprised to see so many well-dressed and obviously well-to-do people present . . . I went to other Month's Minds with my father – to Merchant's Quay, John's Lane and other city churches. For us young people these Masses were occasions for quite spontaneous demonstrations, shouting insults at the Dublin Metropolitan Police who were always around but, having learned their lesson during the 1913 strike, were anxious to avoid trouble . . .'

C.S. Andrews, *Dublin Made Me*

THE REVIVAL OF SINN FÉIN

Britain had regarded the 1916 Rising as a Sinn Féin rebellion. Its leader, Arthur Griffith, was placed under arrest. However, Sinn Féin was not directly involved in the Rising but it benefited from being associated with its dead martyrs. Those who sympathised with the Rising came to rally around Sinn Féin, and the party grew steadily.

The rebels who arrived home from internment camps in 1916-17 quickly joined the ranks of Sinn Féin and the reorganised Volunteers. In October 1917, Eamon de Valera, the senior survivor of the 1916 Rising, took over the leadership of the new Sinn Féin and the Volunteers.

Republican prisoners receiving an enthusiastic welcome home after their release from internment camps in England.

The increased support for Sinn Féin was clearly seen in a number of by-election victories. Count Plunkett, the father of the executed 1916 leader, won a seat in North Roscommon in February 1917. In July of the same year, de Valera himself won a by-election in East Clare. Neither of them took his seat at Westminster.

WORLD WAR I ENDS

While the events recorded in this chapter were taking place in Ireland, around 300,000 Irishmen were fighting for Britain in World War I. Of these men, 50,000 were killed in action. Although all those soldiers had volunteered for service, an attempt was made to bring conscription into Ireland in 1918. Sinn Féin organised an anti-conscription campaign which further increased their popularity. As a result, the government dropped the scheme.

An anti-conscription meeting, 1918. Sinn Féin was prominent among the groups which organised opposition to conscription.

The war finally ended in November 1918. Those returning home found conditions in Ireland totally changed. Back in 1914, most Irish people had supported Home Rule but now, more and more people wanted a separate Irish Republic.

This important change was very clearly shown in the results of the general election of December 1918. Out of 106 seats, Sinn Féin won seventy-three while the Irish parliamentary party, now under the leadership of John Dillon, won a mere six. The Unionists won twenty-six seats. The newly-elected Sinn Féin MPs refused to attend the Westminster parliament. The scene was now set for a clash between Sinn Féin and the British government.

These two bar graphs clearly show the changes in strength of the main Irish political parties between 1910 and the general election of 1918.

1910
- Home Rulers: 83
- Sinn Féin: 0
- Irish Unionists: 19

(seats)

1918
- Sinn Féin: 73
- Home Rulers: 6
- Irish Unionists: 26

(seats)

TEST YOUR KNOWLEDGE

1 What was the first popular view of the 1916 Rising?

2 How was this view to change in the succeeding months?

3 Why do you think the death sentences imposed on de Valera and Countess Markievicz were changed to life imprisonment?

4 In what way did Sinn Féin benefit from the 1916 Rising?

5 Name two by-election victories secured by Sinn Féin throughout 1917.

6 What role had Irishmen played in World War I?

7 What was the result of the 1918 general election? What do you think was so revolutionary about this result?

Chapter 22: Review

- The IRB welcomed the outbreak of World War I, as they saw it as an opportunity to stage a rebellion against British rule in Ireland – 'England's difficulty is Ireland's opportunity'.

- P.H. Pearse (1879-1916) became a leading member of the IRB. He had earlier been editor of the Gaelic League newspaper *An Claidheamh Soluis*. He was very interested in education and opened his own school, St Enda's.

- The Supreme Council of the IRB settled on Easter Sunday, 1916, as the date of a rising. Connolly and the Citizen Army were persuaded to join forces with the IRB.

- Roger Casement, who had arranged the delivery of arms, was arrested in Co. Kerry. MacNeill now decided to withdraw from the Rising and cancelled all Volunteer activities arranged for Easter Sunday.

- The IRB now decided to hold the Rising on the following day, Easter Monday. The rebels took over various buildings in Dublin including the GPO, the South Dublin Union and Boland's Mills. Patrick Pearse, as Commander-in-Chief, read the Proclamation of the Irish Republic outside the GPO – the rebel headquarters.

- By the end of Easter Week, the rebels were hopelessly outnumbered by British troops. Much of the city centre lay in smoking ruins. On Saturday, 29 April, Pearse surrendered unconditionally to General Maxwell, the British commander.

- In the beginning the people of Dublin were very angry with the rebels. However, this anger soon changed to sympathy after fifteen of the rebel leaders were shot between 3 and 12 May. Most of those who had taken part in the Rising were sent to internment camps in Great Britain.

- When the 1916 rebels were released from imprisonment, they rallied around the Sinn Féin party and chose Eamon de Valera, the senior surviving officer of the Easter Rising, to be their leader. The re-organised Sinn Féin party grew quickly and in the 1918 general election, it won seventy-three out of the 106 Irish seats in the British parliament.

ACTIVITIES

1 *Multiple choice*
  (a) *The older Fenian who helped re-organise the Irish Republican Brotherhood after 1900 was: (i) Seán MacDiarmada; (ii) Patrick Pearse; (iii) Thomas Clarke; (iv) Joseph Plunkett.*
  (b) *In 1915, a famous speech was made at the graveside of O'Donovan Rossa by: (i) Patrick Pearse; (ii) James Connolly; (iii) Eamonn Ceannt; (iv) Thomas Clarke.*
  (c) *The German boat carrying arms and ammunition to Ireland in 1916 was called: (i) the Lusitania; (ii) the Bismarck; (iii) the Asgard; (iv) the Aud.*
  (d) *The Proclamation of the Irish Republic was read on Easter Monday 1916 by: (i) Thomas Clarke; (ii) Patrick Pearse; (iii) James Connolly; (iv) Roger Casement.*
  (e) *The commandant in charge of the rebel garrison at Boland's Mills in 1916 was: (i) Eamonn Ceannt; (ii) Countess Markievicz; (iii) Eamon de Valera; (iv) Joseph Plunkett.*

2 *True or false?*
  (a) *In 1903, Patrick Pearse became editor of the Gaelic League's newspaper, The United Irishman.*
  (b) *The IRB leaders kept their plans for the rising secret from the Commander-in-Chief of the Irish Volunteers, Eoin MacNeill.*
  (c) *Sir Roger Casement was a former member of the British diplomatic service.*
  (d) *A British gunboat, the Helga, sailed up the Liffey and shelled Liberty Hall.*
  (e) *The first Sinn Féin victory in a by-election after the Easter Rising was achieved by Eamon de Valera in East Clare in July 1917.*

3 *Draw up a time chart on the main events leading up to, during and after the Easter Rising of 1916.*

4 *Read again the account by C.S. Andrews on page 185 concerning his attendance at Mass for the dead leaders of the 1916 Rising. Give three important points which you learn from this account. Say whether you consider it a useful source of information.*

5 *Write a detailed account of the part played by Patrick Pearse in the Easter Rising of 1916.*

TROUBLED TIMES IN IRELAND: 1919-23

THE FIRST DÁIL

On 21 January 1919, an historic event took place at the Mansion House in Dublin. Sinn Féin MPs, having refused to take their seats in the British parliament, met and set up a parliament of their own. This became known as the *First Dáil*. Many Sinn Féin MPs were either in prison or on the run – therefore only twenty-seven of them were present in the Mansion House on that day. This small group met for two hours and made the following decisions:

- They supported the declaration of an Irish Republic made at Easter 1916.
- They agreed to a democratic programme that promised widespread reforms in the areas of economy, education and poor law.
- Sean T. O'Kelly was elected to head an Irish delegation to the Versailles Peace Conference where they hoped to win support for their views.

The meeting of the First Dáil at the Mansion House, Dublin, in January 1919.

Eamon de Valera, the most senior member of Sinn Féin, was in prison when the First Dáil met. In his absence, Cathal Brugha acted as president. However, de Valera escaped from prison the following month and was elected president of the Dáil on 1 April 1919. He appointed a cabinet of ministers to take over the running of the country: Arthur Griffith (Home Affairs), Michael Collins (Finance), Cathal Brugha (Defence), William T. Cosgrave (Local Government), Countess Markievicz (Labour), Eoin MacNeill (Industries), Count Plunkett (Foreign Affairs) and Robert Barton (Agriculture).

The British government soon declared Sinn Féin and the Dáil to be illegal. The stage was set for a war between Britain and Ireland to decide who would govern the country. The War of Independence was about to begin.

THE WAR OF INDEPENDENCE
THE FIGHTING BEGINS

On the same day that the First Dáil met in Dublin, the first shooting of the War of Independence took place in Co. Tipperary A group of Volunteers, in search of arms, attacked a number of policemen of the Royal Irish Constabulary (RIC) near the town of Soloheadbeg in Co. Tipperary. Many of the early attacks were on RIC barracks in search of arms, but later, British soldiers also came under attack.

There followed two and a half years of guerrilla-type warfare between Irish Republicans and the British forces.

MICHAEL COLLINS (1890-1922)

Michael Collins was the most important Irish military leader during the War of Independence. Born in Co Cork in 1890, he went to London at the age of fifteen to work in the British post office. He soon became a member of the IRB and the Irish Volunteers and returned to Ireland for the 1916 Rising.

Michael Collins (1890-1922).

Collins did not make his mark on events until after his release from prison at the end of 1916. He then set about reorganising the Volunteer movement which now became known as the *Irish Republican Army (IRA)*.

During the War of Independence, Collins directed IRA activities. He master-minded his own spy network which successfully countered the British spying system. The British government offered a reward of £10,000 for the capture of Collins. To them he was the most wanted man in Ireland.

GUERRILLA WARFARE IN IRELAND

The War of Independence consisted of attacks and reprisals on the part of the British forces and the IRA. The IRA used guerrilla warfare against the British forces – i.e. small groups carried out surprise attacks and then withdrew quickly. Ordinary people, going about their daily work, were often innocent victims of terror and violence.

THE BLACK AND TANS

In the early months of 1920, law and order was breaking down throughout Ireland. To cope with this crisis, the British government in March 1920 sent over a new force which became known as the *Black and Tans*. Many of these had fought in World War I and could not find employment after the war. They were attracted to Ireland by the high wages of ten shillings (50p) a day. Due to a shortage of police uniforms, this force wore a mixture of dark green and khaki which led to their name, the Black and Tans. Used to war and adventure, they let loose a reign of terror in Ireland.

A smaller force, the *Auxiliaries*, were sent to Ireland in August 1920. These consisted of ex-army officers who were given great freedom in the methods they used. Like the Black and Tans, they used widespread terror against both the IRA and the civilian population.

A group of Black and Tans carrying out a raid on Liberty Hall, Dublin.

The British Viceroy in Ireland, Lord French, inspecting a group of Auxiliaries.

THE FLYING COLUMNS

The IRA was organised in small groups which conducted hit-and-run attacks on the crown forces. Such groups were known as *Flying Columns*. The IRA were not in uniform and were able to escape quickly into the local countryside where they had many supporters among the local people. Famous leaders of Flying Columns included Ernie O'Malley, Liam Lynch, Sean MacEoin and Tom Barry. The Black and Tans and

An IRA flying column during the War of Independence.

the Auxiliaries found the tactics of the IRA impossible to defeat. As a result they carried out acts of revenge on the local civilian population and on public figures who were known to be sympathetic to the IRA.

1920: A YEAR OF TERROR

1920 was the most violent year in the War of Independence.

- In March, Tomás MacCurtain, the Sinn Féin Lord Mayor of Cork, was shot dead in his house by crown forces.
- On 25 October, Terence MacSwiney, the next Lord Mayor of Cork, died in Brixton prison, London, after a hunger strike lasting seventy-four days.
- On 1 November, Kevin Barry, an eighteen-year old university student, was hanged in Mountjoy jail, Dublin, for his part in an IRA ambush.

The funeral of Terence Mac-Swiney passing through Cork.

Kevin Barry, the eighteen-year-old medical student who was hanged in Mountjoy Jail, Dublin, in November 1920 for his part in an IRA ambush.

- Sunday, 21 November, was to become known as 'Bloody Sunday'. Collins had discovered the hide-outs of a number of undercover British agents in Dublin. Beginning at 9 am, his hit squad assassinated fourteen of them. On the same afternoon, the Black and Tans, in an act of reprisal, opened fire on a crowd watching a football match between Dublin and Tipperary at Croke Park. Twelve people, including one of the Tipperary players, were killed and another sixty were injured.

- On the night of 10-11 December, the Black and Tans and the Auxiliaries set fire to a large part of the centre of Cork city. This was a reprisal for the IRA ambush, under the command of Tom Barry, at Kilmichael, Co. Cork, on 28 November.

Crowds gather outside Mountjoy Prison, Dublin, during a hunger strike by IRA prisoners.

TEST YOUR KNOWLEDGE

1 What incident marked the beginning of the War of Independence?
2 Who was the most important Irish military leader during the War of Independence?
3 What new name did the Volunteers take?
4 What type of fighting took place during the War of Independence?
5 Who were the Black and Tans? How did they get their name?
6 Who were the Auxiliaries?
7 What were the Flying Columns? Name one of their most famous leaders.
8 What happened in Dublin on 'Bloody Sunday', 21 November 1920?

WORKING WITH EVIDENCE

Cork in Flames – A Night of Terror

'Cork has never experienced such a night of horror than that of Saturday. The residents in every part of the city were terrified by the rifle and revolver firing, bomb explosions, extensive outbreak of fire, the breaking and smashing of windows and business premises and crashing of walls and buildings . . .

In view of recent occurrences, the principal streets were not paraded by such large numbers as is customary on Saturday nights, but many people were out-of-doors when they were startled by the discharge of rifle and revolver shots . . . As soon as the firing commenced the thoroughfares quickly cleared, pedestrians having proceeded with all haste to their homes, and with the exception of the armed parties, the city presented a deserted appearance in a very brief period of time . . .

It was hoped that when curfew hour was reached (10 o'clock) there would be a cessation of the firing and the explosions, but such hopes were not realised; in fact as the night advanced the situation became more terrifying, and the people, especially women and children, were rendered helpless amidst fire and shot. It was an awful experience and will forever be remembered by those who passed through it . . .

The centre of Cork City after it was set on fire by the Black and Tans in December 1920.

It was only when dawn arrived that an idea of the terrible devastation could be obtained . . . A portion of the city embracing valuable business premises had been devastated and nothing but smouldering ruins could be seen. It was an appalling and terrible spectacle. Fine buildings with highly valuable stock had been wiped out, and thousands of people had been rendered idle. The total loss must reach a few million.'

Cork Examiner

1 On what date was Cork city burned?
2 Why were there so few people on the streets when the firing began?
3 Who were the 'armed parties' referred to?
4 What is a curfew?
5 Describe what the people of Cork saw the following morning.
6 'It was an awful experience and will forever be remembered by those who passed through it.' Imagine that you witnessed the burning of Cork. Describe what you saw.

FROM TRUCE TO TREATY
DEADLOCK: A TRUCE IS DECLARED

By 1921, the War of Independence had almost reached a deadlock. While the British controlled the major towns, the IRA had a firm grip on the countryside.

The Dáil had also set up its own government departments and courts: more and more people were now using these and ignoring the British ones. By the middle of 1921, morale among both the British and IRA had reached a very low point. Ordinary people, both in Britain and Ireland, longed for an end to the violence and the terror. In July 1921, both sides agreed to a truce.

De Valera and Lloyd George, the British prime minister, met in London. While no agreement was reached at this meeting, they did arrange for peace talks to begin in London the following October.

A PEACE TREATY IS SIGNED

In October 1921, an Irish delegation went to London to arrange a treaty with the British government. This delegation consisted of Michael Collins, Arthur Griffith, George Gavan Duffy, Eamonn Duggan and Robert Barton. De Valera, the president of the Dáil, did not go. This caused a major surprise at the time. The Irish group had no experience of talks at this level. They faced an experienced British team which included Lloyd George, Winston Churchill and Austen Chamberlain. The Treaty drawn up by the British contained the following points:

- The twenty-six counties of Ireland were to be given 'Dominion Status'. Under this Ireland, would become a member of the British Commonwealth and would be known as the 'Irish Free State'.
- While the Irish Free State would have its own government, parliament and army, members of the parliament would have to take an oath of allegiance to the king of England.
- The British army was to remain in possession of certain Irish ports which were known as the 'Treaty Ports'.
- This treaty only covered the twenty-six counties of Southern Ireland, as the government of Ireland Act (1920) had set up a separate parliament in Belfast under the British king. However, a boundary commission was to be set up with the task of redrawing the border between North and South.

The Irish delegation, under severe pressure from Lloyd George, signed the Treaty on 6 December 1921. They now had to convince the Irish at home that acceptance of the Treaty was the only way forward.

The Irish delegates at the Treaty negotiations in London in the autumn of 1921.

David Lloyd George, the British Prime Minister who negotiated the Anglo-Irish Treaty.

TEST YOUR KNOWLEDGE
1 *Why did both sides want a truce?*
2 *Name the members of the Irish delegation who went to London to negotiate a treaty on October 1921.*
3 *State two terms of the Treaty.*
4 *Why was the boundary commission set up?*
5 *Do you think the Irish delegation performed well? Give reasons for your answer.*

COUNTRY DIVIDED OVER TREATY

When the Irish group arrived back in Ireland after signing the Treaty, they found a sharply divided country. Most ordinary people were relieved that the war had ended; however, others saw the Treaty as a 'sell-out' to the British.

The debate on the Treaty began in the Dáil on 14 December 1921. De Valera was against the Treaty. He objected to the oath of allegiance and would only accept a full Irish Republic. Those supporting de Valera included Austin Stack, Cathal Brugha and Erskine Childers.

Michael Collins and Arthur Griffith strongly defended the Treaty. They saw it as the best deal there was in the circumstances. The only alternative to acceptance of the Treaty was the renewal of war. They also argued that the Treaty was a good beginning along the road to greater freedom. It would, in Collins' words, give Ireland 'the freedom to win freedom'.

The vote on the Treaty was taken in the Dáil on 7 January 1922: sixty-four voted for it and fifty-seven against. De Valera resigned from the presidency of the Dáil and was replaced by Arthur Griffith. The new Free State government now prepared to take over from the British who were leaving the country.

The IRA was also bitterly divided over the Treaty. While one faction supported Collins and became absorbed into a new national army, another faction prepared to take up arms against old colleagues who supported the Treaty.

THE CIVIL WAR BEGINS

In April 1922, the anti-Treaty IRA or *Irregulars*, under the command of Rory O'Conor, occupied the Four Courts in Dublin.

As tensions were mounting in the city and in the country, both sides attempted to avoid a war which would involve the murder of friends and comrades. They agreed to hold an election in June 1922. This election, however, only increased the tension and the bitterness: fifty-eight pro-Treaty TDs were elected while only thirty-five anti-Treaty TDs were returned. Matters came to a head when Sir Henry Wilson, a hardline Unionist and military adviser to the Northern Ireland government, was assassinated in London by two IRA men.

The shelling of the Four Courts, during 1922.

On 28 June, Michael Collins, under pressure from the British government, ordered the Free State army to shell the Four Courts. The Civil War had begun.

Dublin was the first scene of the fighting. The fierce street battles, which took place around O'Connell Street, ended in the total defeat of the anti-Treaty forces, Cathal Brugha being among the casualties.

After their defeat in Dublin, the Irregulars held out in Munster. By the end of August 1922, after ferocious fighting, all the towns of that province were in Free State hands.

Irregular soldiers surrendering to Free State forces in Dublin during the Civil War.

THE DEATH OF TWO LEADERS

In the meantime, the Free State government had lost its two leading figures. On 12 August 1922, Arthur Griffith died suddenly of exhaustion at the age of 50. Ten days later, Michael Collins was shot dead in an ambush in Co. Cork. His death at the age of thirty-two was a tragic loss to the new state.

The funeral of Arthur Griffith passing through Dublin.

MANY REPUBLICANS ARE EXECUTED

William T. Cosgrave became the new leader of the Free State government. Cosgrave and his leading ministers in the Free State government, Kevin O'Higgins and Richard Mulcahy, were determined to deal severely with the Irregulars. They set up military courts with the death penalty for those found carrying arms. Under these new laws, from December 1922 many Republicans, including Erskine Childers and Rory O'Connor, were executed and some 12,000 others were interned. The Irregulars in turn attacked members of the Dáil and Senate. The Civil War had now entered its bloodiest phase.

THE CIVIL WAR ENDS

By the spring of 1923, the Free State government had gained firm control over the country. General Liam Lynch, the Commander-in-Chief of the IRA, was killed in action on 10 April and was succeeded by Frank Aiken. The Republican leaders now realised that they could not win the Civil War. Stocks of arms and ammunition were very low, and the sympathy of the general public was not with them. The IRA laid down their arms and went into hiding. The Civil War had ended.

Although the war was over, the bitterness and hatred caused by it were to last for many years to come. Some 600 people had died and there had been widespread damage to property and communications. The Free State government under W.T. Cosgrave had a difficult task ahead of them – to restore order and unity to a bitterly divided country.

TEST YOUR KNOWLEDGE
1 Why did de Valera object to the Treaty?
2 How did Collins and Griffith defend the Treaty?
3 What was the view of the IRA on the Treaty?
4 What was the first incident in the Civil War?
5 What two Free State leaders died in 1922?
6 How did W.T. Cosgrave and his ministers deal with the threat to law and order posed by the Irregulars?
7 Why do you think the Irregulars lost the Civil War?
8 State two effects of the Civil War.

Chapter 23: Review

- The Sinn Féin MPs elected in December 1918 refused to take their seats at Westminster but met in the Mansion House in Dublin and set up the First Dáil on 21 January 1919.

- The War of Independence began on the same day that the first Dáil met when the IRA attacked a group of policemen near Soloheadbeg in Co. Tipperary.

- In March 1920 the British government sent the Black and Tans to Ireland to combat the IRA. In August a smaller force known as the Auxiliaries was sent. Both these groups used widespread terror against the IRA and the civilian population.

- The IRA organised themselves into Flying Columns and carried out a guerrilla warfare against the British forces in the country.

- The year 1920 was the worst in the War of Independence. Two Lord Mayors of Cork, Tomás MacCurtain and Terence MacSwiney died, Kevin Barry was executed and on Bloody Sunday, 21 November, the Black and Tans opened fire on a crowd in Croke Park in retaliation for the assassination of British spies at the hands of Michael Collins' hit squad earlier that morning.

- The British parliament passed the Government of Ireland act in 1920 which gave Northern Ireland its own parliament.

- By the summer of 1921 both sides in the War of Independence were anxious for peace. In July 1921 a truce was arranged and de Valera went to London for peace talks. These talks failed but further discussions were arranged for the following October.

- In October 1921, an Irish delegation, including Michael Collins and Arthur Griffith, travelled to London to draw up a treaty with Britain. Under pressure from the British prime minister, Lloyd George, the Irish signed a treaty on 6 December. The twenty-six counties of Ireland were given dominion status as a member of the British Commonwealth under the title the Irish Free State.

- The Anglo-Irish Treaty was debated in Dáil Éireann between 14 December 1921 and 7 January 1922. Michael Collins and Arthur Griffith defended the Treaty, while those against it included de Valera, Cathal Brugha and Erskine Childers. When the vote was taken on 7 January 1922, sixty-four voted for the Treaty while fifty-seven voted against.

- The Anti-Treaty IRA or Irregulars occupied the Four Courts in Dublin in April 1922. On 28 June the Free State army shelled the Four Courts – this was the beginning of the Civil War.

- In August 1922 two Free State leaders, Arthur Griffith and Michael Collins, died and W.T. Cosgrave became leader of the government.

- The Free State government set up military courts with the death penalty for those found carrying arms. Under this new law, many Republicans, including Erskine Childers and Rory O'Connor, were tried and executed.

- By the spring of 1923, the Free State government had gained firm control over the country. The Irregulars lacked the support which the IRA received from the local people during the War of Independence. As a result they laid down their arms and the Civil War came to an end in April 1923.

ACTIVITIES

1 *Multiple choice.*

   (a) 21 January 1919 was an historic occasion because: (i) the Black and Tans arrived in Ireland; (ii) Kevin Barry was executed; (iii) the First Dáil met; (iv) Cork city was burned.

   (b) The War of Independence began in January 1919 with an attack on policemen in: (i) Dublin; (ii) Tipperary; (iii) Cork; (iv) Limerick.

   (c) The Lord Mayor of Cork who died on hunger strike in London in October 1920 was: (i) Terence MacSwiney; (ii) Kevin Barry; (iii) Tomás MacCurtain; (iv) Cathal Brugha.

   (d) A truce in the Anglo-Irish War was declared in: (i) December 1920; (ii) March 1921; (iii) July 1921; (iv) December 1921.

   (e) After the death of Griffith and Collins, the new leader of the Free State was: (i) Kevin O'Higgins; (ii) W.T. Cosgrave; (iii) Erskine Childers; (iv) Robert Barton.

2 *Fill in the blanks with words from the box.*

Michael Collins	**Henry Wilson**
Four Courts	**Irregular**
Free State	**Civil War**
Lloyd George	**Arthur Griffith**
The Free State government	

After the shooting of _____ in London, the British government of _____ put pressure on _____ to attack the _____ forces which had occupied the _____. The _____ began on 23 June 1922 when _____ troops opened fire on the Four Courts. In August, the new Free State suffered a serious loss when _____ collapsed and died and _____ was shot in an ambush in West Cork.

3 *Write a paragraph on two of the following: (a) The First Dáil; (b) The role of Michael Collins in the War of Independence; (c) The Black and Tans and the Auxiliaries.*

4 *List the main points in the Anglo-Irish Treaty (1921).*

5 *Imagine that you were present at the Treaty debates in the Dáil. Write a short speech which you would have made either for or against the Treaty.*

6 *Explain why the Civil War broke out in June 1922. Write an account of its main incidents.*

THE IRISH FREE STATE: 1923-32

After the end of the Civil War in 1923, W.T. Cosgrave and his government faced many problems in building up the new state. In this chapter we will look at the main problems facing the government and the efforts made to deal with them.

W.T. Cosgrave addressing a political rally.

THE GOVERNMENT OF THE FREE STATE

A new set of laws or *Constitution* was drawn up in 1922 which outlined the structures of the new state. The following are the main points of the 1922 Constitution.

- The *Oireachtas* or parliament consisted of two assembles; the *Dáil*, with TDs elected by the people, and the *Senate* which consisted of some members elected by the Dáil and others nominated by the leader of the government.
- Members of the Dáil and Senate were elected by a system of *proportional representation.*
- The head of the government was to be known as the *president.* He was leader of a cabinet of ministers known as the *executive council.*
- All members of the Oireachtas were required to take an oath of allegiance to the king of England as head of the Commonwealth.
- The king's representative in Ireland was to be known as the *Governor-General.*

LAW AND ORDER

Ireland had not experienced peace and order for many years. The Civil War had left behind a deeply divided country. The restoration of law and order was, therefore, a high priority for the new government. This important task was in the hands of Kevin O'Higgins, the young and energetic Minister for Home Affairs. O'Higgins took the following measures to restore law and order.

- In 1923, he set up an unarmed police force known as the *Gárda Síochána* which replaced the old Royal Irish Constabulary.
- He brought in the Courts of Justice Act (1924) which reorganised the system of law courts in the country.
- He introduced harsh laws to deal with the IRA. These included Public Safety Acts which gave wide powers of arrest to the police and provided for the death penalty in certain cases.

Kevin O'Higgins, Minister for Home Affairs in Cosgrave's government.

The Garda Síochána, the police force which replaced the R.I.C. in 1923.

As a result of the steps taken by Kevin O'Higgins, order and stability gradually returned to the countryside. O'Higgins also played a key role in dealing effectively with another threat to the authority of the government. This threat took the form of the so-called *Army Mutiny*.

THE ARMY MUTINY

At the end of the Civil War, the national army consisted of 60,000 men. The government decided to reduce the size of the army once peace was restored. This move was resented by some army officers who were also dissatisfied by the lack of progress towards a republic.

In March 1924, a number of these officers sent an ultimatum to the government insisting that their views be put into operation. O'Higgins acted swiftly to deal with the situation. He demanded the resignation of the senior officers involved. The Minister for Defence, Richard Mulcahy, also resigned. The national army was never again to question the authority of a government.

1 *Who was the leader of the first government of the Irish Free State?*
2 *Name the two houses of the Oireachtas. How were their members elected?*
3 *Who was the Governor-General?*
4 *Who was the Minister for Home Affairs in the Free State government?*
5 *State two measures taken by O'Higgins to restore law and order after the Civil War.*
6 *Why were some army officers dissatisfied with the government?*
7 *How did the attempted army mutiny end? What was its long-term significance?*

IRELAND AND THE COMMONWEALTH

The restoration of law and order was not the only achievement of the government of the Irish Free State. It was to play an important part in gaining more independence for Commonwealth countries by loosening the ties between them and Great Britain. In 1931, an important act was passed known as the *Statute of Westminster*. This stated that Britain and other members of the Commonwealth were now on an equal footing with Britain and that Commonwealth countries had the right to reject legislation passed by the Westminster parliament on their behalf.

Desmond Fitzgerald, Minister for External Affairs in the Cumann na nGaedheal government.

However, for most ordinary people the most pressing concern was whether their living standards would improve under the new Free State government.

THE ECONOMY

Despite all the hopes of a better world with the coming of independence, life for the ordinary citizen remained much as it had been under British rule. For most people, the standard of living remained low. There was a severe housing shortage, wages were low, and public health was a matter of some concern. For many people, emigration remained the only alternative to a life of poverty at home.

As Ireland was a rural country, agriculture was the biggest industry. Patrick Hogan was appointed Minister for Agriculture. He encouraged the export of Irish agricultural produce and took steps to improve the quality of Irish goods. As a result of these policies, Irish agricultural exports greatly increased during the 1920s. Hogan also set up the Agricultural Credit Corporation (ACC) in 1927. This gave loans to farmers who wished to improve their land.

Industry posed a different problem. With the exception of Belfast, Ireland did not have any large-scale industrial centre. In industry, as well as in agriculture, the government favoured the practice of free trade between countries. It was slow to protect Irish industries from outside competition by means of tariffs.

The greatest economic achievement of these years was the establishment of the Electricity Supply Board (ESB) in 1927 and the construction of a hydro-electric scheme at Ardnacrusha on the River Shannon. This was a giant project for the new state. It came into operation in October 1929 at a cost of £5 million. It provided electricity for both Irish factories and homes.

The construction of the Shannon Hydro-electric scheme.

TEST YOUR KNOWLEDGE
1 *What is meant by the Statute of Westminster?*
2 *What do you regard as the greatest economic achievement of the Irish Free State in the 1920s?*
3 *What do you understand by the term 'free trade'?*
4 *Name two organisations set up in 1927. State the purpose of each.*
5 *What problems remained for the ordinary citizen after independence?*

POLITICAL DEVELOPMENTS

Within the Dáil, the Cumann na nGaedheal party formed the government, and the Labour party, together with a large number of independent TDs, became the opposition. Sinn Féin, under the leadership of Eamon de Valera, refused to enter the Dáil. They did not recognise the Irish Free State and would not take the oath of allegiance to the king as head of the Commonwealth.

As conditions in the country returned to normal, de Valera realised that he and his followers had little or no influence as long as they remained outside the Dáil. At the Sinn Féin Ard Fheis in March 1926, de Valera proposed that Sinn Féin TDs should enter the Dáil if the oath of allegiance was abolished. When this proposal was rejected, de Valera resigned from Sinn Féin, taking many followers with him. In May 1926 he founded a new party – *Fianna Fáil*. The new party had three main aims:

- to establish a 32-county Irish Republic;
- to restore the Irish language as the spoken language of the country;
- to make Ireland self-sufficient by protecting native agriculture and industry from outside competition.

1927: A DRAMATIC YEAR

A general election took place in June 1927. As a result, Cumann na nGaedheal won forty-six seats, Fianna Fáil forty-four, Labour twenty-two. The remaining seats went to small parties and independents. Cosgrave, however, had no difficulty in forming a government because Fianna Fáil would not enter the Dáil while the oath of allegiance remained.

A republican election poster in the elections of 1927.

De Valera leading a group of Fianna Fail TDs from the Dáil after their refusal to take the oath of allegiance.

PUT AN END TO IRELAND'S NIGHTMARE.

BREAK THE CONNECTION WITH ENGLAND.

1925

FREE STATE MINISTER HOGAN SAYS : — 'We'll bloody well execute again.'
FREE STATE MINISTER O'HIGGINS SAYS : — '77 Executions, and 777 more if necessary.'
— AND THE NEW COERCION ACT IS DESIGNED TO MAKE THEM 'NECESSARY.'

ON'T HELP TO FORGE A NEW LINK TO THE CHAIN BY VOTIN FREE STATE.
OTE REPUBLICAN—AND GIVE IRELAND A CHANC

On Sunday, 10 July 1927, an event occurred which shocked the Irish Free State and led to important changes. On that day the Minister for Home Affairs, Kevin O'Higgins, was shot dead as he returned home from Mass. Although nobody was convicted, it was generally believed that the IRA was responsible.

As a result of O'Higgins' murder, the government immediately brought in two very important acts:

- **The Public Safety Act**
  This was a very severe measure which gave large-scale powers of arrest to the Gardaí and set up special courts with the death penalty for those found illegally carrying arms.
- **The Electoral Amendment Act**
  This stated that those standing for election to the Dáil or Senate must swear to take their seats if elected, and if they did not take their seats within three months of being elected, they would lose them.

This last act posed a major problem for Fianna Fáil. They were now forced to enter the Dáil even though they had to take the oath of allegiance. Fianna Fáil's entry into the Dáil was followed by another general election in September 1927.

While Cumann na nGaedheal still formed the government with sixty-one seats, Fianna Fáil became the official opposition with fifty-seven seats. The supporters and opposers of the Treaty now faced one another for the first time within Dáil Éireann. All was set for a stormy period in Irish politics.

THE RISE OF FIANNA FAIL: 1927-32

During these years, Fianna Fáil went from strength to strength while support for Cumann na nGaedheal was falling. This growth in support for Fianna Fáil was due to the following reasons.

- Fianna Fáil was a very well organised party and carefully built up support throughout the country. Sean Lemass and Gerard Boland played important parts in this.
- The effects of the Great Depression were felt in Ireland after 1929 and made the Cumann na nGaedheal government very unpopular.
- In 1931, de Valera founded the *Irish Press* newspaper to spread Fianna Fáil ideas.
- The tough security measures taken by Cumann na nGaedheal made the government unpopular. This played into the hands of Fianna Fáil which was especially supported by those who favoured a republic.

All these factors would be of great importance in the run-up to the general election which was due in 1932.

THE 1932 GENERAL ELECTION

The year 1932 opened with a general election in Ireland. The campaign aroused tremendous excitement among the people as the two main parties bitterly fought out the chief issues of the election.

The election posters of the time provide an important source of information on the most hotly-debated issues of this election campaign. Look carefully at these posters.

What message is being conveyed by these Cumann na nGaedheal posters during the 1932 general election?

Fianna Fail election posters from 1932.

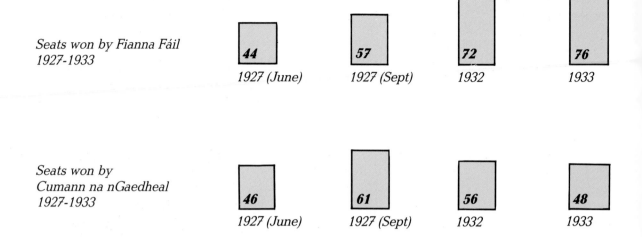

Seats won by Fianna Fáil
1927-1933

44 — 1927 (June)　　57 — 1927 (Sept)　　72 — 1932　　76 — 1933

Seats won by
Cumann na nGaedheal
1927-1933

46 — 1927 (June)　　61 — 1927 (Sept)　　56 — 1932　　48 — 1933

The chart shows us the results of the general election. Although Fianna Fáil won seventy-two seats, the party did not have an overall majority and was only able to form a government with the support of the Labour party. This was to mark the beginning of sixteen years of continuous Fianna Fáil government.

TEST YOUR KNOWLEDGE
1 *What party formed the first government of the Irish Free State after 1922?*
2 *Who formed the opposition in the Dáil from 1922 to 1927?*
3 *Why did Sinn Féin TDs refuse to enter the Dáil?*
4 *What happened at the Sinn Féin Ard Fheis in March 1926?*
5 *Why did the government bring in a Public Safety Act in 1927?*
6 *Why did Fianna Fáil enter the Dáil in 1927?*
7 *State two reasons why Fianna Fáil grew in strength in the years 1927-32.*
8 *State two important issues debated in the 1932 general election.*

Chapter 24: Review

- From 1922, W.T. Cosgrave and his new party, Cumann na nGaedheal, formed the government of the Irish Free State. A new Constitution was drawn up which stated that all members of the Dáil or parliament had to take an oath of allegiance to the king of England as head of the Commonwealth. Because of this, de Valera and Sinn Féin refused to enter the Dáil.

- The new Free State government was very concerned about law and order. The Minister for Home Affairs, Kevin O'Higgins, set up the Gárda Síochána in 1923 and reorganised the system of law courts. He also dealt firmly with a group of army officers in 1924 when faced with an incident called the 'Army Mutiny'.

- During the 1920s Ireland, together with other dominions, tried to achieve greater freedom for themselves within the British Commonwealth. In 1931, an act called the Statute of Westminster was passed. This made each dominion equal with Britain and gave each one the right to reject laws affecting them passed by the Westminster parliament.

- The Cumann na nGaedheal government supported the practice of free trade between countries – it did not favour the protection of Irish agriculture or industry. The great industrial achievement of the 1920s was the setting up of the ESB in 1927 and the construction of the Shannon Hydro-electric Scheme at Ardnacrusha.

- Between 1927 and 1932 Fianna Fáil was the main opposition in the Dáil and grew from strength to strength. They built up support throughout the country and set up their own newspaper – the *Irish Press* – in 1931.

- At the General Election of 1932 Fianna Fáil won 72 seats, Cumann na nGaedheal 56. De Valera did not have an overall majority but was able to form a government with the support of the Labour Party.

ACTIVITIES

1 Complete the following sentences:
   (a) In the Free State, all members of the Dáil and Senate were required to take _____.
   (b) The king's representative in the Irish Free State was known as _____.
   (c) In 1923, the Royal Irish Constabulary was replaced by a new unarmed police force, _____.
   (d) In 1931, an important law concerning the British Commonwealth was passed. It was known as _____.
   (e) The Minister for Agriculture in the Free State government, Patrick Hogan _____.

2 True or false?
   (a) Fianna Fáil won an overall majority in the 1932 general election.
   (b) In 1931, de Valera founded a newspaper known as the Irish Independent to support Fianna Fáil.
   (c) Fianna Fáil entered the Dáil for the first time in 1927.
   (d) In 1924, Richard Mulcahy, the Minister for Defence, resigned from the government.
   (e) The Irish Free State left the British Commonwealth in 1931.

3 Write an account of the Cumann na nGaedheal government under the following headings: (a) law and order; (b) the economy; (c) Ireland and the Commonwealth.

4 Explain why Fianna Fáil came to power after the 1932 general election.

THE AGE OF DE VALERA

A PEACEFUL TRANSFER OF POWER

When the Dáil met on 9 March 1932, many people expected some trouble with the change of government. The wheel had turned full circle – those who had been on the losing side of the Civil War ten years before were now about to take over the government of the country. In fact, some Fianna Fáil TDs had guns hidden in their pockets as they went into the Dáil on that eventful day.

However, people's fears proved groundless as Cumann na nGaedheal peacefully handed over power to Fianna Fáil. This clearly showed that democracy was now firmly rooted in the Irish Free State.

The Fianna Fail government which came to power in 1932.

DE VALERA DISMANTLES THE TREATY

As soon as de Valera came to power, he set about dismantling the Anglo-Irish Treaty. He took the following steps to move Ireland towards a republic.

- In April 1932, he removed the oath of allegiance to the king as head of the Commonwealth. When the British government protested that the abolition of the oath broke the Treaty of 1921, de Valera ignored their protests.
- He set about downgrading the role of the Governor-General, the king's representative in Ireland. De Valera and his cabinet boycotted social functions at which the Governor-General was present and the office was eventually abolished in 1937.
- As the Senate of the Irish Free State opposed these measures, de Valera had it abolished in 1936.
- In the same year, a great opportunity arose for de Valera when King Edward VIII of England abdicated because of his proposed marriage to an American divorcee. De Valera used this crisis to bring in the External Relations Act of 1936, which had the effect of removing the influence of the king from the Irish Free State.

De Valera addressing the League of Nations in Geneva. As well as leading the government, he also served as Minister for External Affairs. At Geneva he called for world peace, disarmament and respect for the rights of small nations like Ireland.

TEST YOUR KNOWLEDGE

1 Why do you think many people expected trouble with the change of government in 1932?
2 How was it clear that democracy was firmly established in the Irish Free State?
3 What was the first step taken by de Valera in demolishing the Treaty?
4 How did de Valera treat the office of Governor-General?
5 Why did he abolish the Senate?
6 How did de Valera use the abdication of King Edward VIII for his own purposes?

A NEW CONSTITUTION

By 1937, de Valera had succeeded in dismantling the Anglo-Irish Treaty and moving Ireland further towards a republic. The next step was taken when a new Constitution was drawn up in 1937. This was to replace the Constitution of 1922. The new Constitution (*Bunreacht na hÉireann*), accepted by the people in a referendum in 1937, contained no references to the king of England and made Ireland a republic in everything but name.

Read the following extracts from the Constitution and then answer the questions which follow.

WORKING WITH EVIDENCE

Bunreacht na hÉireann (The Irish Constitution), 1937

Article 2
The national territory consists of the whole island of Ireland, its islands and territorial seas.

Article 5
Ireland is a sovereign, independent, democratic state.

Article 8

1. *The Irish language as the national language is the first official language.*
2. *The English language is recognised as a second official language.*

Article 40

All citizens shall, as human persons, be held equal before the law . . .

Article 41

1. *The State recognises the family as the natural primary and fundamental unit group of society . . .*
2. *In particular, the State recognises that by her life within the home, woman gives to the State a support without which the common good cannot be achieved.*
3. *The State pledges itself to guard with special care the institution of marriage, on which the family is founded, and to protect it against attack.*

   No law shall be enacted providing for the grant of a dissolution of marriage.

1 *What type of state did the Irish people accept in the 1937 Constitution?*
2 *What was the provision in the Constitution regarding the Irish language?*
3 *Which article of the Constitution guaranteed equality before the law for all citizens?*
4 *Would you agree that the family was singled out for special praise and protection in de Valera's Constitution? Support your answer with quotations.*
5 *Quote the extract from the Constitution which banned the granting of divorce.*
6 *What was contained in the Constitution concerning the role of women in the home?*

THE BLUESHIRTS

Election meetings in Ireland at this time were stormy affairs which often ended in violence. The IRA constantly disrupted Cumann na nGaedheal meetings. In response to this, a group of ex-army officers set up an organisation known as the *Army Comrades Association* to protect these meetings from IRA interference. Because of the uniform they came to wear from March 1933, this group was known as the *Blueshirts*.

The Blueshirt leader was Eoin O'Duffy who had been dismissed by de Valera from his post as commissioner of the Gardaí. The Blueshirts

General Eoin O'Duffy addressing a Blueshirt rally.

A Blueshirt parade.

212

organised meetings and marches throughout the country. Because of their uniform and military-style parades, together with their strong opposition to Communism, many people at the time saw similarities between them and the Fascist movements which were then springing up in Europe.

De Valera was determined, however, to clamp down on the Blueshirts. In August 1933, the government banned a big parade to Leinster House in Dublin which was planned by the Blueshirts to commemorate Michael Collins, Arthur Griffith and Kevin O'Higgins.

In September 1933, the Blueshirts joined Cumann na nGaedheal and a small party called the Centre Party to form a new political party – *Fine Gael*. Eoin O'Duffy became the first leader of Fine Gael.

O'Duffy's extreme views soon embarrassed many within Fine Gael and in September 1934 he was forced to give up the leadership of the party. The Blueshirts eventually declined as a movement and O'Duffy led a group of them to fight on the side of General Franco in the Spanish Civil War.

THE ECONOMIC WAR: 1932-38

When Fianna Fáil came to power in 1932, they were committed to ending the *land annuities* to the British government. These were repayments made by Irish farmers of loans they received from previous British governments for land purchased. Britain responded to de Valera's refusal to pay the land annuities by placing a twenty per cent tariff on Irish agricultural exports. The Irish government responded by placing duties on British goods coming into Ireland. This dispute, which lasted until 1938, became known as the *Economic War*.

The Economic War had disastrous effects for Ireland. Farmers in particular suffered and many of them had to slaughter their cattle because they were unable to sell them. The value of Irish agricultural exports fell from over £38 million in 1929 to £14 million in 1935. The whole Irish economy suffered and unemployment soared.

De Valera on his way to London in 1938 to take part in discussions to end the Economic War.

By 1938, both governments agreed that the Economic War had gone on long enough. Discussions began in London in March 1938 which led to a settlement of the dispute. Under the terms of the Anglo-Irish Agreement, it was agreed that Ireland would pay a once-off payment of £10 million to cover the outstanding land annuity debts. The most important aspect of this agreement, however, was the return of the Treaty Ports (Spike Island, Berehaven and Lough Swilly) to the control of the Irish Free State. Without these, Ireland could not have remained neutral in the war which was about to break out in Europe.

The Treaty Ports

British troops leaving Spike Island.

TEST YOUR KNOWLEDGE
1 *Why were the Blueshirts founded?*
2 *Who was the leader of the Blueshirts?*
3 *Why did many people see similarities between the Blueshirts and continental Fascist movements?*
4 *How did de Valera's government deal with the Blueshirts?*
5 *What were the land annuities?*
6 *What was the Economic War? How did it begin?*
7 *What effect had the Economic War on Irish agriculture?*
8 *What was the most important part of the Anglo-Irish Agreement? Why was this so?*

A STATE OF EMERGENCY: 1939-45

When World War II broke out in Europe in September 1939, the government of the Irish Free State declared that Southern Ireland would remain neutral. Two main reasons were put forward for this decision.

- As a small nation, the Irish Free State was open to attack by stronger powers.
- Partition: the continued division of the country ruled out any possibility that the de Valera government could enter the war on Britain's side.

This policy of *neutrality* was only made possible by the return of the Treaty Ports from Great Britain in 1938.

A *state of emergency* was declared giving the government extensive powers to ensure the maintenance of neutrality. Strict censorship of radio and newspapers was imposed. To meet any possible threat to neutrality from the pro-German IRA, internment was introduced under the terms of the Offences against the State Act (1941). The size of the national army was increased in preparation for a possible invasion and voluntary Local Defence Forces (LDFs) were established.

LIFE IN IRELAND DURING THE EMERGENCY

Rationing of essential items brought home the hardships of war to the ordinary people of Ireland. This was necessary because the disruption of shipping brought about shortages of food and fuel. A new Department of Supplies under the direction of Sean Lemass was established to organise the fair distribution of scarce commodities.

Stockpiling turf in the Phoenix Park, Dublin, during the Emergency.

Sparing the polish: a contemporary advertisment.

Please use sparingly supplies are restricted

NUGGET

The Supreme Polish

★ We suggest its use on alternate days only and a brush up every day

Ration books covering items such as tea, sugar and clothing were issued to each household in the country. Farmers were compelled by law to produce a certain amount of crops. In the cities, gas was strictly rationed and the gas inspector (known as the 'glimmer man') could be seen on his rounds. Trains were largely run on turf, and private motor cars were rarely seen because of the scarcity of petrol.

Look carefully at the cartoons from the Emergency. What can we learn from them about life in wartime Ireland?

"WHERE'S YOUR TEA CANISTER?"

"My husband wants it for the sitting-room. He's been shot three times by emergency coal!"

However inconvenient wartime shortages were, Ireland was spared the horrors of widespread bombing experienced by her European neighbours and Northern Ireland. Southern Ireland's worst experience of civilian casualties occurred when the Germans bombed Dublin in error on the night of 30 May 1941, with the biggest number of casualties occurring in the North Strand.

On the alert: the Irish Army manning anti-aircraft guns in 1940.

The scene of destruction following the German bombing of the North Strand

THE ENDING OF THE WAR

When World War II ended in the autumn of 1945, the Irish Free State had succeeded in maintaining its neutrality. At home, the Emergency produced greater unity and co-operation among people and helped to heal some of the Civil War divisions. To the world at large, neutrality proved Ireland's ability to stand alone as a small nation.

There were also some disadvantages attached to Irish neutrality.

- While other European countries were to take part in the move towards European unity after the war, Ireland was to remain aloof.
- Partition was further strengthened as Northern Ireland, which had taken part in the war, drew even closer to Great Britain.

However, through its policy of neutrality, Southern Ireland had avoided the horrors of war. This was its greatest advantage.

TEST YOUR KNOWLEDGE
1 What made Irish neutrality in World War II possible?
2 State two reasons for Irish neutrality.
3 A state of emergency was declared in Ireland. What forms did this take?
4 What new department was set up during the war years? Who directed it?
5 Who was the 'glimmer man'?
6 State two effects which the policy of neutrality had on Ireland.

Chapter 25: Review

- Once de Valera came to power he set about demolishing the Anglo-Irish Treaty: he abolished the Oath of Allegiance; downgraded the role of Governor-General; and after the Abdication Crisis in Britain he removed the influence of the king from the Irish Free State.

- The Blueshirts grew out of the Army Comrades Association which was set up to protect Cumann na nGaedheal political meetings from IRA interference. Eoin O'Duffy took over the command of the Blueshirts. In September 1933 this group joined with Cumann na nGaedheal and Dillon's Centre Party to form Fine Gael.

- The Economic War was a tariff war between Britain and Ireland which began when de Valera refused to pay the land annuities to the British government. This disagreement had a terrible effect on Irish agriculture. It came to an end in 1938 when the Anglo-Irish Agreement was signed.

- A new constitution was drawn up by de Valera in 1937: this contained no references to the king of England and made Ireland a republic in everything but name.

- For most people living in Ireland in the 1930s life remained harsh – living conditions were poor and emigration continued to rise. Despite this, certain improvements were made – many semi-state companies such as Aer Lingus and the Irish Sugar Company were set up, and the numbers employed in industry increased.

- When war broke out in Europe in September 1939, the Irish Free State declared its neutrality. This policy was only made possible by the return of the Treaty Ports from Great Britain in 1938.

- A state of emergency was declared giving the government extensive powers to ensure the maintenance of neutrality.

- The wartime Emergency resulted in a shortage of essential goods. Ration books covering items such as tea, sugar and clothing were issued to each household in the country. This rationing was directed by Seán Lemass who became Minister for Supplies.

- While neutrality saved the Irish Free State from the horrors of war it also had disadvantages: the country was isolated internationally after the war, and it strengthened the partition of the island.

ACTIVITIES

1 *Match an item in Column 1 with an item in Column 2.*

COLUMN 1	COLUMN 2
The role of the King of England in Irish affairs	The Economic War
The Blueshirts	The Treaty Ports
Land Annuities	Seán Lemass
The Department of Supplies	The External Relations Act (1936)
The Anglo-Irish Agreement (1938)	Eoin O'Duffy

2 *True or False?*
   (a) In April 1932, de Valera removed the oath of allegiance to the British monarch which members of the Dáil and the Senate had to swear.
   (b) De Valera's new constitution of 1937 contained no references to the king of England.
   (c) The Blueshirts were supported by many Fianna Fáil members.
   (d) The Economic War lasted from 1932 to 1938.
   (e) The Treaty Ports were returned to the Irish Free State in 1938.

3 *List the main steps taken by de Valera after 1932 to weaken the links between Ireland and Great Britain.*

4 *Write a paragraph on the Blueshirts.*

5 *Imagine that you lived in Ireland during the 'Emergency'. Write a letter to a friend describing your experiences.*

FROM DEPRESSION TO PROSPERITY: 1945-66

A NEW PARTY IS FORMED

The end of World War II in 1945 was not followed by an immediate ending of emergency conditions in Ireland. Food and fuel were in short supply and large numbers of people continued to emigrate. Many people were tired of Fianna Fáil which had been in government since 1932. The opposition parties – Fine Gael and Labour – were both weak at this time and did not appeal to the voters at large.

A new political party was formed in 1946 – *Clann an Poblachta*. This new party was very republican. It also supported social and economic changes such as a huge housing programme, improved health facilities and free education. Its leader was Seán MacBride, a former chief-of-staff of the IRA. Support for the new party rapidly increased as it promised to tackle many of the country's most pressing problems.

A general election was held in February 1948. Examine the table below closely showing the results of this election.

Seán MacBride, the leader of Clann na Poblachta.

THE FIRST INTER-PARTY GOVERNMENT: 1948-51

After the 1948 general election, the parties opposed to Fianna Fáil agreed to form an *inter-party* or *coalition government*. The main parties in the new government were Fine Gael, Labour, and Clann na Poblachta. John A. Costello of Fine Gael became Taoiseach; William Norton, the Labour leader, became Tanaiste or deputy prime minister; Seán MacBride, the leader of Clann na Poblachta, became Minister for External Affairs.

John A. Costello, who became Taoiseach in the first Inter-Party government.

RESULTS OF 1948 GENERAL ELECTION	
Fianna Fáil	68
Fine Gael	31
Labour	14
Clann na Poblachta	10
Clann na Talmhan	7
National Labour	5
Independents	12

The first inter-party government is remembered for the following achievements.

- In 1949, the *Republic of Ireland Act* was passed which officially declared the twenty-six counties of Ireland a republic and broke the last links with the British Commonwealth.
- Two important semi-state organisations were set up to promote Irish industry and trade – the *Industrial Development Authority (IDA)* and *Coras Trachtala*.
- The Anglo-Irish Trade Agreement of 1948 brought about higher prices for Irish agricultural exports to England.
- A national programme of building was begun. By 1950, 12,000 new houses were being built each year.
- Under the direction of Noel Browne, the Minister for Health, a programme for eliminating the killer disease, tuberculosis, was put into force. At the time, TB caused the deaths of 2000-4000 young people each year. Santoria were built throughout the country to help those with TB.

THE FALL OF THE GOVERNMENT

The Minister for Health, Noel Browne, proposed free hospital and health care for all mothers and their children. This was known as the *Mother and Child Scheme*. The doctors and the bishops strongly opposed this scheme of state medicine for everybody and put pressure on the government to drop it.

When the Taoiseach, John A. Costello, and a majority of the government agreed to abandon the scheme, Noel Browne resigned both from the government and from Clann na Poblachta. Other Clann na Poblachta TDs also resigned from the party. As a result of this, the government lost its majority in the Dáil and a general election was called in May 1951.

For many people, the Mother and Child Scheme crisis had shown the power and influence of the Catholic Church in Ireland.

Dr Noel Browne, a member of Clann na Poblachta and Minister for Health in the first Inter-Party government.

IRELAND IN THE 1950s

Fianna Fáil under de Valera were in power again from 1951 to 1954. Between 1954 and 1957, a second inter-party government under John A. Costello took over, and in 1957 Fianna Fáil again returned to power, this time with a large majority in the Dáil.

Despite the frequent changes of government during the 1950s, there was little change in the living conditions of ordinary people.

A march in protest against unemployment in Dublin in the 1950s.

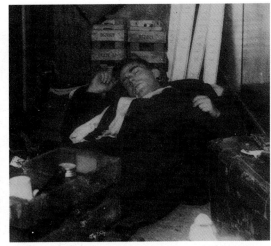

An emigrant on board a ship leaving Ireland in the 1950s.

Unemployment was widespread and the only option open to many young people was to leave Ireland in search of work. During the 1950s, emigration reached huge levels not known since the nineteenth century. Some people wondered if independence was worth the struggle between 1916 and 1921 if, thirty years later, the country could not provide a living for its people.

In 1959 de Valera, who at this time was seventy-seven years of age, resigned as Taoiseach and was elected president of Ireland. Under his successor, Seán Lemass, great changes came about. These changes were to result in a bright new future in the 1960s.

The number of emigrants from Ireland increased steadily during these years.

1946-1951: 120,000

1951-1956: 197,000

1956-1961: 212,000

Emigration from Ireland

Eamon de Valera, President of Ireland 1959-73.

TEST YOUR KNOWLEDGE
1 *What new party was formed in 1946? Who was its leader?*
2 *Name the main parties which formed the first inter-party government.*
3 *What was the Republic of Ireland Act (1949)?*
4 *Why did the first inter-party government fall from power in 1951?*
5 *Why was emigration so high in the 1950s?*
6 *To what office was de Valera elected in 1959?*
7 *Who became Taoiseach in 1959?*

THE 1960s: A TIME FOR PROSPERITY

Seán Lemass, who was Taoiseach from 1959 to 1966, saw a great need for Ireland to industrialise in order to create jobs for her people. He believed that the government had a vital part to play in this.

In 1958, T.K. Whitaker, the secretary of the Department of Finance, drew up a plan known as the *First Programme for Economic Expansion*. Lemass put this plan for the economy into action.

Seán Lemass, Taoiseach 1959-66.

T.K. Whitaker, whose First Programme for Economic Expansion brought about great changes in Ireland in the 1960s.

Under Whitaker's plan, grants were given to farmers and businessmen to help them produce more goods. Big foreign industries were attracted to Ireland by generous grants and tax concessions. A new town was built at Shannon, Co. Clare, where the first industrial estate was developed.

Due to government loans and generous tax-free concessions, many new factories were set up in Ireland during the 1960s.

POPULATION CHANGES IN THE REPUBLIC OF IRELAND

Year	Population	
1951	2,961,000	During the 1950s the fall in population continued. This trend was reversed during the economic prosperity of the 1960s.
1956	2,898,000	
1961	2,818,000	
1966	2,884,000	
1971	2,978,000	

As a result of Lemass' efforts, many new jobs were created in the 1960s. Emigration was greatly reduced and, as the chart shows, the Irish population began to increase for the first time since the Famine. Two other economic plans followed, one in 1963 and another in 1969, but they were not as successful as the first.

Economic progress was not the only type of change experienced in the Lemass era. There were also significant changes in education and in society at large.

GREAT CHANGES IN EDUCATION

One of the main advances in the 1960s came in education. Donogh O'Malley, the Minister for Education, brought in free secondary schooling for all, and free transport for those who lived at a distance from schools. Grants were also provided for the building of new secondary schools.

More and more children availed of secondary education in the 1960s.

All of these changes resulted in a huge increase in the numbers receiving a secondary education. By the late 1960s, 144,000 pupils were attending secondary schools – this was almost double the figure of ten years previously. Comprehensive schools and Regional Technical Colleges were also introduced at this time. These developments in education were to have far-reaching results.

THE 1960s : GREAT SOCIAL CHANGES IN IRELAND

The 1960s were years of great social change throughout the Western world. There were new tastes in music and fashion, new attitudes among young people and massive changes in technology and communication. Ireland was part of this changing world.

In these years, the standard of living of most Irish people rose. This was made possible by greater job opportunities and higher wages. A returning emigrant who had left Ireland some years before would have seen great improvements in housing, sanitation, roads and in the diet and clothing of ordinary people.

On New Year's Eve 1961, Telefís Éireann, Ireland's first television station, began broadcasting. More than anything else, television brought Ireland into contact with the outside world and led people to question old attitudes. Travel opportunities increased for most people during these years. Aer Lingus, the national airline, expanded greatly, and more and more people came to own their own cars.

The Catholic Church in Ireland also changed greatly in the 1960s. After the Second Vatican Council, lay people became more involved in Church affairs and many young people began to question the beliefs of the older generation.

The new technology: the Presentation Control Desk in RTE in 1965

TEST YOUR KNOWLEDGE

1 What great need did Sean Lemass see?

2 Who was secretary of the Department of Finance?
   What plan did he draw up?

3 How was industry attracted to Ireland?

4 What were the results of Lemass' efforts?

5 Name two changes brought about in Irish education in the 1960s.

6 When did television come to Ireland? What effects did it have?

Chapter 26: Review

- Clann na Poblachta, a new political party under the leadership of Seán MacBride, was founded in July 1946. This party stood for great social and economic changes.

- In the general election of 1948, Clann na Poblachta won ten seats in the Dáil. It joined with Fine Gael and Labour to form the first Inter-Party Government. John A. Costello of Fine Gael was the Taoiseach of the new government.

- In 1949, this government passed the Republic of Ireland Act which declared the twenty-six counties of Ireland a republic. A huge housing programme was launched by the government. Noel Browne, the Minister for Health, put a programme for eliminating the killer disease TB into operation.

- Noel Browne proposed a free medical scheme for mothers and their children known as 'The Mother and Child Scheme'. When the doctors and bishops brought pressure on the government to drop this scheme, Browne resigned and at the same time left Clann na Poblachta. As a result the government lost its majority and fell from power in May 1951.

- In the 1950s living standards in Ireland were very low. Unemployment was widespread and emigration reached levels which had not been known since the nineteenth century.

- In 1959 de Valera retired and was replaced as Taoiseach and as leader of Fianna Fáil by Seán Lemass.

- In 1958 T.K. Whitaker, secretary of the Department of Finance, drew up 'The First Programme for Economic Expansion'. Lemass put this plan of industrialisation into operation.

- Industry was attracted to Ireland through grants and tax-free concessions. The first industrial estate was set up at Shannon.

- As a result of Lemass' efforts, many new jobs were created in the 1960s.

Emigration was greatly reduced and, for the first time since the Famine, the Irish population began to increase again.

- There were also important changes in education during the 1960s. Donogh O'Malley, Minister for Education, brought in free secondary schooling, and free transport was provided for students living at a distance from the schools.

- The Sixties was a time of great social change in Ireland. Living standards rose. In 1961, television came to Ireland for the first time. Travel opportunities also increased greatly.

ACTIVITIES

1 Match an item in Column 1 with an item in Column 2.

COLUMN 1	COLUMN 2
Minister for Health	Seán MacBride
An Inter-Party Government	William Norton
Taoiseach	John A. Costello
Leader of Clann na Poblachta	Noel Browne
A Fianna Fáil Taoiseach	Seán Lemass
Leader of the Labour Party	

2 Complete the following sentences.
   (a) The general election of 1948 resulted in the formation of an _____.
   (b) The Republic of Ireland Act (1949) broke _____.
   (c) The first Inter-Party Government (1948-51) set up two important semi-state organisations to promote Irish industry and trade. These were _____.
   (d) The minister in charge of the Mother and Child Scheme was _____.
   (e) In 1959, de Valera resigned from his position as Taoiseach and was succeeded by _____.

3 Write a detailed account of changes in Ireland during the 1960s.

4 Write a paragraph on the career of Seán Lemass as Taoiseach.

IRELAND: 1966-85

A NEW TAOISEACH

Jack Lynch, who succeeded Seán Lemass as leader of Fianna Fáil in 1966.

In November 1966, Seán Lemass retired as Taoiseach and leader of Fianna Fáil. Although only Taoiseach since 1959, he had been involved in politics since the War of Independence. His successor as Taoiseach came from a younger generation of Irish politicians. A majority of Fianna Fáil TDs voted for the Minister for Finance, Jack Lynch, to succeed Lemass as leader of the party.

During his first two years in office, Jack Lynch's government continued to run a country enjoying economic prosperity. However, the rate of economic growth was slowing down and many critics of the government believed that more could have been done to help the under-privileged in society. Following the example of young people in Europe and America, socialism became fashionable among Irish students. The Irish Labour Party gained many new recruits, including some prominent figures from universities and the world of broadcasting.

When Jack Lynch called a general election for June 1969, the Labour Party under its leader Brendan Corish fielded more candidates than usual and campaigned on a slogan 'The Seventies will be Socialist'. Fianna Fáil campaigned on their record, stressing improvements like Donogh O'Mally's Free Education Scheme. Since the main opposition parties, Fine Gael and Labour, failed to co-operate, Fianna Fáil gained an overall majority although the party vote had fallen since 1965. The position of Jack Lynch within Fianna Fáil was greatly strengthened by this victory and it appeared that he was now set for a secure term of office as Taoiseach. However, soon after the election, serious unrest broke out in Northern Ireland in August 1969.

For the previous year, members of the minority Catholic community were campaigning for equal rights with Protestants. This campaign was known as the *Civil Rights Movement*. Some extreme Protestants were prepared to use any methods to stop this campaign. In August 1969, widespread violence erupted in Belfast and Derry, resulting in many injuries and deaths.

This Northern crisis was to have a serious impact on the government and people of the Republic.

THE ARMS CRISIS

In August 1969, in a famous speech, Jack Lynch hinted at help for nationalists in Northern Ireland when he said that 'the government can no longer stand by' as Catholic communities were under attack. At the time there was widespread sympathy throughout the Republic for Catholics in Northern Ireland. Many people held simplistic views on Irish unification which took no account of the feelings of Northern Unionists. Within the ruling Fianna Fáil party there were many who held strong Republican views concerning the Northern problem. Some of these included members of the government. Despite his famous speech of August 1969, Lynch hoped to keep the Northern troubles from spreading into the Republic. Government ministers such as Neil Blaney and Kevin Boland believed that he was neglecting Fianna Fáil's aim of Irish unity.

On 6 May 1970, these divisions became public when Lynch dismissed two of his ministers, Neil Blaney and Charles Haughey, because they did not fully support government policy on Northern Ireland. Another

Newspaper headlines announcing the dramatic departure of three ministers from Jack Lynch's cabinet on 6 May 1970.

RTE
CENTRAL REFERENCE LIBRARY

THE IRISH TIMES

DUBLIN, WEDNESDAY, MAY 6, 1970

PRICE 9d. (1/- in England)   No. 35,547   CITY EDITION

Blaney, Boland, Haughey out of Cabinet

DEEP DIFFERENCES OVER NORTHERN POLICIES

Dramatic announcement by Lynch at 2.50 this morning

By Andrew Hamilton

THREE SENIOR MINISTERS OF MR. JACK LYNCH'S GOVERNMENT HAVE RESIGNED.

In a dramatic announcement at 2.50 this morning, Mr. Lynch said that two of them, Mr. Haughey, Minister for Finance, and Mr. Blaney, Minister for Agriculture and Fisheries, did not subscribe fully to Government policy on Northern Ireland, and he had asked for their resignations.

Mr. Boland, Minister for Local Government and Social Welfare, then resigned in sympathy with Mr. Haughey and Mr. Blaney.

It is clear that the resignations are due to a fundamental difference in the Government and Fianna Fáil in relation to the Northern Ireland situation. Mr. Lynch has publicly said that the Government is not in favour of any armed intervention.

Mr. Blaney has been spokesman for the traditional Republican view that physical force could not be avoided if the Nationalist and Catholic population were under severe attack.

The following statement was issued at 2.50 this morning by the Taoiseach:

"I have requested the resignations as members of the Government of Mr. Neil T. Blaney, Minister for Agriculture and Fisheries, and Mr. Charles J. Haughey, Minister for Finance, because I am satisfied that they do not subscribe fully to Government policy in relation to the present situation in the Six Counties as stated by me at the Fianna Fáil Ard-Fheis in January last. Caoimhghín Ó Beoláin, Minister for Local Government and Social Welfare, has tendered his resignation as a member of the Government and I propose to advise the President to accept it.

"A special meeting of Fianna Fáil deputies will take place at Leinster House at 6 p.m. today to consider the position that has arisen."

An emergency Cabinet meeting is being held this morning and tonight there is a special meeting of Fianna Fáil T.D.s. At both meetings, Mr. Lynch will try to salvage the party from total disarray. A general election in the near future cannot be ruled out.

In the Cabinet, Mr. Lynch is expected to have support for

MR. LYNCH ... faced with major crisis.

O'Malley for Department of Justice today?

The three Ministers who have left the Government: Mr. Blaney, Mr. Haughey and Mr. Boland.

GENERAL ELECTION MUST FOLLOW

Most serious crisis since Costello's fall in 1951

By Dick Walsh

THE SACKING of Mr. Haughey and Mr. Blaney and Mr. Boland's resignation seem this morning almost certainly to lead to a General Election.

The division inside Fianna Fáil, which led to Mr. Lynch's action and Mr. Boland's reaction, is the most serious to strike a Government since the fall of Mr. John A. Costello's coalition in 1951.

The first hint of drama came at half-past twelve this morning when the head of the Government Information Bureau, Mr. Frank Nolan

Always the same at the Spring Show

By Maeve Binchy

AT THE R.D.S. Spring Show in Ballsbridge, Dublin, you walk through the first hall and we old friends of stands that seem to have been the same for ever. It gives you a great feeling of the permanency of life as you walk out to the fresh air near the judging rings. But there the picture changes.

A huge crowd seems permanently gathered around something that you can't see because of the crowd's density, and you wonder how

NIXON PLEDGES—OUT AGAIN IN 7 WEEKS

Thant calls for conference as offensive intensifies

PRESIDENT NIXON yesterday gave U.S. Congressional leaders what was described as a "firm commitment" that American forces will not penetrate beyond an 18-22 mile limit into Cambodia, and that all troops will be pulled back within seven weeks. As he spoke, U.S. and South Vietnamese troops pushed deeper into Cambodia and thousands more joined a fresh offensive.

The United Nations Secretary General, U Thant, criticised the expansion of the Vietnam war into Cambodia and supported the French call for an international conference of all parties involved in the Indo-China conflict.

New venom in protest at

minister, Kevin Boland, resigned in sympathy with his dismissed colleagues. On 28 May, both Haughey and Blaney were arrested and charged with attempting to import arms and ammunition for use by the IRA in Northern Ireland. The trial which followed became known as the *Arms Trial*. Both of the ex-ministers were found to be not guilty, Blaney in July and Haughey in the following October.

Charles J. Haughey, one of the ministers dismissed from office by Jack Lynch in May 1970.

The Arms Crisis caused a sensation in the country and led to deep divisions within Fianna Fáil. Both Blaney and Boland left the party, but Haughey remained on and worked his way up to eventually succeed Lynch as leader in 1979. However, just after the Arms Crisis, Jack Lynch succeeded in remaining in control of Fianna Fáil. Over the following two years, against a background of increasing violence in Northern Ireland, Lynch and the Minister for External Affairs, Dr Patrick Hillery, prepared for an event which would shape the country's future destiny – Ireland's entry into the European Economic Community.

TEST YOUR KNOWLEDGE
1 *When did Jack Lynch succeed Seán Lemass as Taoiseach?*
2 *Name the political belief which became popular among Irish students in the 1960s.*
3 *What was the slogan of the Irish Labour Party for the general election of 1969?*
4 *What did the Taoiseach, Jack Lynch, hint at in his famous television speech of August 1969 concerning the Northern 'Troubles'?*
5 *Why were there divisions in Fianna Fáil in 1969 over Northern Ireland policy?*
6 *Name the two former government ministers involved in the Arms Trial of 1970.*
7 *What was the outcome of the trial?*
8 *Who was Minister for External Affairs in 1970?*

IRELAND JOINS THE EEC

As far back as 1961, the Irish government of Seán Lemass had applied for full membership of the *European Economic Community* at the same time that Great Britain applied. However, when the French president, General de Gaulle, blocked British entry in January 1963, Ireland could no longer attempt to join because both British and Irish economies were so closely linked. However, in 1969, the new French president, Georges Pompidou, withdrew any objections to British entry and both Ireland and Great Britain re-applied for membership.

Farmers and businessmen were among those most in favour of Irish entry to the EEC. They argued that it would bring a better market for both agricultural and industrial exports and lead to a greater number of jobs in Ireland. Many trade union leaders were against entry because they believed that jobs would be lost when cheaper goods from Europe replaced home-produced products in Irish shops. Although entry did not involve joining any military alliance, some people believed that Ireland's neutrality would be endangered as all of the other EEC states were members of the North Atlantic Treaty Organisation (NATO). When a referendum was held on the question in May 1972, Fianna Fáil and Fine Gael advised the people to vote 'Yes' while the Labour Party called for a 'No' vote.

The result of the referendum was a massive eighty-three per cent vote in favour of Irish entry to the Common Market. This decision confirmed the conditions of entry negotiated by Dr Hillery which had been signed as a Treaty of Accession in January 1972. All was now in place for Ireland to enter the EEC on 1 January 1973. Shortly after this historic occasion, Jack Lynch called a general election to be held the following month.

THE COALITION IN POWER: 1973-77

Fianna Fáil entered the election campaign highly confident of victory. However, the fact that the party had been in power continuously since 1957 and the divisions during the Arms Crisis encouraged the opposition parties to come to an agreement. Fine Gael under Liam Cosgrave and Labour under Brendan Corish produced a Fourteen Point Manifesto and they agreed to form a coalition government if they had enough seats in the Dáil after the election.

Although Fianna Fáil's share of the vote increased slightly since 1969, it lost six seats and fell from power. With a high level of vote transfers between them, Fine Gael and Labour together won an overall majority in the Dáil. The Fine Gael leader, Liam Cosgrave, became Taoiseach and Brendan Corish, the Labour Party leader, was appointed Tánaiste and Minister for Social Welfare. There were ten Fine Gael and five Labour ministers in the new government.

Liam Cosgrave, Taoiseach 1973-77.

Dr Garret FitzGerald of Fine Gael, as Minister for Foreign Affairs, represented Ireland in the EEC. Another important Fine Gael minister was Richard Ryan who was in charge of the Department of Finance at a time when the economy suffered because of a huge increase in oil prices in the Middle East.

The Minister for Posts and Telegraphs, Dr Conor Cruise O'Brien, was the most controversial member of the coalition. He frequently spoke out on the problem of Northern Ireland and condemned the attitudes of many southern Irish people as being close to the beliefs of the IRA.

Throughout the four years that the coalition was in power, the 'Troubles' in Northern Ireland continued to influence people in the Republic. In 1973, Liam Cosgrave signed an agreement concerning Northern Ireland with the British prime minister, Edward Heath. Known as the *Sunningdale Agreement*, it was destroyed by extremists in Northern Ireland within a year. In May 1974, the violence spread to Dublin and Monaghan when several people were killed and injured in a number of horrific car bombings.

In response to the continuing violence, Cosgrave's government introduced a number of strict laws against members of the IRA and other illegal organisations. Members of these groups were banned from national television and radio channels run by Radio Telefís Éireann (RTE).

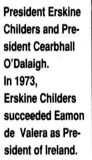

President Erskine Childers and President Cearbhall O'Dalaigh.
In 1973, Erskine Childers succeeded Eamon de Valera as President of Ireland.

Following Childers' sudden death in December 1974, he was succeeded in office by Cearbhall O'Dalaigh. O'Dalaigh resigned in 1976 and was succeeded by Dr Patrick Hillery, who was to serve as President until 1990.

When Cosgrave called a general election for June 1977, the coalition parties, Fine Gael and Labour, believed that they would win. However, many people feared that the government was becoming too strict and they believed that the economy had disimproved.

Fianna Fáil entered the election with a manifesto promising many improvements, including the abolition of rates on houses and of tax on private cars. The election resulted in a landslide victory for Fianna Fáil. They won an overall majority of twenty seats in the Dáil and Jack Lynch became Taoiseach once again.

GENERAL ELECTION RESULTS 1969-1977			
	1969	1973	1977
Fianna Fáil	75	69	84
Fine Gael	50	54	43
Labour	18	19	17
Independents	1	2	4

Jack Lynch receiving his Seal of Office from President Hillery following Fianna Fáil's landslide election victory in 1977.

TEST YOUR KNOWLEDGE

1 *When did the Irish government first apply for membership of the EEC?*
2 *What groups supported Irish entry into the EEC?*
3 *Which political party campaigned against Irish entry to the Common Market? Why?*
4 *What was the result of the referendum of May 1972 on Irish entry to the EEC?*
5 *Who became Taoiseach in 1973?*
6 *Name three ministers in the coalition government, 1973-77.*
7 *How did the government respond to the threat of violence from Northern Ireland?*
8 *Describe the results of the general election of 1977.*

THE RISE OF CHARLES J. HAUGHEY

The first two years of the new government appeared prosperous. Many new jobs were created, especially in the public service in areas like teaching, nursing and the civil service. Included in the government were George Colley as Tánaiste and Minister for Finance, and Charles Haughey as Minister for Health.

Despite their huge majority, some Fianna Fáil TDs were afraid that they would lose their seats in the next general election. Fine Gael was becoming increasingly popular under its energetic new leader, Dr Garret FitzGerald, and in 1979 a new oil crisis in the Middle East damaged the Irish economy. After Fianna Fáil lost two by-elections in the summer of 1979, some of the party's TDs declared their dissatisfaction with Jack Lynch as leader. Therefore it came as no surprise to many people when he resigned suddenly in December 1979, hoping that his Tánaiste, George Colley, would succeed him in office. However, a majority of Fianna Fáil TDs chose the Minister for Health, Charles Haughey, as party leader. He was duly elected Taoiseach by the Dáil.

The new Taoiseach was fifty-four years of age and had a reputation for hard work and for making firm decisions. He appeared to have left the troubled times of the Arms Crisis behind him in the distant past. However, many people in his own Fianna Fáil party, including his former rival, George Colley, were suspicious of him and would have preferred another leader.

Charles J. Haughey giving a press conference following his election as the fourth leader of Fianna Fáil in 1979.

In January 1980, Charles Haughey went on television to warn the people that the government was borrowing too much money and that hard decisions would have to be made. However, few cutbacks in expenditure were made before the approaching general election which was held in June 1981.

GARRET FITZGERALD AND THE COALITION

Fianna Fáil under Charles Haughey lost the election and were replaced by a Fine Gael-Labour coalition with Dr Garret FitzGerald (Fine Gael) as Taoiseach and Michael O'Leary (Labour) as Tánaiste. Soon after taking office, the Minister for Finance, John Bruton of Fine Gael, warned the public that the amount of money owed by the government was a very serious problem.

Dr Garret FitzGerald succeed Liam Cosgrave as leader of Fine Gael in 1977. He served two terms as Taoiseach during the 1980s.

Throughout the 1980s, successive governments had to deal with this situation by increasing taxes and reducing government spending in areas like health and education. FitzGerald's first government was actually defeated in the Dáil when trying to raise a tax on children's shoes in January 1982.

In the general election which followed, Charles Haughey and Fianna Fáil were returned to power, but without an overall majority. They too faced the problem of reducing the massive public debt. Their attempts to do this partly by cutbacks in health care led to their defeat in the Dáil in October 1982.

The third general election within eighteen months resulted in the return to power of Garret FitzGerald at the head of a Fine Gael-Labour coalition. This time, the government had an overall majority and remained in power until the spring of 1987.

Fitzgerald's government met with failures in some areas and successes in others. Because of disagreements between Fine Gael and Labour, it failed to take the harsh action needed to solve the debt problem by reducing government spending sufficiently. There was a global economic depression taking place at the same time which further damaged the Irish economy.

Soon after becoming Taoiseach, Dr FitzGerald expressed the hope that he could lead a 'Constitutional Crusade' to make the constitution of the Republic more acceptable to Northern Protestants. However, during his period as Taoiseach, a majority of the people voted against his advice in a referendum on the Right to Life of Unborn Children (1983) and on Divorce (1986). On the divorce issue, a majority of the voters decided to keep the ban on divorce contained in the Irish constitution.

Although largely unsuccessful in his treatment of the economy and in his 'Constitutional Crusade', Garret FitzGerald proved himself a statesman in his dealings with the government of Great Britain.

Former Fianna Fáil minister, Desmond O'Malley, launching a new political party – the Progressive Democrats – in 1985.

TEST YOUR KNOWLEDGE

1 Who was Tánaiste in the Fianna Fail government elected in 1977?
2 What position did Charles Haughey hold?
3 Why were some Fianna Fáil TDs worried about their future in 1979?
4 Who succeeded Jack Lynch as Fianna Fáil leader in December 1979?
5 What warning did Charles Haughey give on television in January 1980?
6 Explain the outcome of the general election of June 1981.
7 What was the main problem facing successive governments during the 1980s?
8 How did the coalition government of 1982-87 succeed in managing the economy?
9 What was Dr FitzGerald's 'Constitutional Crusade'? Did it succeed? Explain.

THE ANGLO-IRISH AGREEMENT (1985)

During 1983 and 1984, Irish nationalists of all non-violent political parties from North and South met in Dublin to discuss possible solutions to the continuing crisis in Northern Ireland. They called their meetings the *New Ireland Forum*. Politicians, church leaders, professors and others from Ireland and Britain spoke at these meetings and over three hundred groups or persons sent in their views in written form. However, when the Report of the New Ireland Forum was published, the British prime minister, Mrs Margaret Thatcher, rejected all of the proposals. Dr FitzGerald continued to express his views to the British government and after long, patient negotiations, a historic agreement was reached in November 1985. Known as the *Anglo-Irish Agreement*, it gave the Irish government a say in government action in Northern Ireland and a right to represent the views of the nationalist minority there. Under its terms, closer links were set up between the Irish government and the British cabinet minister in charge of Northern Ireland so that they could work together to bring peace and prosperity to the whole island.

A meeting of the New Ireland Forum in 1984.

Garret FitzGerald and Margaret Thatcher signing the Anglo-Irish Agreement in November 1985.

Chapter 27: Review

- In November 1966, Seán Lemass was replaced by Jack Lynch as Taoiseach. Fianna Fáil was returned to power under Jack Lynch in the general election of 1969.

- The outbreak of violence in Northern Ireland in 1969 had a serious impact on

the government and people of the Republic. In May 1970, Lynch dismissed two of his ministers because they did not fully support government policy on Northern Ireland.

- On 28 May 1970 the two sacked ministers – Charles Haughey and Neil Blaney –

were arrested and charged with attempting to import arms for use by the IRA in Northern Ireland. Later in the year, both were found not guilty.

- On 1 January 1973, Ireland became a member of the EEC. Dr Patrick Hillery became the country's first commissioner in Europe.

- An election in 1973 saw the end of sixteen years of Fianna Fáil power by bringing a coalition of Fine Gael and Labour into government. Liam Cosgrave, the leader of Fine Gael, became the Taoiseach.

- During the four years of coalition, the economy suffered because of the huge increases in oil prices in the Middle East.

The general election of 1977 resulted in a landslide victory for Fianna Fáil and Jack Lynch once again became Taoiseach.

- In 1979, Jack Lynch resigned as Taoiseach and was replaced by Charles Haughey. By this time there was a huge national debt, but Haughey's government failed to tackle it. During the decade of the 1980s, successive governments tried to reduce this national debt by increasing taxes and reducing government spending.

- From 1983 to 1987, Garret FitzGerald was the leader of a Fine Gael-Labour coalition. This government is most remembered for negotiating with Britain the Anglo-Irish Agreement in relation to Northern Ireland.

ACTIVITIES

1 Multiple choice.
   (a) In November 1966, Seán Lemass was succeeded as Taoiseach by:
      (i) Liam Cosgrave; (ii) Donogh O'Malley; (iii) Jack Lynch; (iv) Charles Haughey.
   (b) The Minister for External Affairs who prepared Ireland's entry into the EEC was:
      (i) George Colley; (ii) Patrick Hillery; (iii) Kevin Boland; (iv) Neil Blaney.
   (c) The Republic of Ireland joined the EEC in: (i) 1969; (ii) 1973; (iii) 1975; (iv) 1979.
   (d) The Minister for Foreign Affairs in the coalition government (1973-77) was: (i) Brendan Corish;
      (ii) Liam Cosgrave; (iii) Garret FitzGerald; (iv) Conor Cruise O'Brien.

2 Complete the following sentences:
   (a) The Sunningdale Agreement (1973) was _____.
   (b) In the general election of 1977, Fianna Fáil under Jack Lynch _____.
   (c) In December 1979, Jack Lynch resigned from his position as Taoiseach and was succeeded
      by _____.
   (d) One of the main problems facing all governments during the 1980s was the level
      of _____.
   (e) The Anglo-Irish Agreement (1985) was _____.

3 Write an account on the career of Jack Lynch as Taoiseach.

4 Show how the troubles in Northern Ireland affected life in the Republic from 1969 onwards.

5 Write a paragraph on the Anglo-Irish Agreement (1985).

NORTHERN IRELAND: 1920-63

THE FOUNDATION OF NORTHERN IRELAND (1920)

The state of Northern Ireland consisting of the six north-eastern counties of Antrim, Armagh, Derry (or Londonderry), Down, Fermanagh and Tyrone was set up under the Government of Ireland Act which was passed by the British parliament in 1920. A Northern Ireland parliament and government were established in Belfast. Although the Six Counties remained part of the United Kingdom under the king of England, British governments did not interfere in the affairs of the province between 1922 and 1969.

King George V opening the first Northern Ireland Parliament on 21 June 1921.

Unionist workers in a Belfast shipyard demonstrating against Sinn Féin during the 1918 General Election.

From the start, the Unionist party was in complete control of the government. You have seen already how Sir Edward Carson and Sir James Craig tried hard to prevent Home Rule coming to Ireland. Although they would have preferred to keep all of Ireland under the rule of the Westminster parliament, when this proved impossible they agreed to a divided or partitioned Ireland with the Protestant north-east forming a separate state. Although only four counties had Protestant majorities, the Unionists were friendly with the British government and succeeded in having Fermanagh and Tyrone, with their slight Catholic majorities, included in Northern Ireland.

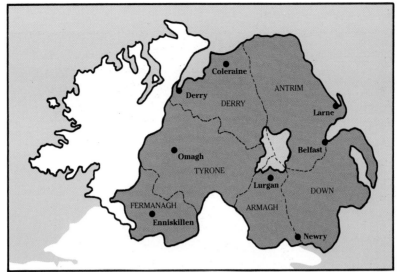

Northern Ireland

The Ulster Unionist Party consisted almost completely of Protestants and had very close links with the Orange Order, an extreme Protestant organisation. James Craig, later Lord Craigavon, who was prime minister of Northern Ireland from 1921 until 1940, once remarked: 'All I boast is that we are a Protestant Parliament for a Protestant People'.

However, one-third of the population of Northern Ireland consisted of Catholics. Most of them were nationalists who believed in a united Ireland. They were seriously distrusted by the Unionist majority and were never given a share in the running of the country.

Stormont Castle, the home of the Northern parliament from 1932.

Lord Craigavon, Prime Minister of Northern Ireland 1921-40.

A ONE-PARTY STATE

The state of Northern Ireland was designed so that the two-thirds Unionist majority would have a majority in parliament. Take a look at the chart of election results in Northern Ireland between 1921 and 1969.

General Elections in Northern Ireland				
	Unionists	Nationalists	Others	Total
1921	40	12	0	52
1925	36	12	4	52
1929	40	11	1	52
1933	39	11	2	52
1938	42	8	2	52
1945	35	10	7	52
1949	39	9	4	52
1953	39	9	4	52
1958	37	8	7	52
1962	34	9	9	52
1965	36	9	7	52
1969	39	6	7	52

You can clearly see how the Ulster Unionist Party always had a huge majority, unlike government parties in Great Britain or in the south of Ireland which were frequently turned out of office by the voters. As they had no fear of losing power, Unionist governments were not likely to listen carefully to criticism or to bring about badly needed improvements in the running of the country.

With no hope of gaining power, the large Catholic minority community was hostile to the new state of Northern Ireland. Unionists in turn saw Catholics as a threat to the state and were determined to secure their position by enforcing strict law and order.

TEST YOUR KNOWLEDGE
1 What act of parliament established the state of Northern Ireland?
2 What party controlled the government there?
3 How many counties had Protestant majorities? Name them.
4 Who became the first prime minister of Northern Ireland?
5 Why were Catholics distrusted by the Unionist majority?
6 What was the response of Unionists to the threat to their position posed by the minority?

LAW AND ORDER

The early years of the new state of Northern Ireland were marked by widespread violence and disorder. The IRA were active, especially in border areas. Thousands of Catholics were driven from their jobs and homes. After an inflammatory speech from Sir Edward Carson near Belfast on 12 July 1920, all of the Catholic workers in the city's shipyards were expelled from their jobs.

Against this background of violence and intimidation, the new government set up a police force, the *Royal Ulster Constabulary (RUC)*, and a reserve force known as the *B Specials*. While Protestants regarded these forces as their protectors, they were never accepted by Catholics as fair upholders of law and order.

British troops manning the barricades in Belfast in 1921.

B Specials on patrol on the Border during the 1920s.

In 1922, the Northern parliament passed the *Special Powers Act* which gave the government extensive powers, including the use of the death penalty and internment without trial.

The most serious threat to the survival of Northern Ireland was removed when Sinn Féin and the IRA split over the Anglo-Irish Treaty of December 1921. The Civil War which followed in the South gave the Unionist government in the North a welcome opportunity to strengthen its control over the Six Counties without fear of intervention by republicans from the South.

However, although law and order was restored in Northern Ireland by 1923, the government presided over a deeply divided society.

DISCRIMINATION IN NORTHERN IRELAND

From the outset, the Unionists favoured their fellow Protestants and acted against the interests of Catholics. This policy was known as *discrimination* and was evident in the following areas:

- *In housing*, Catholics were frequently discriminated against by Unionist-controlled local authorities.
- *In employment*, Protestants tended to be favoured with jobs and more Protestants than Catholics were found in better-off jobs, in proportion to their numbers.
- *In the civil service*, the number of Catholics in the higher-up positions was very small indeed.
- *In elections*, the Ulster Unionist Party increased its control by two means:
  1. The abolition of proportional representation (PR) in elections, as this had been fairer to minorities than the straight vote.
  2. *Gerrymandering* – this was the rigging of constituencies and was most blatant in Derry where, despite a Catholic majority of voters, the corporation was controlled by Unionists.

As the years went by, Northern Ireland remained a divided society. Protestants and Catholics attended separate schools, separate churches, and for the most part did not mix socially. After boycotting the parliament for a number of years, the Nationalist Party under Joseph Devlin took their seats in 1926. However, they were always a small minority and their demands for change were ignored.

TEST YOUR KNOWLEDGE
1 Who controlled the state of Northern Ireland after it was set up in 1920?
2 Who was its first prime minster?
3 What percentage of the total population was comprised of Catholics? What was their attitude to the new state?
4 What police force was set up in Northern Ireland?
5 Who were the B Specials?
6 State three forms of discrimination practised against Catholics in Northern Ireland.
7 In your opinion, why were Unionists suspicious of the Catholic minority?

A TIME OF DEPRESSION

In common with the rest of Europe, Northern Ireland was badly hit by the Great Depression of the 1930s. Many jobs were lost in the famous Belfast shipyard of Harland and Wolff, while the second shipyard in the city, Workman and Clark, closed down in 1934.

Harland and Wolff shipping was badly hit during the Great Depression of the 1930s.

Unemployment levels were very high, reaching a peak of 100,000 in 1938. To make matters worse, there was very little assistance available from the state for the unemployed. In housing, medical services and public health there had been hardly any improvements since Northern Ireland was set up in 1920. Even the welfare payments which did exist were only about half the size of those available in the rest of the United Kingdom.

As a result of severe hardship, both Protestant and Catholic workers took to the streets of Belfast in 1932 to protest against their living conditions. However, Unionist leaders became alarmed at the solidarity of Protestant and Catholic workers and in various speeches they encouraged Protestant employers to employ Protestants in preference to Catholics. In March 1934 Basil Brooke, who later became prime minister of Northern Ireland, remarked:

> 'I recommend those people who are Loyalists not to employ Roman Catholics, 99% of whom are disloyal . . . If you don't act properly now, before we know where we are, we shall find ourselves in the minority instead of the majority.'

Basil Brooke later Lord Brookeborough, Prime Minister of Northern Ireland 1943-63.

The protests of the poor against the government soon changed into sectarian riots between Protestants and Catholics, reaching a crisis point in July 1935. Fighting broke out during the Orange parade in Belfast on 12 July. This led to riots which lasted for three weeks and claimed the lives of eleven people, with nearly 600 injured. The British army was called in to restore order as the RUC could no longer control the situation.

Tension between Protestants and Catholics remained high throughout the remainder of the 1930s. However, when Northern Ireland entered World War II along with Great Britain in September 1939, a period of economic prosperity was about to begin.

TEST YOUR KNOWLEDGE
1 *Why was there widespread poverty in Ireland during the 1930s?*
2 *What sort of assistance was available from the state?*
3 *Why did both Catholic and Protestant workers take to the streets of Belfast in 1932?*
4 *What advice did some Unionist leaders give to Protestant employers?*

THE WAR COMES TO NORTHERN IRELAND

The Unionist leaders immediately pledged their loyalty to the king of England and willingly entered the war. They believed, correctly, that with the Irish Free State remaining neutral, the war effort of Northern Ireland would lead to closer links with Great Britain.

The economy of the Six Counties improved steadily during the war years. The farmers got good prices for their produce in Britain, while in Belfast, the shipyards and other heavy industries were busy producing materials needed in the war. When large numbers of British and American troops were stationed in Northern Ireland, local trade benefitted as a result.

Thousands of American troops were stationed in Northern Ireland during World War II.

Belfast and other towns were to suffer from German bombing raids. In April 1941 when the worst raids took place, thirteen fire brigades were sent to the assistance of Belfast from the Irish Free State by the Taoiseach, Eamon de Valera.

Belfast suffered badly from German bombing raids during World War II.

As in England, the shared experience of wartime suffering brought all sections of the Northern community closer together. The widespread destruction of poorer areas of Belfast exposed the terrible living conditions in the slums and paved the way for improvements once the war was over.

THE WELFARE STATE

The Welfare State which was introduced in Britain after 1945 by the Labour government was also extended to Northern Ireland. It included the following improvements:

- A comprehensive scheme of insurance covering sickness and unemployment.
- A free health service for all and a serious campaign to wipe out the dreaded problem of tuberculosis (TB).
- A programme of house building.
- Far-reaching reforms in education, including free secondary education, a raising of the school-leaving age to fifteen, and grants for university students.

The reforms in education improved the position of the Catholic community by enabling future political leaders to receive higher education. In the years ahead, such well-educated men and women would not be willing to accept the status of second-class citizens in Northern Ireland.

Although there were improvements in the economy during the 1950s, politics in Northern Ireland still remained linked to sectarian divisions between Protestants and Catholics. As long as Lord Brookeborough remained as prime minister, there was little hope of an easing of such tensions. However, on his retirement in 1963, he was replaced by a far more open-minded man – Captain Terence O'Neill. It appeared at last that some healing of divisions between Protestants and Catholics might take place.

TEST YOUR KNOWLEDGE
1 *What was the attitude of the Unionist leaders to the outbreak of World War II?*
2 *Why did the economy of Northern Ireland improve during the war?*
3 *List two ways in which the war affected the people of Belfast.*
4 *What is meant by 'The Welfare State'?*
5 *Give three improvements which were introduced to Northern Ireland as part of the Welfare State.*
6 *How did education reform improve the position of the Catholic community?*
7 *Who succeeded Lord Brookeborough as prime minister of Northern Ireland in 1963?*

Chapter 28: Review

- The state of Northern Ireland, consisting of six counties, was set up under the Government of Ireland Act in 1920.

- The Unionist Party, consisting almost completely of Protestants, remained in control of Northern Ireland between 1921 and the abolition of the parliament there by the British government in 1972.

- Catholics, although making up over one-third of the North's population, were not given a share in the running of the state.

- From the beginning law and order was a problem in Northern Ireland. The government set up a new police force – the RUC – and a reserve police force – the B Specials.

- From the outset Catholics were discriminated against in housing, employment and politics.

- In the 1930s, depression and unemployment hit Northern Ireland.

However, its economy greatly improved during the war years.

- After World War II, a welfare state was set up in Northern Ireland.

- In 1963, Captain Terence O'Neill became prime minister of Northern Ireland. He wanted to end discrimination against Catholics. Many Unionists were dissatisfied with his talk of reform.

ACTIVITIES

1 Multiple choice.
  (a) The first prime minister of Northern Ireland was: (i) Lord Brookeborough; (ii) Sir James Craig; (iii) Sir Edward Carson; (iv) Terence O'Neill.
  (b) The practice of gerrymandering involved: (i) denying people jobs; (ii) rigging constituency boundaries; (iii) the lack of proper housing; (iv) internment without trial.
  (c) Unemployment reached a peak in Northern Ireland in 1938 when the following number of people were out of work: (i) 50,000; (ii) 80,000; (iii) 100,000; (iv) 500,000.
  (d) In 1963, a new, forward-looking prime minister came to power in Northern Ireland. His name was: (i) Terence O'Neill; (ii) Joseph Devlin; (iii) Lord Brookeborough; (iv) William Craig.

2 True or false?
  (a) The State of Northern Ireland was established under the Government of Ireland Act (1920).
  (b) From 1922 onwards, British governments in London regularly participated in the affairs of Northern Ireland.
  (c) The Special Powers Act (1922) included the death penalty and internment without trial.
  (d) In 1926, the Nationalist Party under Joseph Devlin took their seats in the Northern Ireland parliament.
  (e) The economy of Northern Ireland disimproved seriously during World War II.

3 List three forms of discrimination practised against the Catholic community in Northern Ireland from 1922 onwards.

4 Write a paragraph on two of the following: (a) Northern Ireland during the Depression of the 1930s; (b) Northern Ireland during World War II; (c) The Welfare State in Northern Ireland.

CAPTAIN TERENCE O'NEILL

Unlike his predecessors such as the Unionist leaders Craigavon and Brookeborough, Terence O'Neill believed in looking for the support of the minority Catholic community in Northern Ireland. He was to be seen visiting Catholic schools and hospitals and he hoped to end anti-Catholic discrimination. O'Neill realised that only by making Catholics contented citizens of Northern Ireland could the Union with Great Britain be made secure in the long term. Unfortunately for him, many of his Unionist colleagues did not share his generous approach.

In 1965, two historic meetings took place, one in Belfast and the other in Dublin, between Terence O'Neill and the Taoiseach of the Irish Republic, Seán Lemass. This was the first time ever that the prime ministers of both states had met. Lemass realised at the time that he was taking a serious risk. The extreme Protestant leader, the Reverend Ian Paisley, organised a protest at the Belfast meeting of the two premiers. He was just becoming well known for his anti-Catholic protests in Northern Ireland, Britain and further afield.

Captain Terence O'Neill succeeded Lord Brookeborough as Prime Minister of Northern Ireland in 1963.

The historic meeting between Lemass and O'Neill in Belfast in 1965.

As O'Neill moved slowly to persuade his own reluctant followers to introduce long overdue reforms, he was to encounter a mass peaceful movement among the Catholic community who took to the streets to demand their rights.

THE CIVIL RIGHTS MOVEMENT

During the 1960s, there were peaceful movements among black people in the United States of America to bring about full civil rights. At the same time, students in many parts of the world were protesting against injustice by taking to the streets in marches and demonstrations. These activities inspired the Catholic minority in Northern Ireland. As their demand for equal rights was ignored in the Unionist-dominated Northern Ireland parliament at Stormont, they too took to the streets to voice their grievances.

In February 1967, the Northern Ireland Civil Rights Association was founded with the aim of securing full citizens' rights for all of the people of Northern Ireland. The first famous incident in the struggle took place at Caledon, Co. Tyrone, in the summer of 1968. Here the young Nationalist MP, Austin Currie, led a protest to a house which had been allocated to a single Protestant girl in an area where there were many large Catholic families on the housing waiting list.

A Civil Rights march in Derry in 1968.

John Hume, one of the leaders of the Civil Rights Movement.

In the following October, events in the city of Derry ensured that the Civil Rights struggle became news all around the world. A peaceful march arranged for 5 October was banned by the Minister for Home Affairs, William Craig. When the march went ahead in Derry, the peaceful protestors, including a number of MPs, were brutally attacked by the RUC. Within hours the events were screened on televisions and described in newspapers around the world. Soon more and more marches were organised and Terence O'Neill's government promised to introduce reforms. However, while he promised too little to please Catholics, he had agreed to too many changes according to many of his own Unionist colleagues.

At many Civil Rights marches, Ian Paisley and his followers organised counter-demonstrations and there was often fighting between both sets of protestors. When O'Neill called a general election in February 1969, Paisley campaigned strongly against him throughout Northern Ireland. Paisley also stood for election in O'Neill's own constituency where he came a close second to the prime minister. This

Ulster Unionists protesting against the reforms proposed by O'Neill's government.

Ian Paisley, an extreme Unionist, was a strong critic of O'Neill's policies.

humiliation of O'Neill and the fact that his party was badly divided over its response to the Civil Rights Movement led eventually to his resignation on 28 April. Ultimately he had failed in his attempt to persuade his Unionist colleagues to offer the hand of friendship to the Catholic community. He was succeeded as Unionist leader by his cousin Major James Chichester-Clark, a landowner from Co. Derry. The new prime minister attempted to restore Unionist unity and introduce gradual reforms. However, events soon got out of hand on the streets of Derry and Belfast and the British government had to intervene directly in Ireland for the first time since 1922.

TEST YOUR KNOWLEDGE
1 *How did Captain Terence O'Neill differ from earlier Unionist leaders?*
2 *What historic meetings took place in Ireland in 1965?*
3 *What movements inspired Catholics in Northern Ireland to struggle for civil rights?*
4 *Explain the Caledon protest conducted by Austin Currie in 1968.*
5 *What took place in Derry on 5 October 1968?*
6 *What was the reaction of Terence O'Neill to the Civil Rights Movement?*
7 *Who succeeded him as prime minister of Northern Ireland in May 1969?*

THE CRISIS OF 1969

In August 1969, serious rioting broke out in Derry and Belfast. It began during the Apprentice Boys' Parade march in Derry on 12 August. This extreme Protestant organisation held a ceremony each year to commemorate the closing of the gates of the city against the attacking Catholic army in the siege of 1689. In the summer of 1969, despite a high level of tension between Catholics and Protestants, the Unionist government refused to ban the march through a city with a majority of Catholics. When the Apprentice Boys reached the Catholic Bogside area, missiles were thrown at them and large-scale fighting broke out. Later in the day, the RUC were prevented from entering the

Bogside area by local people. For over two days a struggle known as 'The Battle of the Bogside' went on between the local people and the police. Bricks, pavement stones and petrol bombs were used against the RUC whose members replied with armoured cars and CS gas. One of the leaders of the people in the Bogside was a twenty-two year old girl from Tyrone, Bernadette Devlin, who had been elected an MP the previous April.

A Civil Rights march in 1969.

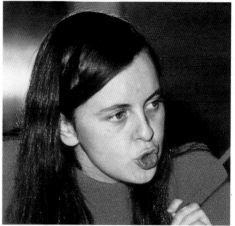

Bernadette Devlin was elected MP in April 1969.

The trouble soon spread to Belfast where some Catholic youths began rioting. Extreme Protestants, angered by the events in Derry, launched wholesale attacks on Catholic areas of Belfast. When the RUC and B Specials were seen to be openly in favour of the Protestants, the British army had to be called in to restore order. By the time they moved in on 16 August, the houses of over 150 Catholic families had been burnt out and six people were dead. Vastly outnumbered by Protestants, the Catholics in poorer areas of Belfast welcomed the British army on to their streets as protectors.

British soldiers on the streets of Belfast in 1970.

When the British home secretary, James Callaghan, visited Northern Ireland at the height of the crisis, he promised that the Labour government of prime minister Harold Wilson would ensure that all people in Northern Ireland, Catholics as well as Protestants, would be given full rights as British citizens. However, the hopes of many people for a brighter future were soon dashed when violent men on both sides of the divide began a campaign of shooting, bombing and destruction.

REPUBLICAN VERSUS LOYALIST

Extreme Protestants were known as *Loyalists* because of their loyalty to the British monarch. Various British governments were to discover that these Loyalists would only follow instructions from London when it suited them. In particular, they were prepared to use violence to prevent the granting of civil rights to Catholics or the sharing of power between Protestants and Catholics. Various secret Loyalist paramilitary or violent organisations were set up. The most powerful was the illegal *Ulster Volunteer Force (UVF)*.

While extreme Loyalists were arming themselves secretly, they also set up a public organisation called the *Ulster Defence Association (UDA)*. Many Unionist politicians encouraged Protestants to hold extreme anti-Catholic views. The most famous of these was the Reverend Ian Paisley who also ran his own religion, the Free Presbyterian Church. From 1969 onwards, Paisley went from strength to strength, winning seats at elections for himself and his followers and doing everything in his power to block concessions to Catholics such as 'One Man, One Vote' or 'Power-Sharing'.

On the Catholic or Nationalist side in 1969, the IRA was almost non-existent. However, in December of that year it split into two groups – the *Official IRA* and the *Provisional IRA*. Each had a supporting political movement, Official Sinn Féin and Provisional Sinn Féin. While the Officials had Socialist and Marxist views, the Provisionals wished to concentrate on removing Unionist and British control over Northern Ireland by means of violence.

Throughout 1970 and the first half of 1971, the level of violence increased greatly. In Catholic working-class areas in Belfast and Derry, people began to turn against the British army and to come under the influence of the Provisional IRA. The IRA shot soldiers or policemen

Troops in riot gear on the streets of Belfast during a demonstration in 1970.

Members of the UDA on patrol.

or bombed Protestant-owned businesses. The Loyalist paramilitaries in turn shot Catholics and bombed Catholic-owned businesses.

The Unionist prime minister, Brian Faulkner, who had succeeded Chichester-Clark in March 1971, decided on a new policy to reduce the level of violence. He persuaded the British government to allow him to introduce internment without trial in August 1971.

TEST YOUR KNOWLEDGE
1 *Why did rioting break out in Derry in August 1969?*
2 *What was 'The Battle of the Bogside'?*
3 *Why was the British army placed on the streets of Belfast in 1969?*
4 *What promise did the British home secretary, James Callaghan, make on visiting Northern Ireland?*
5 *Explain the meaning of the term 'Loyalist'.*
6 *What were paramilitary groups?*
7 *Name one Loyalist and one Republican paramilitary group.*
8 *Who became prime minister of Northern Ireland in March 1971?*

INTERNMENT WITHOUT TRIAL

An aerial view of the Maze Prison near Belfast where many Catholics were interned.

Around four o'clock on the morning of 9 August 1971, the British army arrested over 300 people. After careful examination, 240 of them were interned without trial. Although internment had helped to defeat earlier IRA campaigns, its use in 1971 proved a disastrous mistake for the Unionist government.

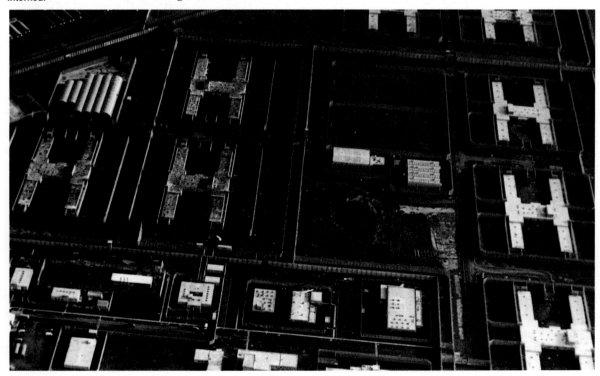

250

When it emerged that very few Loyalist suspects had been interned, Catholics of all shades of opinion united in anger. Many totally innocent men were interned and most of the IRA leaders escaped capture. In the months after internment, there were widespread protests throughout nationalist areas of Northern Ireland and IRA violence increased dramatically. Already since internment, the IRA was receiving greater sympathy and support. Events in Derry in January 1972 were to increase this support further and to pave the way for the fall of the Unionist government at Stormont.

BLOODY SUNDAY: DERRY, 30 JANUARY 1972

On 30 January 1972, thirteen civilians were shot dead by the British army at the end of an illegal anti-internment march. While the army claimed that it was shot at first, the local people strongly denied this.

Civilians are held against a fence by British troops during the banned protest march in Derry on 20 January 1972.

The day soon became known as 'Bloody Sunday' and it caused deeply-felt anger among Catholics in Northern Ireland. In the Republic, a huge wave of anti-British feeling spread over the country and protestors burned the British Embassy in Dublin to the ground. Relations between the Irish government under Jack Lynch and the British Conservative government of Edward Heath reached an all-time low.

It was clear that the Unionist government in the North could not control the situation and Edward Heath demanded that the London government should take over full control of law and order in Northern Ireland.

THE FALL OF STORMONT
DIRECT RULE COMES TO NORTHERN IRELAND

When Brian Faulkner and his government refused to give up control of law and order, the British government was forced to act. On 30 March 1972, the British parliament suspended the parliament and government of Northern Ireland. Instead, the province would be ruled directly from London. A member of the British government known as the Secretary of State would be in charge. On 1 April 1972, William Whitelaw became the first such Northern Ireland Secretary of State.

Edward Heath, the British Prime Minister whose government introduced direct rule to Northern Ireland from 1 April 1972.

Protestants in Northern Ireland were shocked and horrified at the suspension of their Unionist-controlled parliament. On the other hand, most of the Catholic minority were pleased as they believed that they would receive fairer treatment from the British government.

The suspension of Stormont marked the end of an era in the history of Northern Ireland. It did not end the violence, however, as extreme Loyalists and Republicans continued their campaigns. Once the Stormont parliament was abolished, successive British governments made it clear that they would only return power to Northern Ireland if Protestants and Catholics agreed to a power-sharing arrangement.

TEST YOUR KNOWLEDGE
1 *When was internment without trail introduced in Northern Ireland?*
2 *Why were Catholics particularly angry concerning internment?*
3 *What effect did internment have on the IRA?*
4 *Explain the events of 'Bloody Sunday' in Derry on 30 January 1972.*
5 *What was the reaction to 'Bloody Sunday' in the Irish Republic?*
6 *What action was taken by the British government on 30 March 1972?*
7 *Name the first secretary of state appointed to Northern Ireland.*

Chapter 29: Review

- In 1963, Captain Terence O'Neill became prime minister of Northern Ireland. He wanted to end discrimination against Catholics. He also had two historic meetings with Seán Lemass in 1965. Many Unionists such as the Reverend Ian Paisley were dissatisfied with his talk of reform.

- In 1968, Catholics began the Civil Rights Movement and took to the streets in an effort to draw attention to their grievances.

- In 1970, the IRA began operations again in Northern Ireland. In 1971, internment without trial was brought in to deal with the mounting violence. However, this only served to embitter many Catholics.

- On 30 January 1972, thirteen civilians were shot dead by the British army at the end of an illegal anti-internment march. This was known as 'Bloody Sunday' and caused great anger among Catholics in Northern Ireland.

- In March 1972, the British government abolished the Northern Ireland parliament and brought Northern Ireland under direct rule from Britain.

ACTIVITIES

1 Match an item in Column 1 with an item in Column 2.

COLUMN 1	COLUMN 2
An extreme Protestant leader	Brian Faulkner
A British Prime Minister	Austin Currie
A Unionist Prime Minister	William Whitelaw
A Civil Rights leader	Ian Paisley
The first British secretary of state for Northern Ireland	Harold Wilson

2 Complete the following sentences.
   (a) In 1965, two historic meetings took place between _____.
   (b) On 5 October 1968, a famous Civil Rights march took place in _____.
   (c) In August 1969, serious rioting broke out in _____.
   (d) The Ulster Volunteer Force (UVF) was _____.
   (e) In December 1969, the IRA split into two groups, _____.

3 Choose four scenes of the 'Troubles' in Northern Ireland from this chapter and state what you learn from each one.

4 Draw up a time chart on the situation in Northern Ireland between 1967 and January 1972.

5 Write a paragraph on two of the following: (a) The Civil Rights Movement; (b) The Loyalist reaction to the Civil Rights Movement; (c) The abolition of the Stormont parliament and government.

A DIVIDED PEOPLE

THE SUNNINGDALE AGREEMENT

In June 1973, a new assembly was elected in Northern Ireland. It included Unionists and members of two newer parties. One was the largely Catholic Social Democratic and Labour Party (SDLP) which had replaced the old Nationalist Party in 1970. The other was the small Alliance Party which drew support from both Protestants and Catholics. In November, these parties agreed to the British government's demand that they share power between them. As a result, a power-sharing executive or government was set up in Belfast with the Unionist leader Brian Faulkner as leader and the head of the SDLP, Gerry Fitt, as deputy leader. Both these parties, together with Alliance, had members in the executive.

In order to secure the agreement of the Catholic community to this arrangement, the British government under Edward Heath negotiated ties between North and South. This was known as the *Irish Dimension* and involved the setting up of an advisory Council of Ireland which would include politicians from both North and South of the border.

These provisions were contained in an agreement signed at Sunningdale in England in December 1973 between the leaders of the Northern Ireland parties, Edward Heath, the British prime minister and Liam Cosgrave, the Taoiseach of the Fine Gael-Labour coalition government in power to Dublin.

The signing of the Sunningdale Agreement in December 1973.

The power-sharing executive began running Northern Ireland on 1 January 1974. Although the British government continued to take charge of law and order, the new executive had power in many areas of government. There were high hopes that it would mark the beginning of a solution to the conflict in Northern Ireland.

From the outset, however, extreme Protestants such as Ian Paisley and Loyalist paramilitary groups were determined to wreck the power-sharing arrangement. Indeed many members of Brian Faulkner's own Unionist Party were opposed to sharing power with nationalists. In particular almost all Unionists regarded the proposed Council of Ireland as the first step on the road to a united Ireland.

Power-sharing received a serious setback in March 1974 when eleven out of the twelve Northern Ireland seats at the Westminster general election were won by Unionists who opposed the new executive.

On 28 May, the power-sharing arrangement collapsed due to a general strike organised by Loyalist workers. The British Labour government of Harold Wilson had refused to use the army to keep essential services running. However, even without the strike it is difficult to see how power-sharing could have continued when most Unionist supporters were opposed to it.

With the fall of the power-sharing executive, Northern Ireland was placed under direct rule from London once again.

THE VIOLENCE CONTINUES

For the remainder of the 1970s, Northern Ireland experienced a continuation of violence resulting in many deaths and injuries. As one secretary of state was replaced by another, it appeared that the British government now hoped merely to keep the level of violence down and that they had no real hope of a better future for Northern Ireland.

Members of the IRA manning the barricades in Derry in 1976.

The British army during a searching operation in Belfast, 1976.

Both the IRA and Loyalist paramilitary groups continued to carry out shootings and bombings. In 1974, the IRA was responsible for a series of horrific bombings in England, including attacks on public houses in the city of Birmingham and the town of Guildford. Later on, it was claimed that the wrong people had been imprisoned for these crimes. Such miscarriages of justice, added to the terrible loss of life and injury of ordinary English citizens, led to further misunderstanding and tension between the governments and people of Great Britain and Ireland.

In another terrorist incident, the IRA killed the British ambassador in Dublin, Sir Christopher Ewart Biggs, in 1976. During these years there were various attempts by the British government to set up another power-sharing arrangement in Belfast. However, they all failed as the Unionists refused to share power with the Nationalist minority.

In May 1979, a new Conservative government was elected in Great Britain under Mrs Margaret Thatcher. A few months previously, her close friend and adviser, Airey Neave, the spokesman on Northern Ireland, had been killed in a car bomb attack near the House of Commons in Westminster. Mrs Thatcher was determined to do all in her power to defeat the IRA.

The scene of the assassination of the British ambassador to Ireland, Sir Christopher Ewart Biggs, in 1976.

Mrs Margaret Thatcher. Her government was determined not to compromise with the IRA.

In the summer and autumn of 1979, it became clear that the IRA had no intention of ending their violent campaign. In August they carried out an attack in which eighteen British soldiers died at Warrenpoint in Co. Down. On the same day, the IRA killed Lord Mountbatten, a close relative of the British royal family, by placing a bomb in his boat off the coast of Sligo.

A month later at the end of September 1979, Pope John Paul II made a strong appeal to the IRA to end the violence. He was speaking at Drogheda during his visit to Ireland. However, the IRA ignored the pope's plea and continued with their campaign.

They were now to enter into a bitter struggle with the Thatcher government over the conditions of Republican prisoners in Northern Ireland.

TEST YOUR KNOWLEDGE
1 *Name the three main parties elected to the Northern Ireland Assembly in 1973.*
2 *Who became leader of the new power-sharing executive?*
3 *What was the 'Irish Dimension' in the Sunningdale Agreement?*
4 *Who were the enemies of power-sharing in Northern Ireland?*
5 *How did the power-sharing arrangement come to an end?*
6 *Who became prime minister of Great Britain in May 1979?*
7 *What was the reaction of the IRA to appeals for peace by Pope John Paul II in September 1979?*

THE IRA HUNGER STRIKES

Some years earlier, Roy Mason, secretary of state for Northern Ireland in the Labour government, had put an end to special status for IRA prisoners. The British government claimed that shootings and bombings were criminal activities and that those responsible for them should be treated like other criminals and wear ordinary prison dress. The IRA, on the other hand, believed that their members were prisoners of war and entitled to wear their own clothes.

When the British government refused to meet these demands, IRA prisoners carried out various protests, including refusing to wear prison clothes and wearing only a blanket and dirtying their cells. When these measures failed, they turned to a form of protest with a long history in Ireland – the hunger strike.

Because the prisoners were housed in H-shaped compounds in Long Kesh prison, their campaign became known as the H-Block Protests. Mrs Thatcher's government was determined not to compromise with the IRA. The hunger strike proceeded during the spring and summer of 1981 and ten IRA prisoners died before it was called off.

The 'dirty protest' of IRA prisoners in the H-Block of Long Kesh prison in 1979.

Bobby Sands, who died on hunger strike in 1981.

The most famous of the hunger strikers to die was Bobby Sands who was elected an MP for Fermanagh-South Tyrone in a by-election while on hunger strike. Hunger strikers also took part in the general election in the Republic in June 1981 and two of them were elected as TDs. To many people among Nationalists in the North, the reaction of the British government was harsh and unyielding. As a result, the IRA and Sinn Féin gained increased support and sympathy in the years ahead.

During the early 1980s, further attempts were made to set up a power-sharing settlement in Northern Ireland. When these were unsuccessful, the British government moved towards an understanding with the government of the Irish Republic in order to bring peace to Northern Ireland.

THE ANGLO-IRISH AGREEMENT (1985)

The signing of the *Anglo-Irish Agreement* in November 1985 marked the greatest change in the government of Northern Ireland since the suspension of the Stormont parliament in 1972. This was an international agreement between the British and Irish governments. The British hoped for greater security co-operation with the Irish Republic, while the Irish government wanted to improve the conditions of the Nationalist minority in Northern Ireland.

Under the terms of the Anglo-Irish Agreement, two groups were set up:

- *The Inter-governmental Conference:* A meeting of ministers from both governments to discuss Northern Irish affairs;
- *The Anglo-Irish Secretariat:* A group of British and Irish civil servants based near Belfast.

The Unionists bitterly opposed the Anglo-Irish Agreement. They objected to the role given to the Irish government in Northern Ireland affairs and felt that they had been betrayed by the British government. They organised huge protests against the agreement and refused to take part in any discussions as long as the agreement remained. Most Nationalists in Northern Ireland welcomed the agreement as an important advance. However, the IRA ignored the agreement and continued their campaign of violence.

For both governments, the Anglo-Irish Agreement was not a final solution to the Northern Ireland problem. They hoped rather that it would provide a framework for peace and reconciliation in the future.

This banner on Belfast City Hall summarised Unionist reaction to the Anglo-Irish Agreement.

TEST YOUR KNOWLEDGE

1 *Why did the British government and the IRA come into conflict over prisoners in Northern Ireland?*
2 *List two forms of protest carried out by IRA prisoners.*
3 *What were the H-Blocks?*
4 *Who was the most famous of the hunger strikers to die in 1981?*
5 *How did the Hunger-Strike Campaign influence Nationalists in Northern Ireland?*
6 *Explain the functions of: (a) the Inter-governmental Conference; (b) the Secretariat set up under the Anglo-Irish Agreement of 1985.*
7 *How did the Unionists react to the signing of this agreement?*

Northern Ireland 1968-1985

1968	Civil Rights movement begins
1969	British army deployed on the streets
1971	Internment without trial
1972	'Bloody Sunday' in Derry
	Fall of Stormont government: direct rule from London
1973	Sunningdale Agreement
1974	End of Sunningdale Agreement
1981	IRA hunger strike campaign
1985	Anglo-Irish Agreement

Chapter 30: Review

- In 1970 a new party called the SDLP came into existence in Northern Ireland and represented nationalists.

- A power-sharing executive came into operation on 1 January 1974 as part of the Sunningdale Agreement. This had been negotiated between the Northern Ireland parties, the British government and the Irish government.

- From the beginning extreme Protestants were determined to wreck this power-sharing arrangement and it eventually collapsed when Loyalist workers organised a general strike.

- For the remainder of the 1970s, Northern Ireland experienced a continuation of violence resulting in many deaths and injuries.

- In May 1979, a new Conservative government came to power in Britain under the leadership of Margaret Thatcher. Thatcher's government refused to give in to the demands of IRA prisoners for special status. A series of hunger strikes followed and ten IRA prisoners died before it was called off.

- The signing of the Anglo-Irish Agreement in 1985 marked an important change in the government of Northern Ireland. Most nationalists welcomed the agreement while Unionists bitterly opposed it.

ACTIVITIES

1 *Complete the following sentences.*
  (a) *The Unionists reacted to the Anglo-Irish Agreement (1985) by* _____.
  (b) *A power-sharing executive was set up in Northern Ireland in 1973 under the* _____.
  (c) *The power-sharing executive came to an end as a result of* _____.
  (d) *In September 1979, the IRA ignored an appeal to end their campaign of violence. This appeal was made during a visit to Ireland by* _____.
  (e) *During 1981, there was a high level of tension in Northern Ireland because of* _____.

2 *Outline in detail the Sunningdale Agreement (1973) and explain why it failed.*

3 *Write a paragraph on the IRA Hunger Strike Campaign.*

4 *Describe the workings of the Anglo-Irish Agreement (1985) and state why both governments negotiated it.*

IRELAND AND THE USA – SOCIAL CHANGE IN THE TWENTIETH CENTURY

LIFE IN TOWN AND COUNTRYSIDE

IRELAND AND THE UNITED STATES OF AMERICA

In this section, we will look at the lives of ordinary people in both Ireland and the United States of America. From 1900 to the present, many changes took place in both countries in areas such as travel and transport, work and leisure, life in the countryside and the towns, and the role of women.

While there were often vast differences between developments in Ireland and in America, there were also close links between both countries. From around the time of the Great Famine onwards, millions of Irish people emigrated to America. They often left a life on the farm to begin a new life in the expanding cities of America.

Although most of the Irish emigrants struggled to survive in their new environment, many of them became rich and powerful. Some close links between Ireland and America have remained up to the present day.

In this chapter we will travel back in time and look at some of the important changes in the towns and countryside in both Ireland and America from 1900 onwards.

THE IRISH COUNTRYSIDE IN 1900

In 1900, the great majority of the Irish people lived in the countryside where they worked on the land. Look carefully at the following pictures which tell us about the different groups of people living in rural Ireland.

The magnificent residence and estate of a wealthy land-lord. A large number of servants and labourers were needed on vast estates such as these.

A wealthy landlord and his family

A farmer's kitchen around 1900.

Many labourers and small farmers lived in appalling conditions in cottages like this one in Donegal around 1900.

At this time, the population in the Irish countryside was falling. As you can see from the chart, the number of people on farms in Ireland fell continuously from the time of the Great Famine onwards. Because only the eldest son could inherit the family farm, the younger sons usually emigrated. Often only the eldest daughter on a farm could get a dowry in order to marry. This left the other daughters with the choice of remaining on the farm as unpaid labourers or of boarding the emigrant ships.

POPULATION OF IRELAND 1851-1911	
1851	6,552,000
1861	5,798,000
1871	5,412,000
1881	5,174,000
1891	4,704,000
1901	4,458,000
1911	4,390,000

In 1900 there was very little machinery in use on Irish farms. As you can see from the pictures of work at that time, horses were still widely used and both men and women spent long hours toiling on the land.

Carrying turf in the West of Ireland.

Farmers bringing milk to the creamery.

From around 1920 onwards, improvements came about slowly in living and working conditions in the Irish countryside.

A CHANGING COUNTRYSIDE

In general, Irish farmers were conservative and slow to change. Fathers were reluctant to hand over the land to the eldest son. By 1946, in fact, a third of all farmers were over sixty-five years of age.

Despite the fact that rural Ireland contained an ageing conservative population, important improvements took place from around 1922 onwards. The arrival of machinery marked an important change for the better. Up to 1960, over 40,000 tractors were put into use on Irish farms. The arrival of electricity during the 1940s and 1950s improved living conditions on many an Irish farm. At around the same time, many rural homes got running water for the first time.

The arrival of the tractor made work easier on the Irish farm.

Rural electrification improved living and working conditions on Irish farms.

WORKING WITH EVIDENCE

Read the following account of life on an Irish farm in the 1940s.

'The day on the farm started at about 7.00 am with a quick cup of tea. Then, when the cows had been milked and my father had gone to the creamery, the rest of us sat down to a long, leisurely breakfast. Preparations for dinner meant going to the field where the potatoes and vegetables grew and digging a bucket of potatoes and cutting some heads of cabbage; a big black pot of potatoes was boiled every day and whatever was left went with the other scraps to feed the farm dogs and the pigs. Dinner itself was at one o'clock, and a shrill iron whistle that hung beside the kitchen door summoned us. At four o'clock we had afternoon tea, and whatever time the cows were milked in the evening was supper time.

The evening milking was a restful moment. Men and women, tired after their work, slapped their little milking stools on the ground beside the cows.

In early spring or late autumn when milk production was at its lowest, we separated our own milk and made butter. The crops we had planted in spring grew through the summer months. Cutting the corn in the autumn meant the winding down of the year's work, and it was a task in which the neighbours came together and helped each other out. The threshing was one of the biggest events of the farming year. The wheat was threshed into grain, which would in turn be ground into flour to give us our daily bread.'

Alice Taylor, *To School through the Fields*

1 *What was the first task carried out on the farm every morning?*
2 *What preparations were made for the dinner each day?*
3 *What activity was carried out on the farm in autumn?*
4 *Describe what was done to the wheat.*
5 *What impression of farm life do you get from this extract?*

Despite various improvements, emigration from the Irish countryside continued. As you can see from the chart, emigration reached an all-time high during the 1950s, resulting in widespread rural depopulation.

EMIGRATION 1946-1966
(average figures for each year)

Period	Figure
1946-51	24,384
1951-56	39,353
1956-61	42,401
1961-66	16,121

As indicated in the chart over 400,000 people emigrated from the Irish Republic during the 1950s.

During the 1960s, some hope returned to the Irish countryside. Along with the rest of the population, farmers benefited from a general improvement in economic conditions. Bigger and better machines were in use and farmers received higher prices for their goods. However, the big breakthrough for Irish farmers came in 1973 when the country entered the European Economic Community (EEC).

THE COUNTRYSIDE TODAY

Up to 1973, farmers had received grants and other assistance from the Irish government. From then on, they also received grants from the EEC. As well as this, farmers enjoyed guaranteed prices for their products under the *Common Agricultural Policy* (CAP). Many increased the size of their holdings and modernised them. As you can see from the picture, the most modern machinery increased production and efficiency on the larger farms. However, a lot of small farmers, particularly in the West of Ireland, continued their struggle to survive on uneconomic holdings.

Despite the fact that change was usually slow and undramatic, it is clear that life in rural Ireland today is very different from what it was in 1900.

Modern machinery increased production and efficiency on Irish farms

TEST YOUR KNOWLEDGE
1 Name the main groups of people living in the Irish countryside around 1900.
2 Why was the population in rural Ireland falling at this time?
3 Describe work on the farm around 1900.
4 Name two improvements in the Irish countryside between 1922 and 1960.
5 What changes came about during the 1960s?
6 How did Irish entry to the EEC in 1973 affect life in the countryside?

IRISH TOWNS IN 1900

Today, most Irish people live and work in towns and cities and enjoy a standard of living far beyond the dreams of their grandparents' generation. In 1900, fewer Irish people lived in the larger towns and cities. At this time, Belfast was a booming industrial city which owed its prosperity to heavy industry such as shipbuilding and engineering.

Dublin, unlike Belfast, had few large industries with the exception of Guinness and Jacobs. However, it was a centre of trade and commerce, banking and law, and the headquarters of the British government in the country.

Most of the other larger towns, such as Cork, Galway, Limerick and Waterford, owed their importance mainly to their functions as ports.

Dublin around 1900.

Market day in an Irish town around 1900.

WORK IN THE TOWNS

Within the towns and cities there were great differences between rich and poor. People's standard of living depended largely on their occupation and particularly on whether they were skilled or unskilled. There were four main classes of occupation in the larger towns of Ireland around the year 1900.

UNSKILLED WORKERS

A majority of urban workers were unskilled manual labourers, such as dockers, carriers and general labourers. Because of a surplus of these workers, wages were low – about £1 per week – and steady employment was not guaranteed. Labourers were hired and fired at will. Dublin dockers, for example, were taken on every morning as casual labourers, but few were assured of continuous employment.

For women, domestic service in the houses of the well-to-do was the major source of unskilled work. This work was mostly done by country girls who earned about four shillings (20p) per week. However, they were better fed than their equals in other occupations.

Unskilled workers were not protected by trade unions at this time.

SKILLED WORKERS

These consisted of tradesmen or artisans such as plumbers or carpenters who had served their time in various trades. In Dublin, at the turn of the century, about one in every five workers was skilled. Protected by their trade unions, tradesmen earned about twice as much as unskilled workers.

SMALL TRADERS AND CLERICAL WORKERS

Around 1900, the number of small shopkeepers and publicans was increasing. In the towns, shopkeepers and publicans were richer than the population which they served. Clerical workers and teachers also occupied a middle place in society between rich and poor. Large numbers of clerical workers were employed in the civil service, the post office, the banks and in general offices. Such employment was regarded as respectable and secure.

BIG BUSINESS AND THE PROFESSIONS

The richest section of society earned its living either from big business or the professions, especially medicine and law. These groups had a high standard of living and many employed domestic servants in their large, comfortable homes.

HOUSING CONDITIONS IN THE TOWNS AND CITIES

WORKING-CLASS HOUSING

In Dublin around 1900, the typical unskilled worker and his family were housed in a tenement – i.e. one or more rooms in a large house which was occupied by many families. Most of the tenements were located in the centre of the city. About one-third of Dublin's population lived in them. The situation was similar in other towns such as Cork, Galway and Limerick, although small cottages rather than tenements were more typical there. In Belfast, as a result of higher wages and more secure employment, housing conditions were better.

Tenements in Dublin around 1900.

POOLE ST. DUBLIN. 7880. W.L.

WORKING WITH EVIDENCE

Read the following extract from James Plunkett's novel, *Strumpet City*, which is set in Dublin around 1913.

'*In the mornings, just at the breakfast hour, the poor searched diligently in the ashbins of the well-to-do for the half-burnt cinders and carried sacks and cans so that as much as possible of the fuel might be salvaged. The ashbin children were pinched and wiry and usually barefooted. They lived on the cast-offs. They came each morning from the crowded rooms in the cast-off houses of the rich; elegant Georgian buildings which had grown old and had been discarded. The clothes they wore had been cast-off by their parents, who had bought them as cast-offs in the second-hand shops in Little Mary Street or Winetavern Street. If the well-to-do had stopped casting off for even a little while, the children would have gone homeless and fireless and naked.*'

from James Plunkett, Strumpet City

1 Why did the poor search in the ashbins of the wealthy each morning?
2 Describe the children involved in this activity.
3 How does the author refer to the tenements?
4 What is the main point which the author wishes to convey concerning the children's clothes?
5 How accurate an impression of conditions at the time is given in this work of fiction?

THE GROWTH OF SUBURBS

By 1900, the larger cities had expanded outwards to include suburbs. These suburbs were mainly inhabited by the better-off sections of society. A typical suburban house consisted of a front sitting room, dining room and kitchen downstairs, and three or more bedrooms upstairs – some even included a bathroom. The development of suburban housing was made possible by cheap and efficient transport to the city in the form of railways and trams. There was a great contrast between the terrible poverty of the inner-city and the relative comfort of the suburbs.

TEST YOUR KNOWLEDGE
1 What were the four main classes of occupation in the larger towns around the turn of the century?
2 What type of work was carried out by the unskilled workers?
3 What was the major source of female employment at this time?
4 Which groups occupied a 'middle place' between rich and poor?
5 How did the richest section of society earn its living?
6 Describe the housing of the typical unskilled worker.
7 Describe a typical suburban house of this time.
8 What development greatly helped the growth of suburbs?

IMPROVEMENTS IN THE TOWNS

During the 1920s and 1930s, serious efforts were made to tackle the slum problem in Irish towns. Corporations began to build housing schemes for people who had been removed from the inner city. In Dublin, Cork and other towns, this led to the demolition of many tenements near the centre of town. The people were housed instead in new housing schemes such as Marino and Crumlin in Dublin or Gurranabraher and Ballyphehane in Cork.

The buiilding of Corporation houses in Ballyfermot, Dublin, in the late 1940s.

A street in Dublin's inner city around 1960.

The introduction of children's allowance payments and better medical facilities were intended to improve the lives of children living in poverty. In particular the dreaded disease tuberculosis (TB), which attacked adults and children alike, was successfully eliminated during the 1940s and 1950s.

As long as unemployment and emigration remained high, however, Irish towns, like the Irish countryside, could not hope to enjoy any real or lasting prosperity.

TOWNS AND CITIES IN MODERN IRELAND

The economic prosperity of the 1960s had far-reaching influences on life in Irish towns. With more money in people's pockets, businesses responded accordingly. Supermarkets made their first appearance around this time. Local corner shops saw their trade decline as people were attracted by the cheaper prices in supermarkets.

Many publicans and shopkeepers began to modernise their premises during the 1960s. Lounge bars replaced traditional public houses and impressive hand-crafted shop fronts were often torn down and replaced by ugly plastic fittings and glaring neon lights.

Despite the growing prosperity of Irish towns from the 1960s onwards, not everyone fared equally well. Thousands continued to live in poverty in urban ghettoes. These were vast housing estates of working-class homes with very few leisure facilities in the area. Often they were built miles from the centre of town where the grandparents and other relations of their young families continued to live.

By the 1980s, crime had become a very serious problem in most Irish towns. Elderly people felt unsafe, even in their homes, and car theft had become a serious problem.

Unlike 1900, rich and poor people in towns in modern Ireland can rarely be precisely distinguished by their dress. However, deep divisions between rich and poor have continued. Despite various improvements, poverty and unemployment remain serious threats to the well-being of all who live in towns in Ireland at the close of the twentieth century.

TEST YOUR KNOWLEDGE
1 *What action was taken from the 1920s onwards to tackle the slum problem in Irish towns?*
2 *Name a disease which constantly threatened people in Irish towns up to the 1940s.*
3 *How did the economic changes of the 1960s affect Irish towns?*
4 *Show how the appearance of Irish streets changed around this time.*
5 *Did all town dwellers share equally in the prosperity of the 1960s? Explain.*

THE UNITED STATES IN 1900

Unlike Ireland, the United States of America in 1900 was a country with a rapidly expanding population. It was a vast continent containing huge farms or ranches on the one hand and growing industrial cities on the other. In Ireland, there was a serious unemployment problem leading to massive emigration at the time. The US, on the other hand, needed many workers for its expanding industries. Consequently it encouraged the arrival of millions of immigrants from Europe. Many Irish people were among these immigrants.

Immigrants' first view of New York city around 1900.

Society in America in 1900 was far more mobile than in Ireland and other European countries. This means that, if people worked hard, they could rise up in society and others would admire them. It mattered little to people what type of work their parents or grandparents had carried out. This was definitely not the case in Ireland at the time, where most people continued to follow the occupations of their parents.

271

Unlike Ireland, where most people earned their living on the land, towns and cities were very important in the US. But American agriculture still had an important part to play.

AGRICULTURE IN THE UNITED STATES

In some respects, agriculture in the US was like that in Ireland. Farmers received uncertain and often falling prices for their goods. At a time when industry was thriving, this led to a decline of the importance of agriculture in the economy as can be seen from the following table.

PERCENTAGE OF NATIONAL INCOME RECEIVED BY FARMERS IN THE US		
1860	–	30%
1890	–	19%
1920	–	13%
1933	–	7%

If American farmers suffered like Irish farmers from uncertain prices, many of them also suffered from a backward standard of living. As a result, many sons and daughters of American farmers left the land to seek their fortunes in the city. Between 1870 and 1930 the rural population declined from eighty per cent to less than forty per cent of the total.

As the population living in the countryside continued to decline, the political influence of farmers in the US also declined. This was evident during the 1920s when the US government did little to help them during a period of crisis. Between 1920 and 1932, total farm income declined from $15½ billion to $5½ billion. In 1933, as part of the *New Deal* of President Franklin D. Roosevelt, assistance was given to farmers to prevent them from going out of business.

Because of falling prices in the 1930s, American farmers pour their milk away.

During and after World War II, American farmers enjoyed widespread prosperity. However, after the establishment of the European Economic Community (EEC) in 1957, American farmers faced stiff competition from the products of their European counterparts on the world market.

TEST YOUR KNOWLEDGE

1 *List two ways in which the United States differed from Ireland around the year 1900.*
2 *What was the attitude of the US government to immigration?*
3 *Would you agree that society was mobile in America at the time? Explain.*
4 *State two difficulties which faced farmers in both Ireland and America.*
5 *How did the falling numbers in the countryside affect the political influence of American farmers?*
6 *Show how the 1920s was a period of crisis in American agriculture.*
7 *What threat to American farmers began in 1957?*

TOWNS AND CITIES IN 1900

Around 1900, a majority of Americans were living in towns and cities for the first time in the country's history. Huge businesses were run by very wealthy people. A study undertaken in 1896 calculated that one per cent of the national population owned nearly half of the country's wealth.

The Statue of Liberty was the first sight seen by many immigrants on their arrival in New York.

Between 1880 and 1900, the population of New York city, the country's largest city, had increased from 2 million to 3½ million. In the same period, Chicago's population had risen from ½ million to 1½ million, making it the second largest city in the land. Therefore the two largest US cities in 1900 between them would have equalled the entire population of Ireland.

A room in a tenement flat in New York in 1900. Many immigrant families first lived in this type of accommodation.

Life in the big cities of America was often tough and difficult. People who arrived there from American farms or from foreign countries had to give up their old way of life and learn to adapt to the new situation. They faced a choice between hard work or poverty. There was no unemployment benefit or other welfare payments available at the time.

Very often, vast numbers of newcomers to American cities were exploited by corrupt politicians. Having got these people's votes, such politicians did little to improve living conditions; instead they used their power and influence to make themselves wealthy.

FROM EXPANSION TO DEPRESSION: 1920-40

During the 1920s, the cities of America were at the forefront of the modern movement known as the 'Roaring Twenties'. Cities stood for excitement and adventure where the latest fashions in music, dress and behaviour could be found. Suburbs outside cities expanded rapidly as the motor car enabled people to commute from home to work.

The 1920s was also the era of *Prohibition* in America. Alcoholic drink was banned by law. However, the law was openly flouted and many American cities witnessed violent feuds when the police raided illegal drinking places which were frequently run by criminal gangs.

This was also the era of gangsters and their mobs in the US. The most famous of these men was Al Capone whose gang terrorised the people of Chicago until he was shot in an encounter with the police in 1933.

The *Great Depression* followed the collapse of the American Stock Market at Wall Street, New York in October 1929. This had a devastating impact on the lives of people in the towns and cities of the US. By 1933, the number of jobless people stood somewhere between twelve and fifteen million. There were pathetic scenes witnessed in city streets as people who had lost vast fortunes threw themselves from high-rise buildings. Huge queues formed outside food depots where relief was handed out.

Panic spread as people lost their fortunes because of the Wall Street Crash in 1929.

Describe this scene of Prohibition in America in the 1920s.

Under the New Deal programme of President Roosevelt, the economy gradually recovered from depression. But not until after the end of World War II in 1945 did an air of hope for the future return to the towns and cities of America.

THE MODERN CITY

From the 1950s onwards, American cities continued to expand. Much of the new space required for homes and businesses came in the form of high-rise skyscrapers. However, many of the city dwellers now chose to live in suburbs. As a result, the census of 1960 showed that in eight of the ten largest cities, the population had fallen since 1950 due to people moving out to the suburbs. At this stage between forty and fifty million Americans were living in suburbs.

As a result of this movement, many central city areas became ghettoes where the poor lived. Not surprisingly, many ghetto areas had high levels of poverty, unemployment and crime. Crimes including murder, violent attacks, drug pushing and robbery have become part and parcel of everyday life in large American cities.

New York – a city of skyscrapers.

Black children pose for the camera in a New York ghetto.

By 1970, nearly seventy per cent of the American population lived in or near big cities. At the same time, the total farm population was less than it had been in 1830.

At the end of the twentieth century, the US clearly faces some of the same problems as Ireland. In both countries there has been a continuous flight from the land. As Dublin has expanded, so too have American cities with all the problems that the separation of people into wealthy and poor areas has brought about.

1 Show how wealth was unevenly distributed in the US around 1900.
2 Name the two largest cities in the US in 1900. Show that their populations were increasing rapidly.
3 Why was life often difficult for newcomers to American cities?
4 What were the 'Roaring Twenties'?
5 Explain what was meant by 'Prohibition'.
6 When did the Great Depression begin?
7 Show the impact of the Depression on life in American cities.
8 Why had the population of many American cities fallen by 1960?
9 List some of the problems found in modern cities in the US.

Chapter 31: Review

- Historically there have been many close links between Ireland and America which have remained strong up to the present day.

- In 1900, most Irish people lived in the countryside where they worked on the land. Emigration remained very high from the time of the Great Famine onwards.

- Some important changes have taken place in the Irish countryside since 1922. The introduction of tractors and the arrival of both electricity and running water improved life and work on many Irish farms.

- The great change for Irish farmers came in 1973 when the country entered the EEC. As a result of grants and an increase in prices, many farmers modernised their holdings.

- Fewer Irish people lived in large towns and cities around 1900. Within the towns and cities there were great differences between rich and poor. The majority of workers were unskilled, while the richest section of society earned its living from big business and the professions.

- In Dublin around 1900, the typical unskilled worker and his family were housed in a tenement, while the better-off sections of society lived in the suburbs.

- During the 1920s and 1930s, many slums were cleared and people were housed instead in new housing schemes away from the city centres.

- From the 1960s onwards, city life in Ireland underwent many changes. Supermarkets and lounge bars became common. Thousands continued to live in poverty, and crime became a serious problem.

- Unlike Ireland, the US in 1900 was a country with a rapidly expanding population. While most people at that time earned their living on the land in Ireland, towns and cities were very important in the US.

- During the 1920s and 1930s, the population living in the US countryside continued to decline, while big cities expanded.

- While cities stood for excitement and adventure, those living in them often experienced tough and difficult circumstances. The 1920s was era of the gangsters in cities like Chicago, while the Great Depression had a devastating impact on people living in the towns and cities.

• From the 1950s onwards, American cities continued to expand so that by 1970, nearly seventy per cent of the American population lived in or near big cities.

ACTIVITIES

1   Match an item in Column 1 with an item in Column 2.

COLUMN 1	COLUMN 2
Al Capone	Dublin
brewing and distilling	New York
Franklin Roosevelt	Chicago
Wall Street	Belfast
shipbuilding	The New Deal

2   Complete the following sentences.
(a) In 1900, the great majority of the Irish people lived _____.
(b) Life on farms in Ireland improved during the 1940s and 1950s because _____.
(c) A big breakthrough occurred for Irish farmers in 1973 when _____.
(d) From around 1870 onwards, the proportion of Americans living on the land declined because _____.
(e) After 1957, American farmers faced stiff competition from Europe because _____.

3   Write a paragraph on the changes in life in the Irish countryside between 1900 and 1980.

4   Write an imaginary dialogue between a young person and a grandparent in which the young person praises life in Irish towns today, while the grandparent prefers conditions when he or she was young.

5   Show how people in Irish towns followed many of the customs of American towns from the 1960s onwards.

CHAPTER 32

LEISURE AND PASTIMES

IRELAND AROUND 1900

Unlike today, most people in Ireland around 1900 provided their own entertainment. In the absence of television, radio or videos, live home-based entertainment was the norm.

In both towns and countryside, people visited one another's homes in the evening to enjoy conversation, music and card playing. In many parts of the country, a local story-teller known as a *seanchaí* entertained his listeners with tales of long ago.

In Irish towns and cities, many people enjoyed musical evenings. Friends and neighbours would gather around the piano in the candlelight to entertain one another by singing and playing.

Wren boys in Co. Kerry around 1900.

There were many outdoor pastimes in Ireland around 1900. Hunting and horse racing were very popular among the rich. Sports such as rugby and soccer had grown in popularity. However, since the foundation of the Gaelic Athletic Association (GAA) in 1884, hurling and Gaelic football had become very popular throughout the country.

In both towns and cities, a visit to the theatre was a popular way of spending an evening. In 1904, the famous Abbey Theatre opened in Dublin. Here people came to see the work of great playwrights such as Yeats, Synge and O'Casey.

The poor of Dublin look on as the rich make their way to a banquet in Dublin Castle.

A scene from one of Seán O'Casey's plays, 'The Plough and the Stars', which was first staged at the Abbey Theatre in 1926.

THE ARRIVAL OF RADIO AND CINEMA

The arrival of the cinema in Ireland was one of the greatest changes in the world of entertainment. Although some small cinemas had been set up before 1914, it was during the 1920s and 1930s that cinemas became extremely popular throughout the country. In the days before television, thousands of people flocked to the cinema each night to see their heroes and heroines on the big screen.

Another great breakthrough in entertainment in Ireland took place in 1926 when the country's first radio station, 2RN, was set up. This later became known as Radio Éireann. By 1940, not only news programmes and music but also Sunday matches were being broadcast throughout the country on radio.

Radio's first announcer in the studio of 2 RN in 1926.

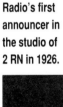

Radio broadcasting for children in the 1940s.

THE BALLROOM OF ROMANCE

Dance halls were another popular form of entertainment in Ireland. Although some catered for Irish music and céilí dancing, jazz, swing and other forms of modern music were played in most dance halls.

During the 1950s, dance halls were at the centre of the new rock and roll craze as Irish people enthusiastically took to the new dance forms popularised in Britain and America.

Many romances had their beginnings in the dance halls throughout the country. These centres of entertainment became even more popular during the 1960s.

Dancing to the music of the 1950s and 1960s.

TEST YOUR KNOWLEDGE

1 *What forms of entertainment were popular in Ireland around 1900?*
2 *Explain the role of the seanchaí.*
3 *Name the main outdoor pastimes in Ireland around 1900.*
4 *What theatre was opened in 1904?*
5 *When did cinema become popular in Ireland?*
6 *Name Ireland's first radio station and state when it was opened.*
7 *What type of dancing became popular in Ireland during the 1950s?*

THE AGE OF TELEVISION

On 31 December 1961, Ireland's first television station, Telefís Éireann, began transmitting for the first time. Within a short period, television became the most popular form of mass entertainment in the country. Television opened up Irish society to many outside influences. Programmes such as the Late Late Show started discussions on issues which had never been publicly debated before. Television also led to a decline in many traditional pastimes such as storytelling, card playing and music in the home.

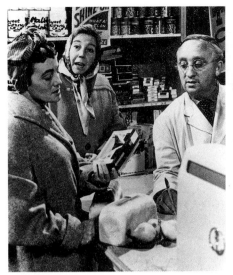

A scene from Tolka Row, a popular television soap opera of the 1960s, set in Dublin.

The Late Late Show, hosted by Gay Byrne, was first broadcast in the 1960s.

The cinema also declined in popularity in the 1960s and 1970s with many of the larger cinemas closing down as more and more people chose to stay at home watching television. During the 1980s, many families became owners of video recorders in addition to their televisions.

Popular music underwent great changes from the 1960s onwards. Young people everywhere danced to the music of the showbands during the 1960s. During the 1970s and 1980s, these were replaced by other forms of music, especially rock. The dance halls were largely replaced by the loud music and flashing lights of discotheques.

Irish traditional music experienced a revival from the 1960s onwards. Groups like the Chieftains, Planxty and Horslips made this form of music popular with the younger generation.

A DIFFERENT WORLD

Leisure activities have changed dramatically in Ireland during the twentieth century. Today, people have more money to spend on entertainment, as well as much more free time than their ancestors a century ago. In 1900, most of the entertainment was centred around the home and provided by the people themselves. In today's Ireland, entertainment has become a multi-million pound industry. There is now a great variety of entertainments to choose from. However, it is also true that some people regret the passing of many of the old forms of entertainment once provided by people in their own homes.

TEST YOUR KNOWLEDGE
1 When was Ireland's first television station opened?
2 How did television affect traditional pastimes?
3 How did popular music change from the 1960s onwards?
4 State two ways in which entertainment in Ireland has changed between 1900 and 1990.

THE UNITED STATES AROUND 1900

As can be expected in such a vast continent, a wide variety of leisure activities were open to Americans around 1900. Outdoor sports included hunting of all types, rodeo racing, horse racing and the two popular team games, American football and American baseball.

As with transport, inventions were just beginning to have an impact in the world of entertainment. The earliest form of record, the phonograph, had arrived as had the first silent movies. However, such novelties as yet posed no serious threat to the live theatre.

The most famous centre of live theatre in the US was Broadway in New York city. There, shows of different types might be seen, ranging from opera and classical drama to the music hall style theatre known as vaudeville. It was still the era of the travelling theatre companies which moved from town to town throughout the country, bringing Shakespeare and the classics as well as more modern plays to local audiences.

Unknown to the wider world, a new type of music was becoming popular at this time in the Deep South of the United States. Centred on the city of New Orleans, this new type of music was known as jazz. It began among black musicians in that area. Within a short period, it became famous the world over.

The United States of America

THE ROARING TWENTIES

After the sacrifices and difficulties of the war years, many Americans were determined to enjoy themselves during the 1920s. Fashions and general behaviour became more daring, and new and exciting dances such as the Charleston were the order of the day. Jazz became more popular and bands were formed to play the latest music.

Unlike their parents, Americans in the 1920s did not have to play the music themselves or leave their homes in order to enjoy it. Gramophone records were becoming widely available and more and more families became owners of wireless or radio sets.

The 1920s, the Age of Jazz

Dance bands became popular in the USA during the 1930s and 1940s.

However, the most popular of all the new forms of entertainment was the cinema.

TEST YOUR KNOWLEDGE
1 *List some outdoor pursuits in America around 1900.*
2 *Name two inventions which became popular at the time.*
3 *What was the most famous centre of theatre in the US at the time?*
4 *Where did jazz music originate?*
5 *What was the Charleston?*
6 *List two inventions which enabled people to hear the latest popular music in America during the 1920s.*

THE MOVIES

From the 1920s onwards, the US became the leading country in the world in the making of motion pictures, or movies as they were popularly known.

During World War I, a studio had been established at Hollywood in California for the making of silent movies where a huge film industry sprang up.

During the 1920s, the silent movies were the great form of entertainment. Stars like Charlie Chaplin, Mary Pickford and Rudolf Valentino entertained millions the world over.

From 1927 onwards, silent movies were replaced by the 'talkies' and in 1939 colour films made their first appearance. Film stars were hero-worshiped by millions of loyal fans and different studios were in strong competition with one another.

Filming at MGM studios in 1936.

Charlie Chaplin in the 'Great Dictator'.

Laurel and Hardy, a great comic duo in the early days of cinema.

Fred Astaire and Ginger Rodgers filming in 1949.

FROM SWING TO ROCK AND ROLL

As well as in cinema, America led the world in the area of popular music. During the 1930s and 1940s, jazz and swing music were all the rage. It was the era of the big bands which played to vast live audiences or to millions over the radio.

When World War II broke out, many of these bands went on tours to entertain the troops. One of the greatest of all big band leaders, Glenn Miller, joined the American air force and was killed on active service in 1944.

In the 1950s, a new craze hit popular music in America – rock and roll. Young people deserted the big bands in favour of new idols such as Buddy Holly or Bill Hailey and the Comets. Rock and roll also involved new forms of dancing. Many older people were shocked by the new fashions in music and dancing. However, the rock and roll craze went from strength to strength and paved the way for the emergence of 'pop music' during the 1960s.

Louis Armstrong, one of the great jazz musicians of his time.

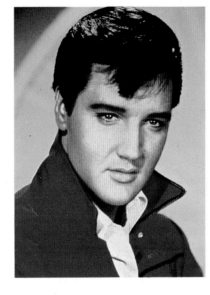

Elvis Presley became a legendary rock and roll star.

MODERN TIMES

As in Ireland, entertainment in the United States from the 1960s onwards was greatly influenced by television and radio and by new inventions such as transistor radios and video recorders. People depended more and more on machines for their enjoyment and the level of live entertainment decreased.

Pop music led on to rock and other types of contemporary music. The films shown in cinemas often reflected the growing level of violence in society. By the 1980s, it was clear that leisure time would be even longer in the future, with many labour-saving inventions in the home, as well as in factories and offices. As a result, more and more leisure centres were built and courses were set up to guide people in the use of their leisure time.

TEST YOUR KNOWLEDGE
1 *Name the main centre of the American film industry.*
2 *Name two stars of the silent movies.*
3 *What improvement took place in film-making in 1939?*
4 *Who was Glenn Miller?*
5 *Name a famous star of rock and roll.*
6 *What trends took place in entertainment in the US from the 1960s onwards?*

Chapter 32: Review

- Most people in Ireland around 1900 provided their own entertainment. Storytelling, music, card playing, sports and a visit to the theatre were widely enjoyed.

- The arrival of cinema and radio marked important advances in entertainment in Ireland.

- During the 1950s and the 1960s, dance halls were very popular places of entertainment in Ireland. During the 1970s and 1980s, the dance halls were largely replaced by discotheques.

- From the 1960s onwards, television became the most popular form of mass entertainment in Ireland. It also led to a decline in many traditional pastimes.

- A wide variety of leisure activities were available in the US around 1900. One of the most popular forms of entertainment was the live theatre. The most famous centre of live theatre was Broadway in New York City.

- During the 1920s, jazz became a very popular form of music. This was also the age of the cinema with stars like Charlie Chaplin and Rudolf Valentino.

- During the 1930s and 1940s, big bands like Glenn Miller's entertained huge audiences. During the 1950s, rock and roll became all the rage, while the 1960s saw the emergence of 'pop' music.

ACTIVITIES

1 *Multiple choice*
   (a) *Broadway, the headquarters of live theatre in the US, is in: (i) Washington; (ii) New York; (iii) Los Angeles; (iv) Chicago.*
   (b) *Telefís Éireann, the Irish television service, began broadcasting in: (i) 1956; (ii) 1966; (iii) 1951; (iv) 1961.*
   (c) *The popular American music form known as jazz originated in the city of: (i) Boston; (ii) Washington; (iii) New Orleans; (iv) Charleston.*
   (d) *The American entertainer Glenn Miller was: (i) an actor; (ii) a band leader; (iii) a rock and roll singer; (iv) a film star.*
   (e) *The famous film studios in the US at Hollywood are in the state of: (i) New Jersey; (ii) Louisiana; (iii) Boston; (iv) California.*

2 *True or false?*
   (a) *The local story-teller in Ireland was known as a seanchaí.*
   (b) *In 1904 the famous Abbey Theatre was opened in Galway.*
   (c) *Ireland's first radio station, 2RN, was established in 1926.*
   (d) *During the 1920s in America, the Charleston was a famous film.*
   (e) *Buddy Holly and Bill Hailey were stars of the silent movies.*

3 *Choose one form of entertainment in Ireland discussed in this chapter and write a short account on it.*

4 *Write a paragraph on the following forms of entertainment in America: (a) 'the movies'; (b) popular music.*

YOUTH AND EDUCATION

IRELAND AROUND 1900

Young people in Ireland today are very much a group apart. They have their own tastes in dress and music and a particular outlook on life. They often question the values of the older generation. The average young person in Ireland today completes second level education and many advance to further study. Young people today bear little resemblance to their counterparts a hundred years ago.

Young people in Ireland around 1900 did not enjoy many of the freedoms taken for granted today. The vast majority attended primary school only and began work by the age of fourteen. Only a privileged minority attended secondary schools and fewer still went on to university.

A typical schoolroom scene in Ireland around 1900.

Unlike today, young people in 1900 could not be so easily identified by their style of clothes or their tastes in music. Many children at the time wore clothes similar to those worn by adults. For the most part they did not challenge their parents or teachers, and discipline was harsh in both home and school.

EDUCATION AROUND 1900

By 1900, the vast majority of children attended primary schools in their local parish. Here they were mostly taught reading, writing and arithmetic (the 3Rs).

WORKING WITH EVIDENCE

Read the following description of life in a Dublin primary school around 1920.

'The desks in First School were long wooden affairs and very shaky. One shake from a boy at one end put blots on twelve copies. The ink wells were filled with a homemade black concoction, and the ink was used for more purposes than writing.

There was no formal teaching done, as we know it now, simply because the room was too crowded. There were three monitors and one brother. The monitors were 'five bob a week' ex-pupils, whose job it was to examine the boys in home tasks. The tasks were allotted each afternoon for homework, and these were examined the following morning. We had no fully qualified lay teachers. A failure at lessons meant a chalk mark on the desk in front of the boy who failed. For each chalk mark a scholar received one 'biff' from the brother, but we always managed to lighten our troubles by rubbing out some of the marks before his tour began. The brother used a leather, which we all preferred to the sticks used by the monitors when the brother left the room.'

Paddy Crosbie, *Your Dinners Poured Out*

1 What reason does the writer give why no formal teaching was done?
2 Who were the monitors?
3 What happened when a boy failed at lessons?
4 What method of punishment was used by the brother?
5 What impression do you get from this account of school life in the 1920s?

Secondary schools were usually run by religious groups. Catholic secondary schools were controlled by bishops or religious orders, while Protestant schools were run by the Protestant churches. Only the sons and daughters of the better-off people could afford to attend secondary schools. A system known as *payment by result* was operated in these schools: the sizes of grants and teachers' salaries were linked to student performance in examinations. This led to a great emphasis on the importance of written examinations and to pressure on students to perform well.

Only the rich could afford to send their children to university where they prepared to enter professions such as medicine and law. From 1900, the numbers attending secondary schools and universities increased steadily.

INDEPENDENT IRELAND: 1922-60

After the achievement of independence from Great Britain in 1922, the first government of the Irish Free State introduced important changes in education. Two new examinations were introduced – the *Intermediate Certificate* and the *Leaving Certificate*. The Irish language was given a central place in the curriculum in both primary and secondary schools. It was also made a compulsory subject in the Intermediate and Leaving Certificate examinations and for entry to the civil service.

From 1922 onwards, the numbers attending secondary schools steadily increased and in 1930 a system of vocational schools was set up. These catered for practical subjects and were controlled by local *Vocational Education Committees* (VECs).

Young people growing up in Ireland between the 1920s and 1950s were similar to their counterparts in 1900. They generally accepted the views of the older generation. They had not as yet developed distinct ways of dressing or special values of their own. At the time, films and books were strictly censored and priests spoke out against modern dancing and 'company keeping' between young men and women.

A classroom in a Dublin school during the 1940s.

During these years, many young Irish people could not find employment at home and had to emigrate to England and America. The 1950s in particular were depressing years for a young person growing up in Ireland as unemployment and emigration reached very high levels. However, the 1960s saw a new period of hope and challenge for Irish society as a whole. During this decade, young people as a group really came into their own.

TEST YOUR KNOWLEDGE

1 State two differences between the lifestyle of young people today and that of young people in 1900.
2 What type of school was attended by most Irish people around 1900?
3 Who attended secondary schools at that time?
4 What system of payment existed in these schools?
5 State two important changes in education introduced by the first government of the Irish Free State.
6 What was life like for young people in Ireland between the 1920s and the 1950s?

MODERN TIMES IN IRELAND

During the 1960s, young people the world over displayed a restlessness and a new questioning spirit. During this time especially, the terms 'teenager' and 'adolescent' were widely used and showed that young people had emerged as a distinct section of society. In Ireland, as in other countries, this challenge was expressed in new forms of dress and music. The terms 'teddy boy', 'hippy', 'bootboy' and 'punk' refer to different phases in fashion among young people from the 1960s onwards.

During the 1960s, young people in Ireland tuned in to the latest pop music from Britain and America. More than any other pop group, the Beatles represented the new restless spirit of the 1960s.

There were far-reaching changes in education in Ireland beginning in the 1960s. In 1967 the Minister for Education, Donogh O'Malley, introduced a scheme of free second level education. This led to a huge increase in the numbers availing of secondary and vocational education. Around the same time, a new curriculum was developed for primary schools. This was more child-centred than the old curriculum and catered more for the personal development of each individual pupil.

Donogh O'Malley.

Second-level students in a modern Irish classroom.

During the 1960s, there was a great increase in the provision of third level education. Universities were expanded and new types of institutions such as regional technical colleges were established. At the same time as the introduction of free secondary education, a system of grants was established to enable more students to go on to third level.

During the 1970s and 1980s, young people became a much more influential sector in Irish society than previously. In 1972, the voting age was reduced from twenty-one to eighteen years of age. Political parties realised the importance of young people's votes and set up special youth sections such as Ogra Fianna Fáil and Young Fine Gael.

Young people enjoying a pop concert in Ireland.

By 1980, with a growing population, Ireland had one of the highest proportions of people under twenty-five in all of Western Europe. While this represented a great human resource, it also presented society with a challenge to provide proper education facilities and good jobs for the growing population.

TEST YOUR KNOWLEDGE
1 How did young people display their challenge to society during the 1960s?
2 Name a famous pop group which had many fans in Ireland during the 1960s.
3 What important reform was introduced by Donogh O'Malley in 1967?
4 What improvements were introduced in third level education?
5 Explain the change in the voting age which took place in 1972.
6 How did political parties respond to the growing importance of young people in the 1970s and 1980s?

THE UNITED STATES OF AMERICA IN 1900

There were many contrasts in the situations facing young people in Ireland and in the US around 1900. While Ireland was suffering from high levels of unemployment and emigration, America was a land of hope and opportunity. With its economy expanding rapidly, there were many employment opportunities open to young people.

Unlike Ireland, America had two strong systems of education, the state system and the voluntary system run by various churches. No grants were paid out of public funds to church-run schools. However, because most of them had a high reputation, many parents willingly paid fees for their children to attend them. Because the Catholic Church in particular believed that their children should attend Catholic schools, a wide network of Catholic voluntary schools was established by bishops, priests and religious orders in both rich and poor areas throughout the country.

An American classroom during the 1960s.

Even at primary schools, young Americans were taught to have a great respect for the country's flag and laws. After primary school, they went on to second level, either the high schools run by the local state government or a private religious-run school.

Unlike Ireland where the education system was centralised and controlled from Dublin, in the US the federal government in Washington had little control over education. Instead, the state governments and local communities were responsible for the running of publicly-owned schools.

The US in 1900 had several universities and other colleges of higher education catering for both men and women. Some of them like the universities of Harvard and Yale had worldwide reputations for excellence.

Boating Day at a ladies' college in the USA around 1900.

AMERICAN YOUTH: 1920-60

Between the two world wars, young people in the US took part in the general changes in American society. Fewer and fewer of them were willing to remain working on the farm. Instead they moved to the cities in search of work and adventure. They were the first generation in America to grow up in a predominantly urban nation. Most of them adapted readily to new fashions in dress, music and behaviour. They also availed of new time-saving inventions such as vacuum cleaners and electric cookers.

During the 1950s, American education caught the attention of the world when serious disputes broke out over the issue of black and white children attending the same school. Matters came to a head in 1958 in the town of Little Rock in Arkansas. When the local governor refused to protect black children wishing to attend a mainly white school, President Eisenhower sent in troops to enforce a decision of the supreme court outlawing the segregation of black and white school-going children. This was one of the leading events in the movement for full civil rights for black people in the US.

Little Rock, Arkansas. Three of the six black students who were refused entry to school being interviewed by a TV crew.

Black parents demonstrating against school segregation in St. Louis in the 1960s.

TEST YOUR KNOWLEDGE
1 *Contrast the situation facing young people in Ireland and the US around 1900.*
2 *What were the two systems of education in existence in the US?*
3 *How were children in primary schools taught to be patriotic?*
4 *How did the US system of education differ from the Irish?*
5 *Name the town where a dispute over the rights of black people to education took place in 1958.*
6 *Who was the US president who resolved this dispute?*

MODERN TIMES IN AMERICA

From the 1960s onwards, young people in America made their influence felt as never before. They were prominent in the spreading of new movements in pop music, carrying on from the rock and roll craze of the 1950s. The pop singer, Elvis Presley, was a great hero among young Americans at the time. Fashions changed. Girls' skirts became shorter as boys' hair grew longer. All of this was an expression of freedom and individuality as well as a rebellion against the older generation.

Elvis Presley

Cult groups grew up throughout the US. The most widespread of these were the hippies. They wore long hair, brightly-coloured clothes and called for world peace and respect for the environment.

One disturbing aspect of the new youth culture was the more widespread use of drugs. These were smuggled into the US and earned huge profits for the criminal gangs who sold them to young people.

During the 1960s and 1970s, young Americans became deeply involved in the politics of protest. There is no doubt that their support of the Civil Rights Movement greatly assisted in the achievement of more civil rights for black people.

Young black people protesting during the Civil Rights Movement in the US.

Young Americans were also prominent in protests against their country's involvement in the Vietnam war. Many young men faced jail rather than go to fight in Vietnam. Students throughout the country protested vigorously about the war and helped to sway public opinion against it and hasten the day of a settlement.

During the 1970s and 1980s, young people in America continued their involvement in politics. As well as concentrating on issues such as world peace, they turned their attention more and more to the need to protect the environment in order to secure the future of humanity in the world.

Scenes such as this one led many young Americans to protest against their country's involvement in the Vietnam War.

Chapter 33: Review

- Around 1900, the vast majority of children in Ireland attended primary school where they learned the 3Rs. Only the children of better-off people could afford to attend secondary schools.

- After the achievement of independence in 1922, the Intermediate and Leaving Certificate exams were introduced. In 1930, a system of vocational schools was set up.

- While the 1940s and 1950s were depressing years for a young person growing up in Ireland, the 1960s brought a new era of hope and challenge. It was during this time that young people emerged as a distinct section of society.

- During the 1960s, far-reaching changes also took place in education, with the introduction of free education in 1967. Universities were also expanded and Regional Technical Colleges were set up.

- By 1980, Ireland had one of the highest proportions of young people in all of Western Europe.

- Unlike Ireland around 1900, the US at that time had an expanding economy with many employment opportunities open to young people. After primary school, American children went to high schools run by the local state government or to a private religious-run school.

- During the 1920s and 1930s, many young people moved to American cities in search of work. While they were expressing their own identity, it was during the 1960s that young people in America were more influential than ever before.

- During the 1960s and 1970s, cult groups grew up throughout the US. Young Americans became increasingly involved in the politics of protest. However, one disturbing aspect of the new youth culture was the more widespread use of drugs.

ACTIVITIES

1 *Fill in the blanks with words from the box.*

secondary schools	**pressure**
parish	**the 3Rs**
religious orders	**school fees**
payment by results	**primary**

In Ireland around 1900, the vast majority of children only attended _____ schools in their local _____. Here they were usually taught _____. Only a small minority went on to _____. These were usually run by _____ and students attending them had to pay _____. A system known as _____ was in operation at the time which placed a great deal of _____ on teachers and students alike.

2 *Complete the following sentences.*
   (a) *In 1958, the town of Little Rock, Arkansas in the US became famous because _____ .*
   (b) *The central government does not run the education system in _____.*
   (c) *During the 1960s, young people in Ireland tuned in to _____.*
   (d) *In 1967, a system of free second level education was introduced in Ireland by _____.*
   (e) *Under the Vocational Education Act (1930), _____ .*

3 *List four important changes in education in Ireland between 1900 and 1980.*

4 *Write a paragraph on young people in the US from the 1950s onwards.*

THE ROLE OF WOMEN IN SOCIETY

IRELAND IN 1900

A hundred years ago, women played a much more restricted role in public life in Ireland than they do today. Whether rich or poor, they were frequently dependent on their fathers or husbands. The wives and daughters in rich or middle-income families did not go out to work. Instead, they remained at home, waited on by servants. Better-off women often visited one another's houses or became involved in local charities. They were also expected to be accomplished in skills such as drawing or playing a musical instrument. In dress, they followed the latest fashions from London or Paris.

Women's fashions in Ireland around 1900.

Most Irish women in 1900 did not enjoy lives of luxury and ease. In the countryside, the wives and daughters of all but the richest farmers were expected to work hard on the land. The farmer's wife had particular responsibility for the care of poultry. Very often, the money earned from selling eggs was the only income handled by the women on the farm.

Working-class women in towns and cities frequently had to go out to work as well as taking care of the home. In the north of Ireland, such women found steady work in mills and factories. In Derry, they were often the only breadwinners as their husbands were unemployed. In Dublin and the rest of southern Ireland, working-class women had to rely on very badly-paid work such as house-cleaning or street-selling. Even when women did get steady work, their wages were always much lower than men's.

Working-class women at work in Ireland around 1900.

Some Irish women who protested against unequal treatment in the workplace.

Many single working-class girls were domestic servants in the homes of the better-off. Here they worked long hours with little time off and earned very low pay.

Despite the disadvantages facing women in Ireland around 1900, there were signs of improvements for the future. The number of girls in secondary schools and colleges was steadily increasing. As well as this, the type of education available to them was improving thanks to the existence of many excellent Catholic convent secondary schools and Protestant girls' secondary schools.

At the same time, a small group of Irish women was organising to fight for a basic civil right which was still denied to women – the right to vote.

THE SUFFRAGETTE MOVEMENT IN IRELAND

By 1900, although women who owned property were allowed to vote in elections for corporations and country councils, no woman was allowed to vote in parliamentary elections. At the time, Irish MPs sat in the British parliament at Westminster. In Britain, a powerful women's movement was being organised to fight for the right to vote, or *suffrage* as it was called. The more militant members of this movement were known as the *Suffragettes*. Although some working-class women joined the movement, it consisted mainly of middle-class, well-educated women who resented this denial of equality with men.

Although a much smaller organisation than its British counterpart, the Irish Suffragette Movement shared the same ideals. The first group with this aim, the Dublin Women's Suffrage Society, had been founded as far back as 1876 by Anna Haslam. In 1908, a much more militant group, the Irish Women's Franchise League, was founded by Hanna Sheehy-Skeffington. It was modelled on the British Suffragette

Irish suffragettes march to demand the vote for women.

A suffragette meeting in the Phoenix Park, Dublin.

Movement and did not hesitate to use violent methods of protest when the British government continued to deny women the right to vote or to sit in parliament.

Like their fellow suffragettes in Britain, Irish suffragettes broke windows, went on hunger strike in prison and attacked members of the government. The prime minister himself, H.H. Asquith, had a hatchet thrown at him by a suffragette during a visit to Dublin in July 1912.

WORKING WITH EVIDENCE

Read the following contemporary comments on the Suffragette Movement in Ireland and answer the questions which follow.

Extract A. The Reason for Joining
'I was then an undergraduate, and was amazed and disgusted to learn that I was classed among criminals, infants and lunatics – in fact, that my status as a woman was worse than any of these.'
Hanna Sheehy-Skeffington

Extract B
'The police should use whips on the shoulders of those unsexed viragoes.'
A letter writer in the Evening Telegraph, 9 July 1912

Extract C
'That strange tribe, small in number, that has arisen on the horizon in Ireland in quite recent times. They are not men, they are not women. Woman: the idea comprises dignity, self-respect, refinement, reserve. I don't find any of these qualities among the Suffragettes.'
Monsignor Keller of Youghal

The divisions between Nationalists and Unionists which were so deep at the time also affected women's groups. Some gifted women, although fully supporting women's rights, believed that the struggle for independence from Great Britain should come first. By the time women in Ireland got the vote in parliamentary elections in 1918, the country was in the throes of a violent struggle between the British government and Irish Nationalists. Many women took a very prominent part in that movement.

TEST YOUR KNOWLEDGE
1 *Describe the lifestyle of better-off women in Ireland around 1900.*
2 *List two groups of women who frequently had to work outside the home.*
3 *What signs of improvement in the conditions of women were there around 1900?*
4 *What was the main political disability suffered by women at this time?*
5 *When was the first women's suffrage group set up in Ireland and by whom?*
6 *What society did Hanna Sheehy-Skeffington found in 1908?*
7 *List some of the tactics used by Irish suffragettes.*
8 *When were women in Ireland given the right to vote in parliamentary elections?*

IRISH WOMEN IN THE INDEPENDENCE MOVEMENT

From 1900 onwards, women were to play an important role in the movement for Irish independence. Maud Gonne established a special society *Inghinidhe na hÉireann* for women with republican views. Jennie Wyse Power, a supporter of the suffrage movement, was also a vice-president of Sinn Féin, the nationalist organisation founded by Arthur Griffith in 1905.

The most prominent of all women in the independence movement was Constance Gore-Booth, who later became Countess Markievicz. Born into a rich Anglo-Irish landowning family in Co. Sligo, she devoted much of her life to working for the poor. She was closely involved with James Larkin and James Connolly on the workers' side during the strike and lockout in Dublin in 1913. She was also a leading member of the Citizen Army. Countess Markievicz was involved as well as an organiser of the Fianna Éireann, a republican boy scout movement.

Countess Constance Markievicz.

Countess Markievicz was sentenced to death for her prominent part in the 1916 Rising, but this was commuted to a term of imprisonment. In December 1918, she became the first woman to be elected to the British parliament but she refused to take her seat there as she was a member of Sinn Féin. She became Minister for Labour in the first government set up by Dáil Éireann in 1919.

During the 1916 Rising, the War of Independence and the Civil War, women were very active in caring for the sick, carrying messages and providing other back-up services. They had their own organisation known as Cumann na mBan which was banned by the British government.

INDEPENDENT IRELAND: 1922-60

Between 1922 and 1960, women in Ireland were part of a fairly conservative society. Most people continued to believe that a woman's place was in the home and women's pay continued to lag behind that of men. On getting married, women nearly always gave up their jobs and in some areas such as teaching and the civil service, they had no choice but to do this.

In the new constitution adopted by the Irish people in 1937, the importance of the role of the woman in the home was recognised.

'In particular, the State recognises that by her life within the home, woman gives to the State a support without which the common good cannot be achieved.

The State, shall, therefore, endeavour to ensure that mothers shall not be obliged by economic neccesity to engage in labour to the neglect of their duties in the home.'

Bunreacht na hEireann, Article 41

Despite the assurances in the constitution, many Irish women continued to live in poverty which forced them to go out to work.

Despite the existence of poverty and unemployment, the position of women was improving gradually up to 1960. As in earlier times, their increasing access to education was one of the keys to an understanding of this trend. When the economy improved in the 1960s, Irish women, along with women in many parts of the world, made their voices heard in a demand for full equality with men.

Women at work in Jacobs Biscuit factory in Dublin.

Women workers assembling televisions in modern Ireland. From the 1960s onwards, women in Ireland became fully involved in the latest developments in technology.

THE MODERN WOMEN'S MOVEMENT IN IRELAND

From 1960 onwards, women in Ireland have been concerned with bringing about improvements in a number of key areas:
- More equal educational opportunities
- Equal pay for equal work
- Greater involvement by women in politics and public life generally
- Higher participation by women in the top positions in various careers

Continuous efforts have been made since 1960 to improve educational opportunities for women and to enable them to enter courses traditionally dominated by men such as honours mathematics and engineering. In 1974, a law was passed making equal pay for equal work compulsory. Three years later, the *Employment Equality Act* (1977) was passed. This made discrimination on the grounds of sex or marital status illegal. It also set up the *Employment Equality Agency* to act as a watchdog in this area.

From the 1960s onwards, women in Ireland took a more active role in politics and public life. The number of female TDs and senators increased slowly but steadily and women became government ministers.

Gemma Hussey, a government minister between 1982 and 1987.

Mary Robinson was inaugurated as the seventh President of Ireland on 3 December 1990.

The number of women in the top jobs in the country remained extremely small, however. The fact that women are often expected to run a home as well as a career has been blamed for this situation.

Despite the various inequalities between men and women which remained in Ireland, by 1990 no one can deny that Irish women have come a long way since the time of the struggle for the vote at the start of the century.

TEST YOUR KNOWLEDGE
1 *Name the women's republican group founded by Maud Gonne.*
2 *Where was Countess Markievicz born?*
3 *What was her role during the 1913 strike and lockout in Dublin?*
4 *Name the republican boy scout movement which she organised.*
5 *List two important 'firsts' recorded by Countess Markievicz in 1918-19.*
6 *What did the Irish constitution (1937) state about the role of women in the home?*
7 *List three aims of the women's movement in Ireland since the 1960s.*
8 *Explain the Employment Equality Act (1977).*

WOMEN IN AMERICA AROUND 1900

Around 1900 women in the United States of America had one great advantage over women in Ireland – they were needed as workers by an expanding economy. Ever since the foundation of the United States, women had been scarce, especially in the west. Because of this they gained a status still unknown in Europe. Visitors to America from Europe often remarked on the greater freedom enjoyed by American women.

Industrialisation also helped their position. The mass production of cheaper clothes and other goods lessened the load of a woman in running a home. More importantly, there were far more jobs becoming available for women. Telephone operators, typists and clerical workers now took their place alongside traditional women's jobs such as seamstresses, mill workers and teachers. However, although the number of jobs available to women was increasing, wages lagged significantly behind those of men. In 1900, one study in the United States found that, on average, women's wages were only fifty-three per cent of those of men. The main reason for this was that most women worked in the poorer-paid areas of the economy.

A girl working in an American factory around 1900. Women and girls played a vital part in America's industrial expansion. However, most of them were found in lower-paid jobs.

Workers posing for the camera outside their factory in 1913. Women were paid much less than men doing the same work.

LEARNING AND VOTING

The United States had a very good reputation in the area of higher education for women. From the end of the Civil War in 1865, many women's colleges had been founded and some older universities like Cornell and Michigan had become co-educational. It is not surprising that there was this demand because, by 1900, girls outnumbered boys among those who completed second level education.

It was to be expected that well-educated women would demand full civil and political rights. In line with the good record on women's education, some parts of the United States had taken the lead in granting women the vote.

In 1869, the territory of Wyoming granted women the right to vote and the neighbouring territory of Utah followed suit in 1870. However, it was not until 1920 that the right to vote was extended to women throughout the United States by the nineteenth amendment of the US constitution.

CHANGING LIFESTYLES IN AMERICA: 1920-60

During the 1920s, the role of women in the United States was changing rapidly. Many women had worked outside the home during World War I (1914-18). After that war, a new wave of greater freedom in personal lifestyles swept America and greatly influenced the lives of women. Over twice as many women entered the labour force between 1920 and 1930 as had done so between 1910 and 1920. By 1930, the number of women typists had increased tenfold since 1900.

During the 1920s, women's fashions changed with shorter dresses and lighter clothes. At the same time they could be seen drinking and smoking in public, something which 'respectable' ladies would not have done before 1914.

Throughout the 1920s, the divorce rate increased by fifty per cent. This was in marked contrast to Ireland where divorce was not permitted. In the US during the 1920s, over two-thirds of the divorce proceedings were started by women. This was a sign that they were seeking an escape from marriages if they could not secure equality. Even during the Depression decade of the 1930s, the numbers of women entering the workforce continued to rise.

During World War II, almost four million more American women entered the country's offices and factories. Despite the advances made by 1960, women's wages were still a long way behind those of men and many American women believed that vast inequalities between men and women still existed.

American women enjoying themselves in New York during the Roaring Twenties.

Marilyn Monroe, the famous American actress. Acting was one of the few occupations in which women were as successful as men.

TEST YOUR KNOWLEDGE

1 *Why was there a greater degree of freedom for women in America than in Europe around 1900?*
2 *How did industrial expansion assist women?*
3 *What was the result of a survey on women's wages in the US in 1900?*
4 *When were women first granted the right to vote in part of America?*
5 *Give an example of the increased participation of women in the American workforce during the 1920s.*

WOMEN'S LIBERATION

From the 1960s onwards, a powerful Women's Liberation Movement existed in the United States of America. Men and women who are involved in or supporters of this movement were known as *feminists*. Most American feminists agreed on the need for equal pay, better educational opportunities and a shared workload in the home.

However, there were also deep divisions in the women's liberation movement. Some feminists campaigned for the right of abortion and opposed any attempts to restrict abortion facilities by those who wanted to protect the right to life of the unborn child.

Throughout the 1960s, 1970s and 1980s, greater numbers of American women became involved in public life. In 1984, for the first time ever, one of the candidates for vice-president of the United States of America was a woman, Ms Geraldine Ferraro.

The fact that the United States in the richest country in the world explains the strength of the women's movement there. More women than in other countries had the wealth, education and leisure to engage in a campaign for women's liberation.

A Women's Liberation protest in the US during the 1960s.

Chapter 34: Review

- In Ireland around 1900, the wives and daughters of rich people did not go out to work but remained at home where they were waited upon by servants. In contrast, working-class women in towns and cities often had to go out to work as well as taking care of the home.

- In the early 1900s, the Suffragette Movement in Ireland led by Hanna Sheehy-Skeffington campaigned for the right to vote.

- Women also played an important part in the movement for Irish independence, most notably Countess Markievicz.

- Between 1922 and 1960, many people continued to believe that a woman's place was in the home. There were many inequalities between men and women, especially in the area of pay.

- During the 1960s, the modern Women's Movement emerged. Over the years, many of their aims – such as equal pay for equal work and more equal educational opportunities – were achieved.

- In the US, women around 1900 had far greater freedom than their European counterparts. While many more women worked, their wages lagged significantly behind those of men.

- The US had a very good reputation in the area of higher education for women. By 1900, girls outnumbered boys among those who completed second level education.

- Between 1920 and 1960, many changes came about in the lifestyles of American women. However, as in Ireland, the great change came about in the 1960s with the establishment of a powerful Women's Liberation Movement.

ACTIVITIES

1 Match an item in Column 1 with an item in Column 2.

COLUMN 1	COLUMN 2
An Irish Suffragette leader	Countess Markievicz
First woman to be elected an MP	Hanna Sheehy-Skeffington
Founder of *Inghinidhe na hÉireann*	Geraldine Ferraro
An American vice-presidential candidate	Jennie Wyse Power
Vice-President of Sinn Féin	Maud Gonne

2 True or false?
   (a) Despite many disadvantages facing women in Ireland in 1900, there were signs of improvement for the future.
   (b) The Suffragette Movement in Ireland was made up mostly of working-class women.
   (c) Countess Markievicz was sentenced to death for her part in the 1916 Rising.
   (d) In 1900, a study in the US showed that, on average, women's wages were only a quarter that of men.
   (e) In the US by 1900, girls outnumbered boys among those completing second level education.

3 Draw up a chart in which you can contrast the position of women in Ireland today with conditions in 1900. You may use headings such as 'education', 'work', 'wages', 'attitudes'.

4 Write a paragraph on two of the following: (a) the Suffragette Movement in Ireland; (b) women in the Independence Movement; (c) women in modern Ireland.

5 Write an account of the women's movement in the US in the twentieth century.

CHAPTER 35

RELIGION AND SOCIETY

IRELAND AROUND 1900

In 1900, religion had a powerful influence on the lives of most Irish people. The vast majority of the population belonged to the Catholic Church. Most of the remainder belonged to the Protestant Church of Ireland or to the Presbyterian Church.

In both towns and countryside, the Catholic Church was a powerful institution. By this time, the numbers of priests, brothers and nuns was increasing rapidly and many new churches had been built throughout the country.

An open-air mission in Donegal around 1900.

While the Catholic bishops had overall control of the Church, it was the parish priest who had the greatest influence on the local people. Compared with Europe and America, there was a very high level of religious practice in Ireland. Many people not only attended Sunday Mass but also evening devotions or weekday Mass as well. Pilgrimages to shrines like Knock, Croagh Patrick and Lough Derg were also very popular at the time.

Compared with today, religion appeared very strict. For example during the six weeks of Lent, there was strict fasting and entertainments such as dancing were forbidden.

As well as confraternities and sodalities for Catholic lay people, there were charitable organisations such as the Saint Vincent de Paul Society which carried out good work among the poor.

Outside of north-east Ulster, most members of the Church of Ireland in 1900 belonged to the better-off sections of society such as landlords, businessmen, professionals and their families. Like the Catholic Church, members of the Church of Ireland had their own schools, hospitals and charitable organisations.

The vast majority of Presbyterians lived in Ulster, either in the countryside or in industrial towns such as Belfast. Presbyterians had a reputation for being hard workers and good businessmen. While most Catholics in 1900 were nationalists who wanted greater freedom from Great Britain, the vast majority of Presbyterians and Church of Ireland members were Unionists who wished to keep the complete political union between Ireland and Great Britain.

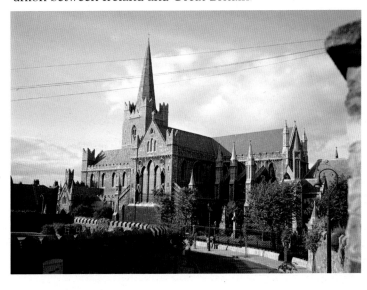

St Patrick's Cathedral, Dublin, the main place of worship for members of the Church of Ireland in the city.

RELIGION AND POLITICS

There were many links between religion and politics in Ireland around 1900. In the northern part of the country, many Church of Ireland and Presbyterian ministers became involved in the Unionist campaigns to prevent the setting up of a Home Rule parliament in Ireland.

The Catholic bishops and priests usually supported nationalist movements as long as these were non-violent. Many priests were involved in the local branches of the Irish Parliamentary Party which raised funds and chose candidates at election time. When the Easter Rising broke out in Dublin in 1916, the Catholic Church was in a difficult position. While condemning the use of violence by the rebels, Church leaders also condemned the extreme reaction of the British government.

During the War of Independence (1919-21), Catholic bishops condemned both the violence of the IRA and that of the Black and Tans and British army. They welcomed the truce of July 1921 and the signing of the Anglo-Irish Treaty the following December.

While the Catholic Church condemned both sides during the War of Independence, it completely supported the Free State government against the Republicans during the Civil War. The bishops regarded the government as the lawful one and condemned the Republicans for rebelling against it.

The role of Church leaders left many Republicans bitter and anti-clerical in the years ahead. After the ending of the Civil War in Ireland the Catholic Church had a profound influence on the lives of the people in the new Irish Free State.

TEST YOUR KNOWLEDGE
1 *Name the three main denominations in Ireland around 1900.*
2 *Show how the Catholic Church was growing in influence at the start of the century.*
3 *Would you agree that religion then was very strict?*
4 *Where did most Irish Presbyterians live?*
5 *What political view was supported by most Catholics?*
6 *What action did the Catholic bishops take during the Irish War of Independence?*
7 *What was the attitude of the Catholic Church to the Civil War?*

RELIGION IN INDEPENDENT IRELAND: 1922-60

In 1922, the Free State government made it clear that Protestants were very welcome in the new state and encouraged them to take an active part in public life. Distinguished Protestants such as the poet, W.B. Yeats, were nominated as senators by the government.

The Catholic Church continued to exert great power and influence in Ireland from 1922 onwards. The Dáil passed a law outlawing divorce and a strict censorship of books and films was introduced.

The attachment of the majority of the people to the Catholic Church was seen when the Eucharistic Congress was held in Dublin in 1932. Five years later, the new constitution drawn up by Eamon de Valera recognised the Catholic Church as the religion of the majority of the people. Although the constitution contained a separation of Church and State, many of its clauses such as the ban on divorce reflected the viewpoints of the Catholic Church.

In 1951, the first Inter-Party government fell after a dispute known as the *Mother and Child Crisis*. The government had refused to support the Mother and Child Free Health Scheme of Dr Noel Browne, the

O'Connell Bridge, Dublin, with the altar for the Eucharistic Congress which was held in Dublin in 1932 in the presence of the pope's representative, Cardinal Lauri. A million people attended a special Mass in the Phoenix Park.

St Patrick's College, Maynooth, the principal seminary for the training of Catholic priests in Ireland. It was here that the bishops held their meetings a number of times each year.

Minister for Health, after objections from doctors and the Catholic bishops. Many people at the time regarded the Mother and Child Crisis as an example of the power and influence of the Catholic Church.

During the 1950s, there was a very high level of religious vocations among young people in Ireland. Each year, hundreds of young people entered seminaries, colleges or convents to train as priests, brothers or nuns to serve in Ireland or in the foreign missions.

In many ways there had been little change in the religion of the people between 1900 and 1960. However, during the 1960s dramatic changes took place in religion as in almost every other aspect of life in Ireland.

Dr John Charles McQuaid, Catholic Archbishop of Dublin from 1940 to 1972, was a powerful and influential Church leader.

THE MODERN AGE

The *Second Vatican Council* (1962-65) brought about huge changes in the Catholic Church throughout the world. These changes deeply influenced the practice of religion in Ireland. The old Latin Mass was replaced by Mass in English or Irish. The priest now faced the people during Mass. The strict laws of fasting were abolished and lay people were more involved in Church affairs. At the same time, the authority of bishops and priests was frequently questioned.

John XXIII was pope from 1958 until 1963. During his short reign, he called together the Second Vatican Council.

The Second Vatican Council (1962-65) in session in St Peter's Basilica, Rome.

During the 1960s, an attempt began to bring Catholics and Protestants closer together by emphasising their common heritage as Christians. This was known as *ecumenism*. From then on, Catholic and Protestant leaders have met for discussions and joint prayer services.

While the influence of the Catholic Church has considerably declined since the 1950s, bishops and priests remained outspoken on certain moral and social issues such as divorce, contraception and abortion. During the 1980s, the Catholic and Protestant churches expressed their views during a referendum on the Right to Life of the Unborn Child (1983) and on Divorce (1986).

The visit of Pope John Paul II to Ireland in 1979 clearly showed that religion continued to play an important part in people's lives. However, despite the enthusiasm displayed on that occasion, religious practice, especially among young people, continued to decline during the 1980s.

The level of vocations continued to decline. However, many religious orders responded by concentrating their efforts in poorer areas. At the same time, the Catholic bishops frequently called for greater justice for the poor in Ireland and in the Third World.

The visit of Pope John Paul II to Ireland in 1979.

TEST YOUR KNOWLEDGE

1 *How did the Free State government prove that Protestants were welcome?*
2 *What great religious event took place in Dublin in 1932?*
3 *Name the Minister for Health involved in the Mother and Child controversy.*
4 *List two changes which the Second Vatican Council brought about in the Catholic Church in Ireland.*
5 *Explain the meaning of ecumenism.*
6 *What religious event took place in 1979?*

CHURCH AND STATE IN THE US

Unlike Ireland, where a majority of the population belonged to one religious denomination, in the United States of America people belonged to several different denominations. The majority of Americans belonged to some form of Protestant Church. Episcopalian churches, rather like the Protestant Church of Ireland, were very strong in the eastern part of the United States. In the southern states, the Baptist churches were strong. These combined a firm attachment to the word of God in the Bible with a deep distrust of the Catholic Church.

Millions of Americans belonged to the Catholic Church throughout the United States. The immigration of vast numbers of Catholic Irish people greatly strengthened Catholicism in America. Some other nationalities who arrived in huge numbers, such as the Italians and the Poles, were also largely Catholic.

The US also had a large Jewish community. At a time when Jews were persecuted in many areas of Eastern Europe, they were pleased to arrive in America where complete freedom of religious practice was allowed.

The US constitution guarantees the free practice of religion throughout the country. At the same time, it lays down a strict separation of Church and State. The US government, or the local state

313

governments, are strictly forbidden to give any money to any religion or to any school controlled by religious groups.

This situation is different from arrangements in Ireland. Although Church and State were separate in Ireland, the government is permitted to give grants to Church-run schools.

The main concern of people involved in the various churches in the US in the twentieth century, however, has been the constant drift away from all religions by millions of American.

A TIME OF GROWING DISBELIEF

During the 1920s, there was a marked decline in the level of religious belief and practice in the United States. This took place against a background of falling moral standards and a huge rise in the divorce rate.

Many Americans blamed the decline of the country and the rise of the cities for this trend. Under the influence of William Jennings Bryan, a believer in the strict interpretation of the Bible, several southern states passed laws banning the teaching of evolution in schools. In 1925 the famous 'Monkey Trial' took place in Tennessee when a biology teacher defied this ban. Bryan died shortly after the trial. The teacher was eventually cleared and the movement for the 'old style religion' of Protestants in America received a severe setback.

RELIGION AND RACISM

Race relations in the US have had a long and difficult history. From the 1920s onwards, this subject posed an increasingly serious challenge for all of the churches.

During the mid 1920s, the extreme organisation, the *Ku Klux Klan*, became very powerful before declining rapidly again by the end of the decade. The Klan was very strong in the southern states where it carried out widespread intimidation against black people. However, it also hated the Catholic Church and stood for a WASP supremacy – that is, White Anglo-Saxon Protestants or the descendants of the original American settlers.

A Ku Klux Klan meeting in the southern United States.

The Reverend Martin Luther King.

Throughout the southern states of America, many Protestant Church congregations were segregated into black and white groups. One effect of this situation was the emergence of powerful leaders from among black Baptist ministers. The most famous of these was the Reverend Martin Luther King, who led the movement for Civil Rights for black people during the 1950s and 1960s.

MODERN AMERICA

From the 1960s onwards, the churches in America experienced many of the changes affecting religion all over the world. The changes brought about by the Second Vatican Council were widely welcomed by American Catholics. However, many priests and religious left their ministries and a serious vocations crisis developed.

On the Protestant side, evangelical leaders remained popular. These were preachers such as Billy Graham who conducted mass rallies and preached that every single word in the Bible must be taken literally. At the same time, many rich Americans funded Protestant missions in Third World countries where no money was spared to win recruits.

During the 1980s, serious disputes developed between church leaders and politicians over areas such as the right to life of the unborn child and the morality of spending billions on nuclear weapons, while people starved in the Third World. While politicians called for a complete separation of Church and State, leading churchmen and women proclaimed that they had a right to speak out when moral issues were involved.

TEST YOUR KNOWLEDGE
1   *How did religion in the US differ from Ireland in 1900?*
2   *List two Protestant churches which existed in the US.*
3   *Explain how immigration had strengthened the Catholic Church in America.*
4   *Why did the Jewish communities wish to emigrate to the US?*
5   *Explain the US practice of separation of Church and State.*
6   *What was 'The Monkey Trial' (1925)?*
7   *Explain the aims of the Ku Klux Klan.*
8   *Name the Baptist minister who became a leader of the Civil Rights Movement.*
9   *What is an evangelical preacher?*
10 *List two issues which caused tension between Church and State in the US during the 1980s.*

Chapter 35: Review

- Around 1900, the Catholic Church had a powerful influence on the lives of most Irish people.

- There was a close link between religion and politics around 1900, with the Catholic Church supporting Nationalist movements as long as they were non-violent while most Protestants were Unionist supporters.

- The Catholic Church continued to exert great power after independence. This influence was seen in the strict censorship laws and the Irish constitution.

- During the 1960s, important changes took place in the Catholic Church under the influence of the Second Vatican Council. The Church remained outspoken on many moral and social issues such as divorce and abortion.

- During the 1980s, there was a continued decline in the number of religious vocations.

- The people in the US do not belong to one religious denomination but to several. There is also strict separation of Church and State in the US.

- During the 1920s, there was a sharp decline in the level of religious belief and practice in the US. The problem of race relations posed a serious challenge for all the churches at that time.

- As in Ireland, the 1960s also brought about many important changes in religion in the US. In more recent times, church leaders have been in conflict with politicians over issues such as abortion and nuclear armaments.

ACTIVITIES

1 *Match an item in Column 1 with an item in Column 2.*

COLUMN 1	COLUMN 2
The Ku Klux Klan	Ulster
The Presbyterian Religion	The Monkey Trial
Billy Graham	Anti-Black Racism
A Church-State issue	An American Preacher
William Jennings Bryan	The Mother and Child Controversy

2 *Complete the following sentences.*
   (a) *Compared with Europe and America, Ireland in 1900 had a high level of _____ .*
   (b) *The two main Protestant Churches in Ireland are _____.*
   (c) *During the Irish War of Independence, the Catholic bishops _____.*
   (d) *During the 1960s, the ecumenical movement became popular in Ireland. This was an attempt _____.*
   (e) *The US constitution laid down a strict separation between _____.*
   (f) *The Reverend Martin Luther King was _____.*

3 *Write a paragraph on religion in Ireland around 1900.*

4 *List some important changes which have taken place in religion in Ireland since 1960.*

5 *Write an account of religion in the US since 1920.*

THE CHANGING WORLD OF TRANSPORT

ON THE MOVE

From around 1900 onwards, there have been vast and exciting changes in travel and transport. These have greatly influenced the lives of ordinary people in both Ireland and America. Pictures taken down through the years provide us with vivid sources concerning these changes. Throughout this chapter we will see for ourselves how transport has progressed from the era of the horse and cart to the modern day Space Age.

A SLOWER AGE

Unlike today in Ireland, in 1900 many ordinary people depended completely on walking in order to travel. There were many people indeed who rarely travelled outside their native parish, village or town. Such people thought little about going on walks of many miles' distance.

At the time a new invention was becoming popular in Ireland – the bicycle.

In both towns and countryside horse-drawn transport was still widely used for work and leisure. Look at the pictures to see horses at work on the farm and drawing goods through the streets of towns. In the early years of the century, horse-drawn transport was widely used, ranging from the carriages of the rich to the pony and trap used by ordinary people.

A Donegal landlord setting off from his residence in 1903.

Many poorer people living in the Irish countryside travelled by donkey and cart.

Horses were also used to carry out work on the farm.

From 1900 onwards, electric trams were beginning to replace horse-drawn vehicles in the main cities.

Electric trams in Dublin around 1914.

At the same time, Ireland had an extensive network of railways. These trains had luxurious first-class carriages for the rich. However, poorer people were also able to use this relatively cheap and comfortable form of transport. Cheap excursions to the seaside by rail helped the growth of seaside resorts such as Bundoran, Bray and Youghal.

TEST YOUR KNOWLEDGE
1 What was the main means of transport for most ordinary people in Ireland around 1900?
2 What new form of transport was becoming popular at the time?
3 How were horses used in the countryside and the towns around 1900?
4 What form of transport was replacing horse-drawn transport in the cities?
5 State two ways in which railways affected the lives of ordinary people in Ireland around 1900.

318

THE AGE OF THE MOTOR CAR

Around 1900, motor cars made their first appearance on Irish roads. At first, only very rich people could afford this new form of transport. By 1914, motor cars were common sights on Irish roads. After World War I, petrol-driven lorries and buses were seen in towns all over Ireland.

During the 1920s and 1930s, road transport competed successfully with the railways and more and more railway lines were closed.

In 1944, a semi-state company known as *Coras Iompair Éireann (CIE)* was set up to take charge of the railways and buses throughout the country. This company controls public transport in Ireland up to the present day.

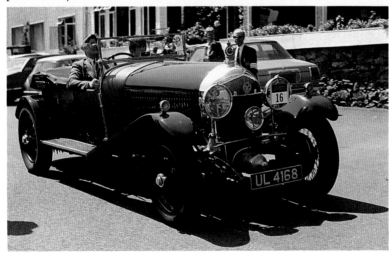

An early Irish-owned car on display many years later.

MODERN TIMES

We have seen already how Ireland experienced major industrial expansion during the 1960s. Travel and transport were a central part of this rapidly changing scene. As people became more affluent, there was a great increase in the number of family cars. At the same time, better roads were being provided throughout the country.

Railway transport also changed as steam engines were replaced by diesels.

One of the great successes of modern Ireland was the national airline company, *Aer Lingus*, which had been founded in 1936. During the 1960s, air passenger transport increased and business expanded at the three main airports of Dublin, Shannon and Cork.

By the 1980s the country had come a long way indeed from the days of the steam engine and the pony and trap.

TEST YOUR KNOWLEDGE
1 What form of transport had become popular in Ireland by 1914?
2 Name the company set up in 1944 to take charge of public transport in Ireland.

Passengers leaving
an Aer Lingus
flight.

From the 1970s
onwards, the
quality of Irish
roads improved
greatly due in
part to the
availability of EC
grants.

3 *Name two important developments in transport during the 1960s.*
4 *What is the national airline company called?*
5 *Write down two ways in which transport in Ireland in the 1980s had improved since 1900.*

THE UNITED STATES OF AMERICA IN 1900

The transport needs of people in the US around 1900 were vastly different from those of people in Ireland. Whereas Ireland was a small country with a declining population, the US was a vast land with a rapidly increasing population, partly caused by a high level of immigration.

A huge railway network criss-crossed the continent from the Atlantic in the east to the Pacific in the west. Many people alive in the US at the time could recall the Pony Express bringing the mail. Indeed trains had arrived in remote western areas only twenty years previously.

A steam train
making its way
through the
western part of
the US around
1900.

Because of the vast populations in American cities, satisfactory systems of transport were required. The Americans were fortunate that many inventors of genius lived in the US at the time. These inventors put their minds to work on transport needs and came up with some impressive results. One of the earliest of these inventions was the cable car developed by Charles Harvey, a New York inventor. By 1900 cable cars were in use in twenty-three American cities where they carried 370 million passengers a year.

In 1880 the famous inventor, Thomas Edison, experimented with a form of electrified railway. This was the forerunner of the streetcar, the American name for a tram. By 1900, many American cities had streetcar systems. Streetcars were faster and cleaner than horse-drawn trams or cable cars. As a result, by 1903, America's 48,000 kilometres of street railways were ninety-eight per cent electrified.

An American streetcar.

As in Ireland, however, great changes took place with the arrival of the motor car.

THE ARRIVAL OF THE MOTOR CAR

In the US, the development of the motor car will always be associated with the name of Henry Ford whose ancestors had emigrated from Co. Cork. Little did people in 1900 realise the revolution which was in store! In October 1899 an American magazine, the *Literary Digest*, contained the following prophecy:

'The ordinary "horseless carriage" is at present a luxury for the wealthy; and although its price will probably fall in the future, it will never, of course, come into as common use as the bicycle.'

Thanks largely to the initiative of Henry Ford in his Detroit Motor Company, the 'horseless carriage' or motor car did come into 'as common use as the bicycle'. In 1908, Ford produced his famous 'Model T' motor car, popularly known as the 'Tin Lizzie'. Its design remained the same for the next twenty years. However, the price continued to drop due to increased efficiency in production. By 1925, Ford was turning out 9000 cars a day or one every ten seconds. Led by Ford, the number of automobiles in the US rose from one million in 1913 to ten million in 1923.

Cars being assembled at the Ford Motor Company in Detroit, Michigan.

These developments in turn led to the construction of lorries and trucks and the building of larger and better roads throughout America. The finances to improve these roads came from taxation on petrol.

As America led the way in road transport in the 1920s and 1930s, it was also to be in the forefront of a transport revolution of a very different kind after 1945 – the Space Race.

Proud owners of Ford's Model-T cars.

TEST YOUR KNOWLEDGE
1 *How were the transport needs of America different from those of Ireland in 1990?*
2 *Who invented the cable car?*
3 *Were cable cars widely used in 1900? Explain your answer.*
4 *What was a streetcar?*
5 *Why were streetcars often preferred to horse trams or cable cars?*
6 *Name Henry Ford's most successful type of car.*
7 *Explain how the car industry in the US was expanding rapidly by the mid 1920s.*

THE SPACE AGE

There was one area of travel where there was no competition between Ireland and America – the exploration of space. Because of its vast wealth, the United States, along with the Soviet Union, became a leading player in the 'space race' in the 1960s.

Indeed America had been a pioneer in terms of air travel. In 1903, two American brothers, Orville and Wilbur Wright, had made the first flight in the world in an aeroplane.

The Wright brothers experimenting with their new invention, the aeroplane.

Charles Lindberg, the first person to fly solo across the Atlantic, standing beside his plane, *The Spirit of St Louis.* The journey, which took place in May 1927, lasted 33 hours.

During the 1920s and 1930s, the American airline industry expanded rapidly. In 1929, the large American company Trans World Airlines (TWA) was established, seven years before Ireland followed suit with the setting up of Aer Lingus. As well as organising international passenger flights, American airline companies built up a huge network of internal flights. By the 1960s, many people in America travelled from city to city by air instead of by road or rail.

It was also during the 1960s that the space programme came into its own. This was a decade of intense competition with the Russians who had been the first to launch a man into space. In 1969, American efforts paid off when the United States became the first country to land a man on the moon. In July of that year, American astronauts Neil Armstrong and

'Man on the moon' – Edwin Aldrin, one of the *Apollo XI* astronauts, walking on the moon in July 1969.

Edwin ('Buzz') Aldrin, members of a three-man expedition on the spaceship Apollo XI, became the first people to set foot on the moon. All around the world, people watched the event on their television screens. By enabling astronauts to travel to the moon, the Americans had shown how incredible had been their progress in transport and travel since the days of the invention of cable cars and streetcars around the beginning of the century.

Chapter 36: Review

- In Ireland around 1900, people largely travelled on foot or by using horse-drawn transport, electric trams and trains.

- During the 1920s and 1930s, motor transport was becoming popular, and in 1944 CIE was set up.

- There were major changes in the area of transport from the 1960s on. In particular, air passenger travel greatly expanded.

- By 1900, the US had a vast railway network. Cable cars and streetcars were also widely used.

- In 1908, Henry Ford produced his famous Model T motor car. By the 1920s the number of cars in the US had greatly increased.

- The US had also been the pioneer in terms of air travel. During the 1920s and 1930s, the American airline industry expanded rapidly.

- During the 1960s, the US was to the forefront in the Space Age. In 1969, the US became the first country to land men on the moon.

ACTIVITIES

1 Complete the following sentences.
   (a) In Ireland around 1900, horse-drawn transport _____.
   (b) During the 1920s, road transport in Ireland _____.
   (c) The Irish national airline company, _____, was established in _____.
   (d) In 1908, Henry Ford first produced _____.
   (e) In 1903, the first aeroplane flight in history was made by two American brothers named _____.

2 Choose four illustrations from this chapter which deal with transport in Ireland and state what you learn from each.

3 Write a paragraph on transport in the US around 1900.

4 Draw up a chart on the main achievements of the US during the Space Age.

COMMUNICATIONS

IRELAND IN 1900

Ireland today is part of a sophisticated world of communications. Radio and television, telephone and telex, computers and Fax machines have all revolutionised communications within Ireland and between Ireland and the rest of the world. As a result of the great changes in communication during the course of the twentieth century, the world has become a kind of 'Global Village'.

Compared with today, Ireland in 1900 had a very simple system of communications. One of the most important ways of communicating news and events to people at that time was the newspaper. Although newspapers had been in existence in Ireland since the late eighteenth century, they had greatly increased in circulation and readership by the year 1900. This was partly due to the marked increase in the numbers of people who were able to read and write by the turn of the century. The *Freeman's Journal* was one of the most popular newspapers at that time.

By the year 1900, Ireland had developed an efficient postal service. In fact the General Post Office in Dublin had been built as early as 1815. In 1840, the 'penny post' was introduced. Under this system, a letter would be delivered to any place in the United Kingdom for the price of one penny. The fee was paid by fixing a stamp to the letter which was then dropped into a posting box. In an age before telephones, the development of a postal service helped Irish emigrants keep in touch with their families at home.

A postman on his rounds, about 1910.

The General Post Office in Dublin.

The invention of the telegraph by Samuel Morse was a very important development in communication. The telegraph allowed messages to be transmitted along a wire in a series of long and short impulses known as 'Morse Code'. In 1858, a transatlantic cable enabled a telegraph message to be sent from Ireland to America. Although the telephone was invented by Alexander Graham Bell in 1876, it was to be a long time before this invention would have an impact on Ireland. While the first telephone exchange was built here in 1880, many parts of the country had to wait a very long time before local exchanges were installed.

Repairing the cable of the transatlantic telegraph on board the 'Great Eastern' steamship

In 1902, an Italian inventor named Guglielmo Marconi opened a radio station in Clifden, Co. Galway, which could transmit signals across the Atlantic without using wires at all. In 1910, Marconi received messages at Buenos Aires from Clifden, a distance of about 9650 km. The invention of the 'wireless' was to have far-reaching effects in the years ahead.

Marconi with an early wireless

1 *Name the most popular newspaper in Ireland around 1900.*
2 *Why was the development of a postal service important for ordinary people?*
3 *What important development in communications took place in the year 1858?*
4 *Did the invention of the telephone have an immediate impact on Ireland?*
5 *What important development occurred in 1902?*

THE AGE OF RADIO

It was not long before the wireless was used for transmitting entertainment and news. With the opening of commercial radio stations, the age of mass communication had surely arrived. Ireland's first radio station – 2RN – opened in 1926. This was later renamed Radio Éireann. The photographs showing the first thirty years of Radio Éireann illustrate the important role it has played in the lives of Irish people.

Kathleen Dolan, the first lady announcer on Radio Eireann.

Eamon de Valera talking on radio to the Irish people in 1941.

'The Foley Family' – a popular radio drama in the 1950s.

Celebrations in O'Connell Street, Dublin to mark the opening of RTE television on 31 December 1961.

Sean Lemass, speaking on Irish television for the first time.

THE MODERN AGE OF COMMUNICATIONS

Ireland's first television station began broadcasting on 31 December 1961. With television, the modern age of communications had begun in Ireland. Television, a powerful medium of communication, has had a great impact on Irish society. It has brought us closer to great events all over the world and has opened up Irish society to a great number of different values and attitudes. In the 1970s, there was widespread demand for the availability of more channels and, in response to this, RTE 2 was launched in 1977.

During the early 1970s, the use of satellites brought about a revolution in television broadcasting.

In businesses and offices, sophisticated computers, facsimile (Fax) and telex machines have greatly extended the powers of communication. In most Irish homes, the radio, television and telephone have brought people into close contact with the outside world. We have come a long way from the days of the penny post and the telegraph.

Zig and Zag were among the most popular characters on RTE children's programmes

American football, a sport made widely popular through television.

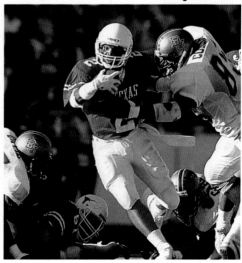

THE UNITED STATES:
DEVELOPMENTS IN THE WORLD OF COMMUNICATIONS

All the developments in communications described above also occurred in America. However, in this huge country, they were far more rapid and on a much grander scale. By 1900, the number of post offices in America stood at nearly 77,000. Today, the United States maintains the largest postal system in the world, handling almost half the world's volume of postal traffic. The first commercial telephone switchboard was opened in New Haven, Connecticut, in January 1878. While Ireland's first telephone exchange was opened in 1880, America had, by then, 139 exchanges in operation with 30,000 subscribers. Within another decade, this figure had risen to nearly 800 main exchanges linking 150,000 subscribers. By 1900, the two cities of Boston and Chicago, nearly 2000 km apart, were connected by telephone.

Alexander Graham Bell (top) lecturing on his telephone while friends in his study in Boston (below) listen.

DEVELOPMENTS IN BROADCASTING

The first known radio programme in the United States was broadcast from an experimental station at Massachusetts on Christmas Eve 1906. The first commercial radio station was KDKA in Pittsburgh which began broadcasting on 2 November 1920. The growth in the number of radio stations was rapid and by 1 November 1922, 564 had been licensed to operate.

The first television stations were set up in America in 1939 and 1940. Their growth was rapid. By 1960 there were fifty million television sets in use throughout America. The use of satellites has revolutionised broadcasting in America and elsewhere. The landing on the moon by American astronauts in 1969 was communicated by satellite to an estimated audience of more than 100 million viewers.

By the closing years of the twentieth century, communications had come a long way in America since 1900, when many people could still remember how the mail was carried by horse and pony-driven vehicles. The inventions of Bell and others around that time laid the foundations for a revolution in communications which not only linked the earth with planets in outer space but also made everyday contact at home and at work easier and more efficient.

Chapter 37: Review

- Ireland in 1900 had a very simple system of communications. The newspaper was very popular at this time. The telegraph was also used, and in 1902 Marconi opened a radio station in Clifden, Co. Galway.

- In 1926 Ireland had its first commercial radio station – 2RN. However, the most significant development in communications came in 1961 with the opening of Ireland's first television station.

- All the developments in Ireland also took place in the US, but on a much larger scale and sooner. The US had a huge network of post offices by 1900 and the first telephone exchange had been opened in 1878.

- The first commercial radio station in the US was opened in 1920, and the first television stations were set up in 1939 and 1940. From the 1960s on, the use of satellites has revolutionised broadcasting in America and elsewhere.

ACTIVITIES

1 *Match an item in Column 1 with an item in Column 2.*

COLUMN 1	COLUMN 2
Samuel Morse	2RN
Guglielmo Marconi	The telephone
An Irish Radio Station	KDKA
Alexander Graham Bell	The wireless
An American radio station	The telegraph

2 *Complete the following sentences.*
   (a) The Freeman's Journal was _____.
   (b) In 1858, a transatlantic cable enabled _____.
   (c) During the 1970s, the use of satellites _____.
   (d) The first commercial telephone switchboard was opened at _____.
   (e) The first known radio programme in the United States was broadcast _____.

3 *Write a paragraph on two of the forms of mass communications which you read about in this chapter.*